Enlightened Journey

ENLIGHTENED JOURNEY

Buddhist Practice as Daily Life

TULKU THONDUP

Edited by Harold Talbott

SHAMBHALA
Boston & London
1995

Shambhala Publications, Inc.
Horticultural Hall
300 Massachusetts Avenue
Boston, Massachusetts 02115

© 1995 by Tulku Thondup Rinpoche
Buddhayana Series: V

9   8   7   6   5   4   3   2   1

First Edition
Printed in the United States of America
on acid-free paper ♻
Distributed in the United States by Random House, Inc.,
and in Canada by Random House of Canada Ltd

Library of Congress Cataloging-in-Publication Data
Thondup, Tulku.
    Enlightened journey: Buddhist practice as daily life /
Tulku Thondup; edited by Harold Talbott.
    — 1st ed.   p.   cm.
    Includes bibliographical references and index.
    ISBN 1-57062-021-0
    1. Spiritual life—Rñiṅ-ma-pa (Sect)   2. Rdzogs-chen
(Rñiṅ-ma-pa)   I. Talbott, Harold.   II. Title
BQ7662.6.T56   1994   94-36154
294.3'444—dc20   CIP

CONTENTS

PREFACE

T HE MOST ESSENTIAL TRAINING in Buddhism, and for
that matter in any spiritual path, is the "skillful means"
that enables the trainees to transmute every aspect of their
daily life into spiritual training. Spiritual training is the exercises that release the intensity of our mental grasping and the
driving force of our craving. Spiritual training eases the pain
and suffering created by our narrow, rigid views and our
burning, confusing emotions.

Spiritual training is crucial to the realization and experience of openness, peace, joy, love, and wisdom. If our mind is
filled with peace, love, and wisdom, our mental and spiritual
energies will be strengthened. If our mental and spiritual
energies are strengthened, the physical elements of our body
become healthy and the events in our life become positive. By
the same token, if our mental energy is strong, our body will
be healthy and our life positive; our mind will be naturally
more peaceful and joyful. The days of our entire life will
flow in a cycle of true happiness. As the third Dodrupchen
Rinpoche writes:[1]

> When your mind is not disturbed, your energy will not be
> disturbed, and thereby other elements of the body will also

not be disturbed. Because of this, your mind will not be disturbed, and so the wheel of joy will keep revolving.

There are two important ways to transmute daily life into training. First, if you have realized the wisdom that transcends mental conceptions, or even if you have not yet transcended mental conceptions but have powerful spiritual experiences such as compassion, devotion, or contemplation, then you can unite or transform all appearances and experiences into a support for the energy of realized wisdom and spiritual experience.

For great adepts, every phenomenal appearance becomes the expression of their inner wisdom itself. All appearances become the power of realization, like the rays of the sun that coax the flowers of happiness to blossom in the hearts of all those around.

Second, for ordinary people like ourselves, whose minds are conceptual, emotional, and unrealized, it is essential to rely on any skillful means—positive and spiritual images, signs, sounds, or sources of power—as the means of generating spiritual energy. If we could see the objects that surround us as a source of inspiration and peace, they will generate peace and joy within us because of the power of our own mental perceptions.

In the same vein, we cannot transform negative situations into positive ones if we see them as negative and react to them with negative emotions. As long as we hold on to negative perceptions, viewing our circumstances through dark shades, the whole world will appear negative, and all our efforts will be one never-ending struggle. So we should lay the foundation of true peace and joy in our own minds by developing the skillful means of spiritual training, not by struggling to ward off adversity. As Shāntideva explains:[2]

> Foes are as unlimited as (the extent of) space;
> They cannot possibly all be overcome.
> Yet if you just overcome the thought of hatred,
> That will be equal to overcoming all foes.
> Where is the leather
> With which one can cover the earth?
> But wearing a leather sandal
> Is equal to covering the earth with leather.

This book contains fifteen of my published articles and transcriptions of talks. It is divided into two parts: an introduction to the Buddhist path and a discussion of meditation practice. The core of this book is the article on the meditation practice of Ngöndro, the essential training of the Longchen Nyingthig[3] tradition of Tibetan Buddhism. The Ngöndro embodies a complete process of training, beginning with inspiring one's mind toward Dharma and ending with unifying one's mind with the enlightened mind of the Buddha, universal enlightenment. The other articles deal with introductory or supportive material which, taken together, constitute a manual on how to turn the various experiences we encounter, whether external or internal phenomena, into spiritual views, disciplines, and experiences.

Part One consists of six articles. They form an introduction to the spiritual view, culture, and life, which are an important means of transmuting our physical and mental life into Dharma training.

1. "Using Daily Life as the Practice of Dharma." This article summarizes some of the fundamental principles of

Buddhism—who we are and why we can turn our daily life into spiritual training and realize Buddhahood, the state of ultimate peace and wisdom.

If we follow the right path of spiritual training, we can overcome all of life's miseries, which are mere illusions of the deluded mind, and be like dreamers waking up from a nightmare. The fully enlightened nature could be spontaneously awakened in us, as we are all Buddha in our true nature. Suffering is the by-product of our mental concept of grasping at "self," fueled by emotions of aggression, greed, and confusion. Training in various meditations such as patience and the beneficial attitude for others pacifies our negative emotions and concepts, and simultaneously generates in us peace, joy, and wisdom.

2. "Opening the Heart with Compassion." Compassion is a caring attitude, an openness of mind. It is also the omnipresent power of Buddhahood. This article explains in simple words what compassion is and how we can develop it. Compassion as a meditation not only generates peace and harmony, but also awakens Buddhahood in us. This presentation on compassion additionally illustrates what kind of results we can expect from various other spiritual trainings, such as devotion, pure perception, and contemplation.

3. "A Spiritual Journey in a Turbulent Life." Using my own turbulent life as an illustration, the insightful teachings of Buddhism are presented. By giving me the strength to bear the calamities and emotional devastation that befell me and many others, Buddhist teachings became my sole means of survival in a turbulent world. If you know how, suffering can

become a more powerful tool than happiness to transform life into the enlightened path.

4. "Buddhist Artifacts as the Support of Spiritual Realization." Using an image of Avalokiteshvara as an example, this article explains the symbolic significance of spiritual artifacts as a source of teaching, inspiration, and power. If we are skilled at perceiving various artifacts as spiritual symbols and sources of power, a time will come when all phenomena, not only spiritual artifacts, will arise before us as the image of teaching and the realization of peace, joy, and wisdom.

It is easier for ordinary people to use objects that have direct spiritual significance and power as a means of inspiration than it is to use ordinary objects. Objects with direct spiritual significance include religious paintings, statues, temples, books, teachers, meditators, and holy places.

5. "Tibetan Buddhist Thangkas and Their Religious Significance." This article outlines Tibetan Buddhist paintings of different traditions, with an emphasis on their religious significance.

For people who are spiritually inclined, religious art in various peaceful and wrathful forms is a powerful tool to develop and strengthen spiritual experience with the various expressions of phenomena. For realized people, spiritual art is power, energy, and light, the extension of their own inner peace, strength, and wisdom. Art can also be wisdom itself arising in the form of images of power and symbols of teachings. So, spiritual art is an important means of turning perceptions of phenomena into the realization of peace, strength, and wisdom.

6. "Preparing for the Bardo: The Stages of Dying and After Death." This article explains in detail the whole process of dying, from the moment death begins to what happens after death. Based on esoteric scriptures (tantra) of Tibetan Buddhism, this chapter outlines the numerous stages involved in living and dying, with teachings on how we should view and experience each step.

Death is a most crucial time for every one of us, a critical opportunity to affect our futures. When we die, all of us, rich or poor, await the same consequences. At death, neither money, power, nor friends, not even our cherished body, can come to our aid. Only the habits and energies—the karma—that have been stored up in our minds will create the manifestations of our next life, our future experiences. So to prepare for death, our most important strategy is to gain spiritual understanding and experience while we are still alive. When death arrives, it will be too late to cry for help.

Part Two consists of nine articles. The main focus of these is the meditation of Ngöndro, the essential training in Dzogpa Chenpo ("Great Perfection"), according to the lineage of the Longchen Nyingthig tradition.

The first three articles are introductions to the Ngöndro practice. They present a brief history of the Nyingma school and an outline of the Ter tradition through which the Ngöndro was revealed and came to us.

7. "The Nyingma School of Tibetan Buddhism." Nyingma or Nyingmapa ("Old One") is the oldest of the four major Buddhist schools of Tibet. This article outlines the unique attributes of the Nyingma school within the literary, spiritual, and social history of Tibet. Longchen Nying-

thig, to which this particular Ngöndro belongs, is one of the prominent lineages of the Nyingma school.

8. "The Terma Tradition of the Nyingma School." Ter or Terma means "hidden treasures." They are spiritual objects, teachings, and transmissions concealed and discovered through enlightened mystical powers by great adepts. The Nyingma school is the richest Buddhist tradition in terms of teachings revealed as Ter. This article summarizes the different classes of Ter discoveries: Earth Ter (*Sa gTer*), Mind Ter (*dGongs gTer*), and Pure Vision (*Dag sNang*) teachings. It details the complete process by which teachings are concealed and then discovered. Longchen Nyingthig teachings were discovered by Jigme Lingpa (1729–1798) as a Mind Ter.

9. "The Empowerments and Precepts of Esoteric Training." This has two aspects: empowerment (Tib. *dBang*, Skt. *abhiṣheka*) and precepts (Tib. *Dam Tshig*, Skt. *samaya*). Empowerment is the entrance to esoteric or tantric training. An aspirant receives this from a tantric master to initiate himself or herself into the training. Empowerments can also be repeatedly received as training in the path. They can also be received as the final attainment.

Precept is the vow, commitment, link, or causation in esoteric or tantric training. This article provides a comprehensive overview of the samayas, the obligations of various levels of esoteric teaching.

To enter into the path of esoteric power and attainments, we have to receive empowerments. To maintain and progress in our esoteric practice, we have to abide strictly by the positive supports of observing the precepts and consistently refraining from negative deeds.

In our true nature we are all one in ultimate peace and wisdom. However, as long as we are trapped in a dualistic mind frame, in emotional struggles and unending sorrow, we must take the right path and stick to it unswervingly. If we are on the right track and move along it with the discipline of the precepts, we can be sure to attain Buddhahood.

The next set of four articles are teachings on the actual practice, which focus principally on the Ngöndro meditation itself.

10. "The Meditation of Ngöndro: The Essential Training of the Longchen Nyingthig Tradition." This article outlines the Ngöndro practice. *Ngöndro* literally means "preliminary." However, the Ngöndro training is in reality far more than a preliminary practice. It is an essential and complete path of meditation training of Dzogpa Chenpo. It starts by generating inspiration toward spiritual training and ends with uniting with or realizing the intrinsic nature of the mind, the Buddha nature that we all inherit.

The Ngöndro meditation involves the following trainings:

1. Prayers to the lineage teachers for the success of the Ngöndro practice.
2. The fourfold preliminary practice to inspire our mind toward Dharma meditation: thinking about the preciousness of human life, the impermanence of life, the suffering nature of the world, and karma, the cycle of causation.
3. The fourfold essential training: going for Refuge to commit our mind to Dharma; developing the mind of enlightenment to lay the foundation of Dharma in us; purification through Vajrasattva to clear our conceptual, emotional, and karmic impurities; and mandala offering to accumulate the forces of merit.

4. The main practice in the Ngöndro: to realize the world as the pure land of Guru Rinpoche, pray with devotion, practice the sevenfold devotional training, recite the mantra, receive the fourfold empowerment, and contemplate the union of one's mind and the enlightened mind of Guru Rinpoche.

5. The conclusion: the dedication of the accumulated merit as the cause of happiness and enlightenment of all beings with all the best aspirations.

The main goal of the Ngöndro meditation is to realize the intrinsic nature of mind by unifying our own mind with the enlightened mind of Guru Rinpoche through the force of devotion. The mind of Guru Rinpoche is the union of all the realized minds of all the Buddhas and spiritual masters, the universal truth. The intrinsic nature of mind is thorough openness without limits, total oneness without discriminations, fully awakened awareness with no ignorance, and fully enlightened wisdom with no confusion.

11. "The Meaning of *The Vajra Seven-Line Prayer* to Guru Rinpoche." In the Nyingma tradition this prayer is considered the supreme, sacred prayer to Guru Rinpoche. Its seven lines are the heart of the prayers of Ngöndro practice. This article is a summary of *Guru'i Tshig bDun gSol 'Debs Kyi rNam bShad Padma dKar Po*, a famous commentary on *The Vajra Seven-Line prayer* written by Mipham Rinpoche (1846–1912), a celebrated scholar and adept of the Nyingma school. It interprets the prayer in seven different levels of outer and inner meaning. This prayer could be practiced as an invocation, an instructional guide on meditation, or an experience of the attainments of different stages of esoteric trainings and realization.

12. "Receiving the Four Empowerments of Ngöndro Meditation." Receiving empowerments is the final stage of the Ngöndro meditation practice. This article summarizes hosts of esoteric trainings and attainments associated with the receiving of the four empowerments, the enlightened blessing powers of body, speech, mind, and wisdom of Guru Rinpoche. Through these blessing powers the mediator realizes and perfects various esoteric attainments. The final attainment is the realization of the union of our own minds and the wisdom mind of Guru Rinpoche, which is the intrinsic nature of mind, the universal truth.

13. "A Brief Meditation on Guru Rinpoche, Padmasambhava." This is a short and simple instruction on meditation for people who have no time or energy to go through the practices of Ngöndro. It is a devotional meditation on Guru Rinpoche, visualizing him with symbols of enlightenment, seeing him as the source of blessings, and receiving blessings in the form of lights. The spiritual energies generated through the power of devotional mind, positive perception, open heart, and awakened awareness transform all expressions into prayers and the power of his enlightened wisdom.

The final two articles relate to the conclusion of the meditation practice. They are instructions on postmeditative training concerning how to maintain a spiritual life, cultivate the meditative experiences acquired in meditation, and continue to progress.

14. "Evaluating the Progress of Dharma Practice." This article discusses how to assess our spiritual strength, dedication, and attainments honestly and gauge true progress in our

daily life and meditation. Before we can find our way out of a city, we need to know where we are.

15. "A Prayer Song to the Absolute Lama." This is a translation of a prayer song to the absolute Lama (supreme master), the intrinsic nature of our own mind, the universal truth. Here the intrinsic nature of the mind is personified by one's spiritual master. This is a prayer of devotional expression to open our minds to the Buddha wisdoms, Buddha manifestations, and Buddha actions. It is a meditative prayer that forces the release of conceptual and emotional stress, opens the eyes and heart to the universal nature, and unifies the whole subjective-objective spectrum in the wisdom of Buddhahood and its natural luminosity.

ACKNOWLEDGMENTS

I WOULD LIKE TO express my gratitude to the following friends and institutions, whose kind contributions made it possible to present this book: Harold Talbott for his skill and dedication in editing the entire book; Michael Baldwin and the patrons of Buddhayana, U.S.A., for their generous sponsorship of my projects for the last thirteen years; Lydia Segal for her editorial help with many articles; Jonathan Miller, Tenzin and Christina Parsons, Paul Levine, Philip Richman, and Martha Hamilton for transcribing and editing some of the talks; David Dvore for his consistent computer help; Victor and Ruby Lam for their lovely apartment for living and writing; the *Bulletin* of the Center for the Study of World Religions of Harvard University and *The Tibet Journal* of the Library of Tibetan Works and Archives for their permission to reproduce articles appearing here as chapters 1 and 8; and the Museum of Fine Arts, Boston, Tabor Academy in Marion, Mass., and Mahasiddha Nyingmapa Center in Hawley, Mass., for their permission to publish the talks presented under their auspices. Finally, my thanks are due to Samuel Bercholz and the staff of Shambhala Publications for publishing this book with great care, to Larry Mermelstein for greatly refining the book with his invaluable editing wisdom, and to Kendra Crossen for lending her professional editing skills to the work.

PART ONE

Introduction

∘ I ∘

USING DAILY LIFE AS THE
PRACTICE OF DHARMA

I WOULD LIKE to present you with a few points on using our
day-to-day activities as Dharma⁴ practice and on making
Dharma practice effective.

According to the esoteric scriptures of Buddhism, the nature of mind, or of the undeluded mind, is Buddhahood. But
the face of the true nature of the mind is obscured by ignorance and defiled emotions, just as the sun is covered by
clouds. Because we do not know the ultimate state of the
mind and cling to illusory, dualistic appearances as true, we
wander in the darkness of saṃsāra⁵ and experience sorrows
and dissatisfaction as if we were in a dream. While we are
having a dream we do not understand that it is untrue. Only
when we have awakened do we realize that the events that
took place in the dream were not real. Likewise, when we
realize the ultimate state, we understand that those happenings within saṃsāra were not real and that the various states
of mental experiences were untrue and were just a reflection

This article was published in the *Bulletin of the Center for the Study of World Religions*, Harvard University, Fall 1980.

in the deluded mind. If the defilements of the mind are cleansed, their nature is perceived as free from conceptualization and as enlightenment. The Buddha said:[6]

> Beings are Buddha in their nature,
> But their nature is obscured by adventitious defilements.
> When the defilements are cleansed, they themselves are the
>   very Buddha.

According to the Dharma, in saṃsāra there is nothing but sorrow and dissatisfaction. Sometimes a person is unhappy from experiencing undesirable things. Sometimes a person is unhappy because of fear of losing what one has. Even the highest state of happiness of which a human being is capable is a state of miserable suffering in comparison to the state of ultimate nature. Saṃsāric happiness is like the enjoyment of an intoxicated mind.

To realize the ultimate nature of Buddhahood, free from elaborations, it is necessary first to cleanse the defiled emotions and perfect the accumulation of merit.

In the absolute, there is no distinction between good and bad or virtuous and unvirtuous actions; nor is there a distinction between positive and negative effects. But for the purpose of achieving freedom from the illusory state of saṃsāra and realizing the ultimate nature, it is necessary to undertake various meritorious practices as a skillful means for cleansing the delusions of the mind.

I am not going to go into the profound philosophical approaches to the absolute truth taught in Buddhism; but I would like to mention some practical aspects to be used in our day-to-day activities and experiences, so that whatever we do, we can transmute those actions into practice.

First, it is necessary to recognize the major defiled emotions, the negative forces that obscure the face of the ultimate nature. Generally, they are classified into three categories, known as the three poisons: ignorance, hatred, and desire. The root of defiled emotions is ignorance. Ignorance is an aspect of the deluded mind—the mind's not knowing the true face of the ultimate nature, but grasping at the illusory appearances of self and objects as dual, real, and valid.

Because a person accepts the subject and object as true and clings to them, there arises attachment to desirable objects and hatred of undesirable ones. By grasping objects that are conceived as real and developing defiled thoughts of liking or dislike for them, the process of karmic[7] forces is built up, and the saṃsāric cycle is set in motion.

What we need at the beginning of our practice, to set ourselves upon the path of liberation from this illusory saṃsāra, is to be mindful—to watch the mind in order to protect it from falling into the defiled emotions and to devote ourselves to meritorious practices.

When a thought of hatred or dislike arises in us toward objects or people, including our enemies, we should reflect that our enemies have been our dearest friends and relatives during our countless past lives, and we should develop compassion for them as ignorant, deluded, and unhappy beings. Anger toward others will produce the worst evil karma, and evil karma is the cause of suffering. If we get angry with someone, we defeat ourselves and afflict ourselves with a grave, negative result in future lives. If, instead, we practice patience when we encounter undesirable elements of experience, we will engage in one of the most effective Dharma practices. The great Bodhisattva[8] and scholar Shāntideva said:[9]

> There is no more harmful enemy than anger;
> There is no more profound austerity than patience.

When the thoughts of desire arise in us, we should also ponder the unworthiness, impermanence, and unreliable nature of the objects of the desire.

When ignorant thoughts arise, that is, when we do not have insight into the absolute nature, we should investigate the meaning of the two truths: the relative and the absolute truth—especially the absolute truth—by means of study, pondering, and meditation.

In relative truth, all phenomenal appearances are conventionally true: that is to say, they are true in the same way that a dream, an illusion, or a reflection is true. They appear and function through the process of interdependent causation devised by the deluded mind. In absolute truth, all phenomena are void, free from conceptualization and elaboration.

There are many kinds of practices that directly or indirectly lead to the same goal of the realization and attainment of the absolute state of Buddhahood. These practices are classified according to two major aspects: the aspect of skillful means and the aspect of wisdom. These two aspects are like the two wings on which a bird flies to reach its goal. Skillful means is an important support practice, which leads to the attainment of the absolute nature. In the aspect of wisdom, the practice is to realize directly that all phenomena appear in the relative state as a dream, and that in their absolute nature they are empty.

At the beginning, one needs to practice skillful means, such as performing devotional practices, giving charity to the poor, observing discipline, being patient, rejoicing in others' well-being, and making offerings. But the most important thing is to develop a compassionate, gentle, and right attitude to others, without having any rigidity or selfishness. That is the essence of the practice of the Mahāyāna tradition.

The three major categories of Buddhism have been described as follows:

> The characteristic of the Common Vehicle (Hīnayāna) is to develop a desire to renounce saṃsāra for one's own sake.
>
> The characteristic of the Great Vehicle (Mahāyāna) is to develop beneficial thoughts toward all beings.
>
> The characteristic of the Esoteric Vehicle (Vajrayāna) is to purify the perceptions and to perceive the world and its beings as the pure land and its deities, in order to attain the absolute nature.

According to Buddhist teaching, the mind is the main factor in all happenings or occurrences. A deluded mind is the cause of experiencing all saṃsāric tastes, that is, the qualities of experience in saṃsāra. Realization of the true nature of the mind is the attainment of absolute nature, Buddhahood. The accumulation of merit and the development of right attitudes are the main aspects of the practice. Physical practices, which are practices using the body and speech, are a support for sustaining the right attitude of mind. Kunkhyen Jigme Lingpa said:[10]

> If the root (of a tree) is medicine, then the fruit will be medicinal.

If the root is poison, then there will be no question about
the fruit.
Meritorious and unmeritorious qualities follow upon one's
attitude;
But they are not derived from the reflection-like physical
practices in themselves.

Thus, whatever we do, as long as we do it with beneficial
thoughts for others and without any selfish attitude, will become a perfect practice. Defiled emotions will be spontaneously reduced. Even if a physical action appears to be unmeritorious, it will be transformed into a meritorious practice,
depending on our intention, just as a few drops of milk make
a cup of tea white. Thus, a person is incapable of performing
unmeritorious action as long as he has a compassionate and
right attitude. It is, therefore, important for anyone who
wishes to be a Dharma practitioner to generate a compassionate or beneficial thought for transforming daily activities into
Dharma practice.

For instance, when we take a meal, if we enjoy it with just
the thought of satisfying ourselves, it will be an unmeritorious action. If, however, we visualize ourselves as divinities
and take the food as an offering, or at least if we enjoy the
food with the intention that we are taking it to protect our
lives in order to serve others and practice Dharma, it is a
meritorious practice. In the same way, we can do whatever
work we do by combining it with Dharma practice. Otherwise, even if we do retreat practice for years in solitude, reciting mantras and visualizing deities, if it is done for the sake
of fame or happiness for ourselves it will not become a pure
Dharma practice.

The beneficial thought for all beings, without partiality and expectations, is called the Enlightened Attitude. The activities generated by enlightened thought are the Enlightened Action. These are the two aspects of the practice of Bodhisattvas. Shāntideva said:[11]

> If Enlightened Attitude has developed, from that very
>   moment
> Those beings suffering in the prison of saṃsāra will be
>   known as the Children of the Buddhas (Bodhisattvas).

Another important element in Dharma practice is confidence. The achievement of results through Dharma practice depends upon confidence—confidence in the teacher, confidence in the teaching, and confidence in ourselves. If we are lacking in confidence, then even if we practice day and night, our practice may produce merits, but it will hardly attain any great results. Until we reach a high stage of attainment, in which there is no effect of worldly happenings or events upon us and no difference between happiness and suffering, we should maintain confidence—which is faith—as the foundation of the practice. Without confidence, no spiritual attainment is possible. The Buddha said:[12]

> In people who have no confidence,
> The Dharma will produce no result,
> Just as a burnt seed
> Will never produce a green shoot.

The point of this is that whatever we do, we should do it with a beneficial thought for all beings. Thereby all our daily activities will become Dharma practice. And we should develop a strong confidence in our practice, in our teacher, and in ourselves, so that the practice of Dharma will be effective.

o 2 o

OPENING THE HEART
WITH COMPASSION

I N THIS CHAPTER I will be talking about compassion and the meditation on compassion. But before going into compassion, I would like to mention a couple of important points, which will make it easy for us to understand what compassion is, how it can be developed, and how it can be helpful.

In Buddhism, the mind is the main focus—the source of all happiness and unhappiness, and the key to enlightenment. Of course it is this emphasis on the mind that causes some to say, "Buddhists are selfish; they live in solitude and meditate alone only to take care of their own minds and achieve personal satisfaction. They don't go out and work in the streets for people who need their service," and so forth.

However, as you know, in Buddhism generally and especially in Mahāyāna Buddhism, the most important part of practice is to develop what we call Bodhichitta, the mind of enlightenment. That is an attitude of taking responsibility

A transcription of a talk given in Marion, Mass., on December 29, 1992.

for helping others, serving others, and putting that into action without any selfish motivation. That is the most important point in Buddhism. Of course, whether a Buddhist is actually pursuing such a life or not is an issue for that individual. But what Buddhism or Buddha'a teachings teach us is that we should dedicate our entire life, our whole attitude, and our every action only to serve others, to open our mind and body to others, the whole universe. When we open ourselves to others we are also opening ourselves and serving ourselves. Thus this attitude of taking responsibility to serve others fulfills a dual purpose.

How do we serve others? The goal is to serve others, but how do we start? We have to start with ourselves. If I am going to serve you, I have to start with myself, by improving my attitude and actions to make myself a good servant for you, to make myself a proper tool to serve you. Otherwise, even if I try to serve you, I will not be able to do so properly. We have to improve ourselves first.

We can improve ourselves only if we can discipline our minds. If my mind is cruel, whatever I say will be words of harshness and whatever I do will be harmful to others and to myself, directly or indirectly. But if I have compassion, gentleness, and wisdom in my mind and heart, then whatever I say will be words of peace, love, and joy, and whatever I do will serve and benefit others. So, in order to serve others, we have to start with ourselves, and to improve ourselves we have to start with the mind, by disciplining it and developing Bodhichitta. And that is the essence of the Buddhist approach.

The next question is, "What is mind?" There are two aspects to the mind: enlightened mind and conceptual mind.

ENLIGHTENED MIND

Enlightened mind, or Buddha nature, is the true nature of every being. Buddhists believe that all beings, not only humans, but also animals, including the tiniest insect, possess enlightened mind. The true nature of the mind is enlightened, and it is peaceful and clear. The clear and peaceful nature of the mind can be understood both through our own daily lives and through Buddhist wisdom.

All of us can probably agree that if the mind is not disturbed by external events, emotional struggles, or conceptual rigidities, it becomes peaceful. The more peaceful our mind becomes, the clearer it gets. It is like water, which is peaceful and clear if it is not polluted or stirred. It is like the sky, which is pure and clear, if it is not polluted or covered by clouds. In the same way, when the mind is not disturbed by our rushing life and turbulent emotions, it is peaceful. The more peaceful it becomes, the more it gains in wisdom and clarity.

Emotions disturb not only our peace, but also the clarity of our minds. That is why we often hear people complain, "I was so angry I couldn't figure out anything," or "I was so upset, I couldn't understand anything; I couldn't see anything." When overwhelmed by emotions or the speed of our busy lives, the mind becomes totally blind or blank, without much wisdom or ability.

Our mind's natural state is peaceful and clear, and bringing it back toward this state is not only possible but important for improving our lives. Buddhism goes even beyond this. Buddhists believe that the true nature of the mind, the actual mind itself, is enlightened. Enlightened mind is open, one, and omniscient.

Regarding the enlightened mind being open, when the enlightened mind sees things, it does not conceptualize in a dualistic manner. It sees everything as one in the natural awareness wisdom itself, like reflections appearing in a mirror.[13] If you do not use dualistic concepts, then you are totally open to the whole universe, like space, which is totally open, without any boundaries or restrictions. We, however, are used to using dualistic concepts. When we see a table, we think, "That is a table," and we see it there as an object. As we think of the table as an object, we position our mind as a subject, and duality is thus established. Duality is followed by thoughts of discrimination—"This is a good table, a bad table, etc."—and from there we build up a rigid world of walls and fences. By contrast, the enlightened mind sees things in a total openness, without any condition.

If there is total openness, there cannot be any boundaries, since there are no divisions of subject and object. Then, of course, everything is one, nondual. If everything is one, there cannot be any conflicts or clashes, because conflicts and clashes exist only if there are two or more positions.

Now you must be thinking, "That means the enlightened mind is a sort of sleeping or blank state, because it does not even see objects." No. On the contrary, the enlightened mind is omniscient. The enlightened mind sees everything. Not only everything, but everything simultaneously. That is the quality of Buddha mind.

In one sense the enlightened mind is so foreign to us it can be hard even to think about it. However, we can get an inkling of it through stories of "near death experiences," which I always love to quote. Of course some of these experiences can simply be hallucinations or induced by drugs. Yet on the whole, there are some amazing things revealed in these experiences.

Even people who have not necessarily realized the enlightened mind have some spiritual or inner experience during the process of death, before coming back to life. According to what I have read in books and heard told, many people experienced traveling through a tunnel and meeting light at the other end. And as soon as they are touched by the light, they feel amazing bliss and peace. But the most amazing thing that they say is that bliss and peace are the light, and the light is bliss and peace. What they are feeling is light, and they are inseparable from the light. So these people are having an experience that is not channeled through the usual dualistic mind. Light is not just a tool to bring them peace. Light is the peace and they are the light, and so the subject, object, and the experience all are one.

Another man tells a story that for a few minutes after he died he saw everything that had happened in his life, from his birth till his death. But he did not simply see one event after another—he saw his entire life all at once. He was not really seeing with his eyes or knowing with his mind, but was just aware of everything vividly.

So, the enlightened mind is not really so foreign. We can all experience it when we realize the truth, or at some important juncture of life. But if you are not a meditator, you may not recognize the enlightened mind when you experience it and will be distracted again by the emotional and conceptual system of the world.

CONCEPTUAL MIND

Conceptual mind is what happens when enlightened mind has been obscured by conceptual and emotional coverings. It is the aspect of mind that experiences things through dualistic concepts, grasping at self, discriminative thoughts, emotions, and experiences of suffering.

When an object—for example, a table—appears before us, we immediately register, "This is a table." In so doing, we conceive of the table as an object, and our mind automatically becomes the subject, and so duality (*gNyis 'Dzin*) is established.

At the very moment dualistic thinking sets in, we "grasp at self" (*bDag 'Dzin*), which means that we grasp at the object as a truly existing entity. In Buddhism, this mental grasping is not just grasping at one's ego or "personhood" (*Gang Zag*), the I, me, or my, but also grasping at "phenomenal existents" (Tib. *Ch'os,* Skt. *dharma*), such as trees, table, friend, or Jack.

DISCRIMINATION

This mental grasping is then followed by thoughts of discrimination—thoughts that the table is bad, ugly, and so on.

Once we have labeled the object in this way, all kinds of emotions (Tib. *Nyon Mongs Pa,* Skt. *klesha*), such as craving or hatred, ensue. We think, "I must have this wonderful table," or "I hate having this table. It is so ugly." Our thoughts and feelings of attachment or craving for the things we have designated as nice and our hatred for the things we have designated as ugly are emotions. Emotions generate and strengthen our dualistic concepts, grasping at self, and our discriminative thinking.

The more we revolve in the cycle of conceptual mind, the stronger our pattern of dualistic thinking becomes, the tighter the grip of our grasping at self, the more pervasive our discriminative thinking, and the more overwhelming our emotions. The result is pain and excitement, the ups and downs of mundane life. The wheel of this mundane life then gains its own momentum, turning without any break. And this is where we are today. All of us ordinary beings are in this cycle of conceptual mind with its dualistic thinking, discriminative mind, emotional struggles, and pain and excitement. This is what our life is.

In my forthcoming book, *Healing Power of Mind*, there is a story illustrating this. When I was little, maybe six or seven years old, we went for a picnic. Since we hardly ever went out of the monastery, this outing was a very rare opportunity. We went for a couple of days to some very beautiful, open green fields in Tibet. In the midst of the high mountains, there was a wide, open green field. The whole field was covered with colorful flowers. I was barefoot, running around here and there, enjoying the touch of the green grass, the view, and the beautiful atmosphere.

Suddenly an excruciating pain shot through my foot. I fell down to the ground, and my entire body rolled up in a ball of pain. It seemed the whole world had become just pain. I did not know what had happened. Eventually a grown-up came over, examined me, and opened my toes. I had caught a bee between them. As the bee started stinging me, my toes tightened up. The more my toes tightened, the more the bee stung me, and the more I was stung, the tighter my toes got. And so it went, on and on. But as soon as my toes were opened and the bee was freed, the pain, at least the excruciating pain, subsided.

In the same way, according to Buddhism, it is our grasping at self, meaning our mental grasping at I, my, me, the table, you, my enemy, and so on as truly existing entities, which is at the root of suffering. As our mind gets tighter and tighter, we feel increasing pain or excitement. But as our mind gets looser and more relaxed, the more peaceful, calm, and clear we become. And so, as we were saying before, the mind is the key, and the most important thing for us is to improve, heal, and enlighten it.

Appearances arise before us whether we are a Buddha or an ordinary person. However, a Buddha can see everything simultaneously without limits, while an ordinary person's view is restricted and distorted and focuses on one thing at a time. A Buddha sees with what is called the two wisdoms: the wisdom of seeing appearance as they are and as they appear. The perception of ordinary people, in contrast, is limited, rigid, and delusory. The root of the difference between a Buddha and ourselves lies in the way we perceive things—whether forms, sounds, feelings, or ideas. Whenever we see anything, we grasp it as if it had a self, a truly existing entity. By so doing, we begin the division of "I" as subject and the appearing "thing" as object. This leads to our intellectual concept of discriminating between things as good or bad. This, in turn, generates the heated emotional afflictions, the flames of so-called experiences of pain and excitement.

A Buddha sees everything simultaneously, in total oneness and openness, without grasping at the self of appearing phenomena. There is hence no division into subject and object, no discriminative mind, no emotional affliction, and no experience of pain or excitement.

The point at which we either fall into saṃsāra or are liberated into the enlightened state is when we grasp or do not grasp at the appearing phenomena as if they had a self. This point is where the switch is turned on or off. It is the source and cause of all the suffering. As Shāntideva says:[14]

> All the violence, fear, and suffering
> That exists in the world
> Comes from grasping at self.
> Then what is the use of this awesome demon for us?
> If we will not let go of the self,
> We will not be able to put an end to our sufferings,
> Just as if we do not let go of fire with our hands,
> We cannot avoid being burned.

Therefore, the main goal of meditative training is to realize and perfect the realization of Buddhahood, free from intellectual obscurations rooted in grasping at self and the emotional obscurations of hatred, attachment, and confusion. This realization will only come through methods that reduce and cleanse emotional afflictions and intellectual concepts of duality through meditative training and meritorious deeds, such as of compassion.

The ultimate goal of meditation is freedom from grasping at appearances, but not by blocking the appearances themselves. As the great ancient Indian adept Tilopa said:

> O son, appearances are not the problem, but grasping at them is.
> O Nāropa, cut off the grasping.

The goal of meditation is not merely to remain without emotions and thoughts, but to realize the true nature, the Buddha mind, which is total freedom from grasping at self and the full attainment of ultimate peace, openness, oneness, and omniscience.

Once, Saraha,[15] the greatest Buddhist adept of ancient India, was pursuing esoteric trainings with his consort in solitude. One day he asked his consort to prepare a radish dish for him. However, when she came to serve it to him, he had gone into meditative absorption where he remained for twelve years. When he finally came out of his meditation, he immediately asked his consort, "Where is my radish dish?" Some time later, Saraha told his consort that he wished to go to the mountains to meditate. His consort rebuffed him, "Physical isolation is not real solitude. The supreme solitude is freedom from (grasping at) characters (or objective images) and mental concepts." She observed, "Although you were in absorption for twelve years, you could not cut off the subtle character of the radish dish from your mind. So what is the benefit of going to the mountains?" According to her clarifications, Saraha meditated not merely on the absence of concepts, but on the realization of the absolute truth (gNyug Ma'i Don), and they both became great adepts.

Stages of Progress

How do we improve or heal our conceptual and emotional mind? Generally it is important to know that there are three stages through which to proceed according to Buddhist wisdom. They are negative, positive, and perfection stages.

For the first of these, if we have a lot of rigid, dualistic concepts, experience strong emotions, and often feel excruciating pain and sorrow, then our life is in the negative cycle of mundane life. So now what should we do? We should move from the negative stage of mundane life to a positive spiritual life, and then from a positive stage to the stage of perfection, the realization of the enlightened mind.

The stage we are at now, whether we accept it or not, is mostly negative. Again, this may prompt some people to say, "Buddhists are pessimistic." But this view is not pessimistic. It is realistic. Many of us do feel pain and sorrow. And even when we fell that life is wonderful and we are happy, it does not last. This feeling often vanishes after a few days, and we do not know what will happen to us after that. Today we might be healthy, but we do not know about tomorrow. Today we are alive, but we have no control over what happens to us tomorrow. Today we may be rich, but tomorrow we may lose everything.

So nothing is certain; everything is changing, hanging by a thin string. Anything that is changing, which has an impermanent character, is negative, unreliable, and not positive or perfect. So we have to progress toward a positive life. Then some time in the future perhaps we can move to perfection.

Any time we develop a concept, attitude, perception, or feeling—it does not matter if it is conceptual or emotional—

that loosens the force and tightness of duality, the grip of grasping at self, emotions, and experiences, that is a positive view and a positive experience. Practices of generosity, discipline, meditation on compassion, devotion, contemplation, and so on will enhance this positive state of mind. We have to use positive thinking and positive emotions to improve our lives and slowly move toward perfection.

The realization of the enlightened mind, Buddhahood, which is total openness, oneness, and omniscience, is the perfection. The perfection stage is beyond positive thinking and positive feeling. However, this should not necessarily be today's goal, but the goal of the future. Today we should try to move from the negative stage to the positive stage.

COMPASSION

What trainings does Buddhism offer to help us go from negative to positive and then to perfection? Of course, all the numerous Buddhist meditation practices are for this purpose. But today we are talking about compassion, so we will take compassion as the means of undoing the cycle of conceptual mind.

Compassion has three aspects. This is not necessarily a strict textual interpretation, but I am trying to arrange it so that it will be easy for us to comprehend. First there is positive compassion, which is limited, emotional, and conceptual, but a positive approach. Second is universal compassion, which although still conceptual, is broader than positive compassion because it is universal. This is the most powerful approach to compassion offered by the conceptual mind.

Lastly is Buddha compassion, the omnipresence or all-pervasive power (*Thugs rJe Kun Khyab*) possessed by the Buddha. This is the perfection of compassion.

To begin, we meditate on positive compassion. To develop it we think one-pointedly about someone who is suffering, and think about his or her feelings of pain over and over again. We feel the person's suffering by putting ourselves in his or her place. As a result, from the depth of the heart, an unconditioned compassion develops, together with a sense of determination of taking the responsibility of alleviating this person's suffering and bringing happiness and enlightenment. This caring and determined attitude should be put into practice through the six perfections (Tib. *Phar Phyin,* Skt. *pāramitā*) such as generosity and tolerance. This compassion is dualistic and conceptual and is driven by emotions, but it is a positive attitude and results in positive actions of trying to do the best we can for others.

Then what happens? Of course you all agree that it is a wonderful thing to care for others. But there is more to it than that. This creates good karma, merit, and benefits for others and ourselves. Also, when we reach out emotionally, we break and crush the barriers of our mental and emotional defenses and the distinctions between me and you, between my friend and my enemy, which divide me from you, us from others, subject from object.

Here, we are not grasping at the labels of I, my friend, and so forth. Our totally open, caring, and loving minds, with our full positive emotional strength, burst out to reach suffering people. We are reaching out from the depth of the heart to the people who are suffering, and then to all without any limits. Besides breaking our mental shells and reaching out without discrimination, this outpouring emotional force of compassion stirs up and releases all the emotional and conceptual garbage and toxins we have been preserving.

Although this kind of compassion is emotional and conceptual, it is positive. And as we are full of concepts and emotions, we should use them to our best advantage to propel us along the positive path. If we could develop such compassion in our minds, then whatever we do will become an action of compassion and a source of happiness for others and ourselves.

Totally opening our minds to the whole universe in compassion is universal compassion. In this, we are not necessarily focusing on just one person or a few people who are suffering, but on all—the entire universe. In fact, all beings are suffering on the roller-coaster cycle of change. Even when we feel happy and that our life is perfect, it will change. So as long as we are in this changing cycle we are in a domain of suffering.

However, we do not have to be depressed about this, since we can improve our future by improving our minds through developing compassion. As mentioned in positive compassion, we should think over and over again about and feel the suffering of the whole universe in order to develop a strong compassion that reaches out to all and takes responsibility for leading all to happiness and enlightenment, without limits or distinctions. Psychologically, emotionally, and physiologically, this opens and expands our minds and energy to others and to ourselves, to the whole universe. It helps us to go beyond the more narrow compassion pinpointed on ourselves, our family, our children, or a particular being in distress. If we can thoroughly open up our minds without any boundaries, limits, or discrimination to the infinite universe, then that is the best compassion and best spiritual training possible with the conceptual and emotional mind. Our minds, energies, and actions will manifest benefits to all, regardless of whether they are so-called friends or enemies, or whether they are outwardly suffering or happy.

The total perfection of compassion is the compassion of the Buddha. Buddha compassion is the aspect of omnipresence or the all-pervading power of Buddhahood. If we realize and perfect the enlightened mind, we will become the Buddha, and the all-pervading power will be our own Buddha compassion. So the all-pervading power of the enlightened mind and of the Buddha is the Buddha compassion.

But, again, this is the final goal, not our immediate goal. Our immediate aim is to generate positive compassion, an emotional and conceptual compassion toward suffering people. We have to start with one suffering person, then extend it to more and more beings and develop a commitment, a determination, from the depth of the heart, "I am going to take the responsibility of helping this person." We should then not just stop with positive thoughts, but should also carry them out with positive deeds.

MEDITATION ON COMPASSION

We can meditate on compassion by thinking about the story of a suffering person—visualizing the image and feeling the suffering. This can be followed by a meditation on compassion itself and on the healing lights of the Buddha of Compassion, Avalokiteshvara, to heal the suffering. Before we begin the meditation, there are three important point to explain.

First is the generation of a strong compassion from the depth of the heart for those who are suffering, so that tears flow from our eyes, hair stands up on our bodies, and if we are sitting we feel we have to stand up and if we are standing we feel we need to sit down. Thinking of and feeling the suffering are the most powerful keys to invoke compassion in us.

Here, some might think, "This is too emotional and painful for me. I cannot even imagine having such a feeling." In the first instant of meditation, we may generate emotions of sadness. But great benefits will follow. This meditation forces us to realize what our mundane life is made of—suffering. It inspires us to get ourselves out of this cycle of misery and to rescue others from it. As we discussed before, this kind of positive conceptual and emotional compassion opens up our rigid and narrow mentalities by breaking our mental and emotional limitations and restrictions. It exposes and releases the garbage we have been protecting within us.

Second is the clear visualization of a particular suffering person and having strong thoughts and feelings about the experiences that this suffering person is going through. We put ourselves in that person's place and feel the pain and fear. Visualizing a particular image and thinking about a true tragedy in detail awakens vivid, real, solid, and powerful feelings of suffering and the suffering nature in us, and that is the key to developing compassion.

Here, some might feel, "Why don't you leave this poor suffering person alone?" According to Buddhist wisdom, if someone causes others to generate meritorious thoughts or perform virtuous actions, that person will earn merit. Also, in the meditation, we do not just think about the suffering of this person, but we bring healing blessings from the Buddha of Compassion and share them with that person for healing. So, we are not simply using a suffering person as a means of achieving happiness and enlightenment for ourselves, but we benefit that person and others.

Third is to visualize the Buddha of Compassion, to develop trust and devotion in him, to pray to him, and to bring his blessing lights that pacify our own sufferings, as well as those of others and of the whole universe.

Some might think that praying to the Buddha of Compassion is idol-worship or relying on external forces. However, Buddhism is not in favor of idol-worship. It believes that the only source of real spiritual attainment is our own mind. Only our own mind is the ultimate source of power, as it possesses the enlightened mind, which is the Buddha. However, Buddhists do use images, among other things, as the source of spiritual teachings, inspiration, and support. This is called skillful means. If we see something as positive and use it in a positive manner, positive results will ensue. When the image used has a spiritual significance, it can greatly help us to generate spiritual benefits. Notwithstanding this, we ultimately receive benefits because of our own mind, our mental attitude and view, not because of the external phenomena.

Buddha himself said that he could only show us the path to Buddhahood, a path he completed. But actually walking that path is totally up to the people, the individual beings. Buddha said:

> I have shown you the path for liberation.
> Now the liberation is up to you to attain.

o 3 o

A SPIRITUAL JOURNEY IN
A TURBULENT LIFE

I WOULD LIKE TO SHARE some of the stories of my own life, because for me it was not only a life of training in how to survive in the darkest situations, but also in how to make the best out of it.

I was born into a nomad family in a tent in the wild, grassy tablelands of Eastern Tibet, among the world's highest mountains. The land was covered with snow for almost eight months of the year. My family belonged to a tribal group that lived in tents with domestic animals, such as yaks, horses, and sheep. Three or four times each year we used to move our camps to different valleys, so that there would be enough fresh grass for the animals to live on.

Then, at the age of five, the first big change in my life took place. I was recognized as a reincarnation or rebirth of a deceased celebrated religious teacher of Dodrupchen monastery, an important monastery in Eastern Tibet. Even though my parents were sad to give me up, since I was their

---

A talk given at Tabor Academy, Marion, Mass., on May 24, 1990.

only child, they offered me to the monastery for good, without hesitation. My parents were proud and privileged because their child had become one of the respected persons in their society overnight.

After I arrived at the monastery, I only visited my parents once every two years for a stay of not more than a week at a time. Suddenly my life had changed. I did not have a so-called normal childhood of playing with other children. Instead, dignified tutors took care of me and served me with respect, as I had been recognized as their teacher's reincarnation. From dawn till dusk, the cycle of time was filled with learning, saying prayers, or contemplation. Life was filled with inner joy and peace, as my tutors were very wise, compassionate, understanding, peaceful, and practical people. They were not strict, rigid-minded disciplinarian monks, as you might imagine, but gentle, humble, and caring human beings, full of life and smiles. After some time I did not feel the urge to play or run around without purpose, and did not even feel the need to look around; I could sit still in peace for hours.

In the monastery I was taught the importance of realizing and maintaining the pure nature of the mind, a spiritual center of wisdom, peace, joy, compassion, and energy within oneself. Buddhists believe that the identity of a being is the mind and that mind in its true nature is pure, peaceful, and perfect. As we know, when our mind remains free from the pressure of external situations and emotions, it becomes more peaceful, open, wise, and spacious.

Even today, after three decades, I feel the peaceful experiences of my monastic life in my heart; and my ears ring with the echoes of the kind, soothing words of the most wise and compassionate monks of my childhood monastery. They have always been the main source of guidance and energy in my life's struggle through confusions and weaknesses.

Until the age of eighteen, I never saw an airplane or an automobile. A wristwatch might have been the most sophisticated product of modern technology that I had ever seen.

Then, at the age of eighteen, because of the most unfortunate political change to take place in Tibet, we had to flee over a thousand miles across the country, escaping into India. When we got to India, I started twenty-two years of a refugee life. Not only did I find myself in a foreign country, but everything was totally new to me, including the identity of myself, which was now that of a refugee, a person who is looking for shelter to survive. I could not mingle with people as I could not speak a word of their languages, and I had no grasp of the new culture. Almost all of the nearly one hundred thousand Tibetan refugees in India got sick, and many died because of the change of food, weather, water, or altitude. The personal experiences, images, stories, and fears about the hellish lives of our loved ones who were left behind, trapped in Tibet, kept haunting and torturing all of us, day and night. For many refugees, life became intolerable, and some were forced even to choose the extreme means to end it.

For us there was only one solution and consolation, and that was to try not to dwell in our worrying, but to remember the words of the great Buddhist writer, Shāntideva, who said:

> If you can solve the problem,
> Then what is the need of worrying?
> If you cannot solve it,
> Then what is the use of worrying?[16]

My attempt was to try to live in the spiritual sanctuary, the peaceful center within myself, which I was taught to cultivate during my monastic life, and to try to stabilize my shaky life by seeing and appreciating whatever positive aspect and goal of life was left in front of me. So, finding spiritual peace in myself as the shelter and using positive attitudes as the means of communication were the two factors that enabled me to handle my life more easily at a most difficult juncture.

Then about ten years ago, I moved to the United States, the land of freedom. And now I live here in Cambridge.

In 1984, after a twenty-seven-year absence, I was able to visit my homeland, Tibet. It was a time of joy to see the few survivors among my old friends and relatives, and a time of sadness to learn that most of my loved ones, whose faces I had been cherishing for years, as well as my respected teachers, whose words were the source of my healing, had perished in the hellish life of the previous two decades there. The monastery, the learning institution of my memory, had disappeared into thin air. Nothing was left but the broken walls of the monastic buildings and the broken hearts of people, which were reflecting each other. However, just about the time of my visit, step by step, the system was starting to allow people to reestablish their traditional family and religious lives and to rebuild the monasteries.

I saw that many of the Tibetans who were victims of imprisonment and torture were friendly with the officers who had victimized them. And one victim told me, "What happened to us wasn't the fault of those individual officers. All of us equally were victims of the system, the negative karma.

It is not fair to blame a few of them for what they had to do." It reminded me of the lines of Shāntideva:

> Even if I am unable to develop compassion
> For people who are forced to harm me,
> Because of their emotional afflictions of ignorance and
> anger,
> The last thing I should do is to become angry with them.[17]

Generally, it is hard to find the peaceful center that is in us, but if we could recognize and appreciate the positive circumstances of our lives, then a spirit of peace and strength will arise in us.

For me, as much as I enjoy the Western modern life, that much I appreciate the earthy and humble but spiritual life of my childhood, and that actually keeps me standing on my own feet throughout the journey of my life. As much as I feel the joy of my spiritual life, that much I appreciate the freedom, wisdom, compassion, and generosity based on the Judaic-Christian values of Western life, which have enriched and ensured my spiritual values.

I am not a wise person from whom you can hear any wisdom, but I am a person who went through a lot of experiences in a short time span, and I do hope that my story may have produced in you, for a moment, a sigh of relief over your own fortunate lives in this land of freedom and plenty. That is an experience of peace and appreciation, and that is the first step of a spiritual journey. Keep it alive.

o 4 o

BUDDHIST ARTIFACTS AS THE SUPPORT OF SPIRITUAL REALIZATION

I WOULD LIKE TO SAY a few words abut the significance of Buddhist art in Tibet. As you might know, in Tibetan art most of the artifacts are representations of Buddhist teachings. Tibetans regard them as objects of homage and sources of inspiration and for making merit, but not as materials to decorate their homes. For Tibetans, the sacredness of the religious objects is so profound that when I was in my teens, my teacher used to tell us, "When you are examining or looking at an image, you are not supposed to think or say, 'this is a good image or this is a bad image,' but you are supposed to think or say, 'the artist was skilled or not skilled,' otherwise you are grading a sacred object as if it were an ordinary object." Their respect for and devotion to religious representations are not just a cultural or intellectual response, but a

A talk given for the Tibetan Art Evening at the Museum of Fine Arts, Boston, on March 1, 1990.

deep-rooted feeling and a spontaneous expression from the heart.

As Buddhism is the heart of Tibetan life, most Tibetan artifacts are representations of Buddhist teachings. That is why religious objects have an unique role and place in Tibetan society. So I would like to talk about how the Buddhist devotees in Tibet use religious objects as tools of their spiritual training and what is the philosophical view behind them.

First, philosophically, the most important point to understand is that Tibetan Buddhists are not idol-worshippers. We do not worship religious artifacts expecting that we will receive attainments from an image of bronze and so on. But we use them as a tool or support to create an inspiration toward Dharma and to generate virtuous experiences, such as devotion, peace, compassion, contemplation, and wisdom. If the religious object becomes a tool to generate virtuous thoughts in our hearts, then that artifact turns out to be a very powerful and beneficial spiritual support for our lives. However, it is not because of the object, but because of our own positive perceptions and devotional feelings, inspired by seeing and being with the religious object. So we are using the object as a key, but the main source of blessing lies within our own minds.

Second, as far as how to use the objects as spiritual supports is concerned, we do not see a religious artifact, such as an image of the Buddha, as just a piece of art. We see or practice seeing it as a living Buddha, in order to generate inspiration, devotion, and pure perception in ourselves. We pay respect to it in order to generate humility. We make offerings to it to develop generosity. We contemplate on it to bring peace and tranquility. And we receive blessings from it, as if from a living Buddha, to make our spiritual experiences progress. Thereby, through the support of the blessed objects, we perfect the two accumulations: the accumulation of merit and the accumulation of wisdom.

We see the image of the Buddha as the true Buddha endowed with all the Buddha qualities, such as compassion for all sentient beings, like that of a mother for her only child, the wisdom of knowing all the happenings and needs of beings simultaneously, as well as the ultimate truth, and the power of pacifying the sufferings of the world and fulfilling all our wishes.

Also, every detail of the artifacts has its own unique significance. Each symbolizes various aspects of Buddha qualities and teaches the meaning of the Dharma. Consider, as an example, a thangka of Avalokiteshvara, the Buddha of Compassion, and I will explain the significance of the details.

His crystal-white complexion signifies that he is pure, unstained by emotional and intellectual defilements.

His sitting firmly in the lotus posture signifies that he dwells in the ultimate nature without changes.

His youthful appearance signifies that he has gone beyond the suffering of aging and decaying.

His loving and unblinking doelike eyes signify that he is watching all the time, without ever ceasing, for all sentient beings to fulfill their needs.

His ever-smiling and peaceful face signifies that he is enjoying the ultimate peace and joy in which suffering is unknown.

His five silken vestments and eight jewel ornaments of the

Sambhogakāya signify that he is in the form of the Sambhogakāya, the subtle form of the two form bodies of the
Buddha.

The folding of his two palms at his heart signifies that he
has united or perfected saṃsāra and nirvāṇa as one in the
ultimate nature.

The wish-fulfilling jewel in his first two hands signifies his
skillful means, which fulfills the wishes of all sentient beings.

The white lotus in his second left hand signifies his wisdom, which is unstained by any intellectual and emotional
defilements, even if his manifestations appear in various
realms, just as a lotus is clean even though it grows in the
mud. It also symbolizes that he belongs to the lotus family
from among the five Buddha families.

The crystal rosary in his right left hand signifies his Buddha activities, which serve sentient beings endlessly, as the
rosary rotates with no end.

If you are trained in seeing and concentrating on the virtuous significance of spiritual objects, you will go through different stages of spiritual appreciation. First, your spiritual
experiences, whatever you have had or are having, will be re-
kindled just by seeing or being in the presence of spiritual
objects. Then, there will come a time when there is no more
need of religious representations to rely on, and every appearance of the universe will become a source of spiritual teaching, inspiration, strength, and experience.

In Tibet the richest religious artifacts are preserved in the
temples of the monasteries, with elaborate offerings and constant prayers and ceremonies. Also, in almost every village
you will find a temple filled with images and scriptures, which

serve as the object of devotion and prayers for the local popu-
lation. Then, in every home, if they have the means, people
reserve a room as a shrine, filled with religious representations. And even in the homes of the poorest families, their
utmost efforts and dreams will be to have a little shrine table
with some religious representations and to arrange at least
some water bowls and a butter lamp as an offering before the
altar, as their spiritual exercise in generosity, devotion, and
meditation.

Through the support of spiritual objects, if the spiritual
experience of peace and enlightenment is born in us, then
wherever we live, our surroundings become a temple of spiritual beauty and joy.

○ 5 ○

TIBETAN BUDDHIST
THANGKAS AND THEIR
RELIGIOUS SIGNIFICANCE

I N COMMON BUDDHISM and especially in tantric (or esoteric) Buddhism, the essential training is to see and experience all phenomena as pure lands, Buddha bodies, teachings,
and enlightened thoughts. If we perfect such training, there
will come a time when the whole universe will arise as the
qualities of the Buddha.

In such training, all forms, expressions, and thoughts are
part of the training in realization. But here I am going to
talk specifically about thangkas, Tibetan Buddhist pictorial
scrolls, and their history, as an example of Buddhist teachings. Thangkas vividly illustrate the different ways of transforming the whole universe into teaching, inspiration, and
realization.

A talk given at the opening of the exhibition of Himalayan Sacred Art at
the Danco Gallery, Northampton, Mass., on October 29, 1981. This
chapter is based on KNR 998/17–1006/4; SG vol. I, 568/21–580/14, &
vol. 2, 247/1–303/11; and TRA 36.

THE HISTORICAL TRADITION OF THANGKAS: THE PICTORIAL SCROLLS OF TIBET

The history of Tibetan art has two stages. The first stage begins in the seventh century and the second stage in the eleventh century. I do not know what kind of art in the form of paintings and sculpture existed in Tibet before the seventh century.

In the seventh century, King Srongtsen Gampo (617–698)[18] married Princess Thritsun, the daughter of King Amshuvarman of Nepal and Princess Wen Ch'eng Kun Chu, daughter of Emperor T'ang T'ai Tsung of China. Both these princesses were devoted Buddhists, and they brought many priceless religious objects with them to Tibet. The most famous and one of the earliest images in Tibet, the Jowo, was brought to Tibet from China by Princess Wen-Ch'eng. Many other precious Buddhist images and paintings by many skilled artists were brought to Tibet from both Nepal and China. In the seventh century, the Jokhang temple in Lhasa and the other 108 Thadul and Yangdul temples were built, and they were furnished with figures of religious importance. Most notably at the end of the eighth century, King Thrisong Detsen (790–858)[19] built the famous Samye monastery, so rich in Buddhist iconography. Until the early ninth century successive kings of the Chögyal dynasty built many religious monuments. Most of the artists of the earlier stage were non-Tibetans. But they selected among the Tibetans handsome men and beautiful women to be the models of the images and paintings of Buddhist male and female teachers and deities. Also, according to historical texts, many beautiful Buddhist images spontaneously arose from the earth and from rocks, and artists used those miraculous images as models for Buddhist pictorial arts. Slowly a new kind of architecture and pictorial art of Tibet emerged. In any case, the influence of Nepalese, Indian, Chinese, and Persian art was great. For example, in the construction of Samye monastery, it is said that each of the three stories of the main temple were built with inspiration from the arts and designs of three different countries: the ground floor is in the style of Tibet, the second floor of China, and the top floor of India.

But during the reign of King Lang Darma in the early ninth century, with the destruction of Buddhism in central Tibet, the artistic life of that part of the country also suffered a total interruption for many decades.

Here it is important to note that not only the visual arts but even the written language was developed for the purposes of the establishment, practice, and propagation of Buddhism. Buddhism had become the basis and means of the life, culture, and literacy of the Tibetan people.

From the eleventh century, with the emergence of different artistic schools, the second stage of Tibetan art developed. There were many schools or traditions, but it seems that there are six major ones that were important and popular at one period or another.

The first one is the Kadam (*bKa' gDam*) school. In the eleventh century the kings of Guge in Western Tibet patronized the Buddhist art of the Tibetan tradition. For geographical reasons this early school was strongly influenced by the art of Kashmir, which itself was influenced by eastern Indian art developed under the rule of the Gupta kings (fourth–

seventh centuries) and Pāla kings (eighth–twelfth centuries) of India. This style of art is found in Spiti, Guge, Purang, and Tsaparang.

The second school is the Palri (*Bal Ris*) or Nepalese school, which developed in the fourteenth and fifteenth centuries. Nepalese tradition was influenced by Pāla art of eastern India. The arts of this school are found throughout Tibet and especially in Tashi Lhunpo monastery and also in some monasteries in eastern Tibet. According to Kongtrul Yönten Gyatso, the Nepalese school was the mainstream of Tibetan painting up to the fifteenth century.

The third school is the Menri (*sMan Ris*). In the beginning of the fifteenth century, Menlha Thöndup, a famous artist from southern Tibet, founded the Menri school, which incorporated the Chinese (of Zi'u-than) style of the Mongol (Yuan) period. There is also a second Menri tradition known as New Menri. In the seventeenth century, Chöying Gyatso, a follower of the Menri school, started his own school. He painted the wall paintings of the Chökhang Shar temple and the stūpa containing the body of the first Panchen Lama (1570–1662) in Tashi Lhunpo.

The fourth school is the Khyenri (*mKhyen Ris*) school. In the sixteenth century Khyentse Chenmo of Gongkar Gangtö started a new tradition of art. But later this school merged with the new Menri tradition.

The fifth school is Karma Gardri (*sGar Bris*). In the sixteenth century Namkha Trashi founded his own school incorporating the Menri, Indian, and Chinese (Zi'u-than) traditions. This tradition was propagated by the artists Chöje Trashi and Karma Trashi.

The sixth school is the Döpal (*'Dod dPal*) school. In the seventeenth century, during the reign of the fifth Dalai Lama (1617–1682), the artists Epa Kugpa (or Hordar) and Tulku Pagtro established their own tradition. A college of art named Döpal (or *'Dod 'Jo dPal 'Khyil*) situated at the foot of the Potala palace in Lhasa follows this tradition. So the tradition of these two artists and of this college became known as the Döpal school.

VARIETIES OF THANGKAS

In Tibet there are rich traditions of various crafts, such as weaving, sculpture, carving, metal work, carpentry, and so forth. But here I would like to explain the significances of thangkas or Tibetan pictorial scrolls as an illustration of these crafts. Thangkas are an upright rectangular form mounted and framed with silk or brocade. They are sacred objects hung on the walls of temples and in shrines as objects of homage and as the support of spiritual practice. But nowadays we also find them as decorations in houses and hotels.

There are two kinds of thangkas; one is called göthang, silken pictorial scrolls, and the other, trithang, the painted scrolls. In terms of fabricating them there are four kinds of silken scrolls: (1) Tsemtrubma is a hand-embroidered pictorial art form using silk threads of different colors. (2) Thagtrubma have figures woven by hand with different colored silk threads. (3) Tretrubma have stitched figures. Many small pieces of silk are cut into shapes and are stitched together for the different designs. (4) Lhenthabma is a glued silk scroll. The different colored silks are cut into designs and glued into figures. The variety of size of the silk scroll can be from 30 by 20 centimeters to 55 by 47 meters.

There are four main categories of painted scrolls, distinguished mainly by the color of the background of the paintings. (1) Tsönthang is a painting having different colors for the background of the painted scroll. (2) Serthang is a painting having gold for the entire background color. The figures and designs are drawn with ink or vermilion on the gold background, and in some cases the figures are painted on the gold. (3) Tsalthang is a painting having vermilion for the background, on which the design is drawn with gold or ink. Sometimes, as with the serthang, figures are painted. (4) Nagthang is a painting having black for the background color, on which the figures are drawn in gold or sometimes with vermilion, and occasionally painted with various colors. The dimensions of painted scrolls can vary from 30 by 20 cm to 3 by 2 m.

There are three other types of painting, which differ from the others in respect to design, size, and use. The first is kyilkhor in Tibetan or maṇḍala in Sanskrit. It literally means the "assemblage." It is mainly a floor plan of the residence of tantric deities, Buddhas, and their retinues. It is an assemblage because it is a place where the deity and his retinue are in assembly. Each deity has a different form of maṇḍala, in which the architectural details and colors symbolize different esoteric wisdoms. Maṇḍalas are a variety of shapes: circle, square, triangle, and semicircle. They are mostly painted on square canvases and are used as objects or supports for meditation, rituals, and empowerments, for which purposes they are spread on the altar. They may also be put in mounts or frames and hung on the wall.

The second type is tsakli. Tsakli are miniature paintings of an upright rectangular shape. Their subjects are mainly figures of various deities and also sacred attributes and objects. They are primarily for use in empowerment ceremonies for the transmission of Buddhist esoteric powers. They are kept on the altar table or on the maṇḍalas. But they can also be put in frames and hung on the wall.

The third type is kyanglha, wall paintings or frescos. They can be of various colors usually painted directly on walls, and sometimes on canvas affixed to the wall. They are mostly square in shape, a number of these squares covering most of the wall space of temples and shrine rooms.

In all Tibetan art forms there are strict and creatively ordered patterns to which the icons must conform. Each of the different figures in sacred art has a clearly defined set of dimensions, forms, colors, positions, gestures, symbols, and significances.

THE RELIGIOUS SIGNIFICANCES
OF THANGKAS

For over twelve centuries Buddhist teachings deeply influenced and guided all aspects of Tibetan life and culture. Eventually the discipline of Buddhism became preeminent in all levels of Tibetan life. Thus, any presentation of the history, culture, literature, life, or fine arts of Tibet has to involve predominantly the teachings and practices of Buddhism. This is very true in the case of Tibetan art, painting, and sculpture, the function of which is the expression and representation of religious themes. In Tibetan art one finds very little that has no religious meaning. In Tibet each well-established home has a separate shrine room with rich religious objects, which are honored with daily offerings. Even in the simplest home or in huts a shrine table will be found displaying some religious objects. These religious symbols are a source of happiness, peace, and energy for those who possess Dharma eyes. Every day the householders say prayers before the sacred objects on the shrine and make offerings of flowers, incense, food, drink, and particularly bowls filled with clean water and butter lamps. This is a means for people to develop generous, peaceful, and clear minds so that they can earn merit, which they believe to be the source of a happy future.

To understand the meaning of Tibetan pictorial art it is important to have some idea of the meaning of Buddhist visualization practices. Among the iconographic figures, there are representations of different male and female Buddhas, sages, and gods. In Buddhism, the scholars classify the bodies of the Buddhas into three categories—the Dharmakāya or "absolute body," Sambhogakāya or "enjoyment body," and the Nirmāṇakāya or "manifested body."

Dharmakāya is the absolute state, which is Buddhahood. It is free from all conceptualizations and has no form or characteristics. But in pictorial art, sometimes it is represented by an image of a naked Buddha, blue in color, symbolizing the fully enlightened state, free from all elaborations, like the sky or empty space.

Sambhogakāya is the most subtle, pure, and supreme form body of the Buddha. The Sambhogakāya can be seen only by those who have attained at least the first stage of the ten stages of the Buddhist goal of attainment. It has numerous forms, details, and significance, but we can classify them into two categories. The first includes the peaceful forms with thirty-two major and eighty minor excellent signs. They are attired in thirteen Sambhogakāya costumes—the five silken articles of vestment and eight ornaments of precious materials, symbolizing the completion or perfection of all the virtues and attainments. But some Sambhogakāya figures are clothed in monastic robes. Those of the second category are the wrathful forms. They have nine wrathful expressions and are attired in eight cemetery costumes, symbolizing the destruction of all the mental demonic forces and the transformation of defiled emotions, such as anger, into the state of wisdom.

Nirmāṇakāya is the manifested body of the Buddha in various kinds of ordinary forms for the sake of beings. They are in the forms and costumes of Buddhas, Bodhisattvas, ascetics, and monks. The forms of the Buddhas who have appeared in this earthly world, such as Shākyamuni Buddha, are called the supreme Nirmāṇakāya, and they are like the peaceful Sambhogakāya forms, distinguished by the one hundred twelve excellent signs; but they are clothed in monastic robes and not ornamented vestments. Most of the Bodhisattvas, such as Mañjushrī, are in princely costumes fully or partially, like the vestments of the peaceful Sambhogakāya form. The ascetics, who follow the esoteric practices, are in the costumes of yogīs— simple and carefree. The representations of the monks, who have renounced their household life, are in monastic robes with shaven heads or monastic hats.

There are also Bodhisattvas, ascetics, and monks who are

not Nirmāṇakāyas but ordinary beings, and the pictorial figures for them are the same as or similar to those of the Nirmāṇakāyas.

Another category of figures are the gods and demons.
Those powerful beings or spirits who are supporters of virtues, the positive forces, are called gods or Dharma protectors, and those who are evil or negative forces are called
demons. In Tibetan the word for god is *lha,* or in Sanskrit,
deva. According to Buddhism, gods dwell mostly in heaven
and enjoy happiness, being fortunate and powerful for the
time being. But they are worldly beings and not enlightened
ones. They have not attained nirvāṇa, freedom from defiled
emotions and their effects, so they are subject to wandering
around the world when their past karmic merit is exhausted.

Each of the different figures and colors of those representations in thangkas has a special meaning and significance for
visual meditation. I will give the significance of two figures as
an example of the symbolism of Buddhist art.

The first is the image of Mañjushrī, the Bodhisattva of
Wisdom. His body of orange color shines like a rising sun,
symbolizing clearness from the clouds of the two obscurations—the intellectual obscuration and emotional obscuration. His five silken vestments and eight jewel ornaments
symbolize that he is adorned with all the virtues of Sambhogakāya. He is sitting in cross-legged posture, symbolizing his
abiding in the absolute state of equanimity without wavering.
His clear eyes are wide open, symbolizing that he has ceaseless love for all and impartial wisdom concerning all as they
are. He is smiling, symbolizing that he is free from suffering
and filled with peace and joy. He is youthful, symbolizing

that he is not subject to old age and sickness, nor to death and birth. In his right hand, he brandishes a blue sword over his head, symbolizing his speech, which cuts the ignorance of beings at its root. In his left hand, he holds a volume of Prajñāpāramitā (transcendental wisdom), symbolizing his mind, which possesses the two wisdoms—the wisdom of knowing all as they are and as they appear. His body is endowed with thirty-two excellent signs and eighty excellent marks, symbolizing his perfection of the virtues of the Buddha.

The second example is Chechog or Mahottaraheruka, a wrathful deity, as described in *Palchen Dupa* of the Longchen Nyingthig tradition. His three heads symbolize the three bodies of the Buddha. His six arms symbolize the six perfections. His four legs symbolize the four boundless attitudes.

His central head is fearsome and in the vajra anger form, symbolizing the destruction of ignorance by transforming it into the sphere of Dharmakāya. His right head is white, thundering with the roar of "ha-ha," symbolizing the destruction of attachment by transforming it into the sphere of the enjoyment body. His left head is red with bared teeth in *am-tsig dam-pa* gesture, symbolizing destruction of anger by transforming it into the sphere of the manifested body of the Buddha. The five-pronged vajra in his first right hand symbolizes the elimination of the five defilements by transforming them into the five wisdoms. The trident in his second right hand symbolizes the transformation of the three poisons into the three bodies of the Buddha. The flame in his third right hand symbolizes the burning of grasping at phenomena as true. The skull in his first left hand symbolizes the transformation of the three poisons into the nectar of wisdom. The plow in the second left hand symbolizes subduing greed by generosity. The scorpion in his third left hand symbolizes the elimination of all the evil forces. The eagle over his head symbolizes his victory over all negative forces. His eightfold cemetery costume symbolizes that he is the destroyer of demonic ego.

Here, it is important to say a few words about the significance of wrathful Buddha images. For us, while it is easy to understand and also inspiring to see peaceful and contemplative images, the wrathful images and images in sexual union are difficult to comprehend as a part of the enlightened path and result. There is not any concept of such images in common Buddhism of the sūtra tradition; it is only in the esoteric (tantric) tradition. According to esoteric Buddhism, which is only for highly accomplished meditators or adepts, there is no distinction of peace or wrath, as all are equal in being illusory and are one in the ultimate state of realization. In the true nature, wrathful form is not excluded as negative, as all phenomenal existents are included as one in peace, joy, and openness.

There are two main purposes in using wrathful images for practice: generating positive energies and taming negative forces. The power or energy of wrathful forms is a great skillful means. It creates and refines the potency of the accomplishment of esoteric experiences and the awakening of the wisdoms—the wisdoms of the union of bliss and emptiness or openness, the union of appearance and emptiness, and the union of clarity and emptiness.

The wrathful forms are powerful tools in taming strong

negative forces. It is not different from a Buddha manifesting in the form of a human being for us and as a monkey for the monkeys. They are not creations or reactions of emotional afflictions or selfish craving. They are reflections of peaceful and enlightened mind in the mold of appropriate form.

The most important point is that though they appear in wrathful form and the sound associated with them is of a fearful expression, they are, or their minds are, peaceful, powerful, and compassionate. Every wrathful deity embodies the following nine main qualities: haughty, heroic, and fearful with respect to body; laughing, threatening, and fierce with respect to speech; and compassionate, powerful, and peaceful with respect to mind.

In Buddhism people do not worship images as the representation of a creator of the world, or as a provider or source of happiness. Instead, they use external objects, such as religious artifacts, as a support or source of inspiration for their spiritual practice. According to the Buddhist conception, the main factor in life is the mind. If the mind has right intention or the right perception of the objects that are being used as a support for religious practice, such as seeing them as Buddhas, it will help to develop faith and other mental virtues. In this way the devotee will achieve merit and gain spiritual strength. The using of objects of sacred art as a support for religious practice does not derive its effectiveness from the power of the objects themselves, but from the attitude of the mind of the practitioner. Of course, using appropriate objects such as religious art forms will have a greater influence on the mind than an ordinary object, such as a table. For example, if one's surroundings are filled with illustrations of passionate figures, by seeing them, hatred or lust will arise in the mind. In the same way, if one's dwelling is filled with religious illustrations, if one has some spiritual experience, it will be a reminder of or will refresh that spiritual experience.

Almost all Tibetan art takes its origin from the Buddhist teachings. It is the support of Dharma practice and the tool of Dharma propagation. It represents and preserves the essence of the Dharma.

o 6 o

PREPARING FOR
THE BARDO

THE STAGES OF DYING AND

AFTER DEATH

*B*ardo in Tibetan means "intermediate state" or "transitional period." In the context of teachings on the bardo, it mainly denotes the period between this life and the next. According to Buddhism, after you die there will be a bardo, a transitional period, and then you will take rebirth in another life. For your present life you have lots of correct and incorrect ideas and information about how you are living and what you are experiencing. But you have no idea about and very little interest in your dying and your future lives. Yet you are here for only a few days, months, or years, and then you will be in the bardo and future lives for ever and ever. At this time, the most worthwhile thing for you to do is to learn how you will be traveling through the bardo to your future

A talk given at Maha Siddha Nyingmapa Temple, Hawley, Mass., on March 22, 1992. This chapter is based on DM, NS (192a/1–195b/3 & 387b/3–396a/3), TRD (vol. Vam, 200a/4–264b/6), GG, BN, KZM, and PM.

lives, and especially how you can turn those lives into ever-lasting joy and wisdom, for yourself and for others.

Before going into a summary of the bardo, I would like to make a couple of points clear. First, in Tibetan Buddhist scriptures there are many detailed descriptions and classifications of the bardo, but it is not necessarily the case that every being will experience the same processes unfolding in the bardo. A few years after birth, a Western child goes to school, then college, then work, then gets married, then has children, and ends with retirement. But not every human being goes through this same life process. The descriptions in the following pages just represent the experiences of a good many average people, most of whom are undergoing a natural death.

Second, in many Tibetan Buddhist scriptures, the bardo is classified into six separate bardos,[20] and in other texts four are given. Here we will be speaking in terms of the four bardo system.

Third, although the actual bardo is the state between two lives, between this life and the next, the scriptures have also considered our present life itself to be a bardo. For while bardo exists between two phases of life, it is illusory in nature and involves wandering without a reliable body and fixed place to stay—characteristics that apply to this life, too, in many ways.

You may think, "I am so and so, and am living in my house with my family," but in fact you are just spending some time in this guest-house-like body of yours, in a bubblelike place. You are gathered with family and friends, like seasonal travelers, because of the forces of your karma, which brought you together like dried leaves collected together in a corner by the autumn wind. Yet soon you will depart to different directions and will never return to each other, not even to these most cherished bodies of yours. So, your present life is akin to a bardo, a dreamlike state, and that is why the scriptures have classified it as a bardo.[21]

Finally, if you recognize the true nature of the mind and appearances in any of the four bardos, you will not go on to the next stage of bardo, as you will be instantly liberated and attain Buddhahood.

The four bardos are the bardo of life, meaning our present life, the bardo of dying, the bardo of ultimate nature, and the bardo of becoming.

THE BARDO OF LIFE

The bardo of life starts from your conception and ends at the beginning of the death process. So your entire life is the bardo of life. If you practice Dharma meditations in general and especially esoteric practices while you are in this bardo, you will be able to attain enlightenment, Buddhahood, possibly even in this very lifetime.

According to Dzogpa Chenpo teachings, in absolute truth the ultimate nature of the whole universe is oneness. It is the union of ultimate nature, total openness, or emptiness, and the five wisdoms with their natural power, the five intrinsic lights. But by not realizing the truth, you discriminate between them as subjects and objects, becoming inflamed with emotions of attachment, aggression, and confusion, rooted in grasping at self. As a result, the whole universe appears before your dualistic mind as the five emotions and five elements in the subjective and objective spectrum, and it becomes the source of pain and excitement.

If you realize and perfect the intrinsic awareness, the true nature of the mind, which is the union of the total openness, the ultimate sphere, and wisdom with its intrinsic lights, then even in this very lifetime you will become a Buddha, and there will be no need to go through the successive bardos. In that case not only has your mind attained the fully enlightened state, but you have also attained an intrinsic light body of wisdom. As a result, if you wish, you can transform your present gross body through various methods into a light body of one kind or another, including what is known in the scriptures as "rainbow body," "light body," and "great transformation." Or else you can go to pure lands without leaving your mortal body behind. But you could also become fully enlightened without any physical display of supernatural signs. Of course, these kinds of attainment are extremely rare, and we are not talking about them lightly.

In the bardo of life of ordinary human beings, you can have both the knowledge and ability to bring about a joyful and peaceful future. But if you do not take advantage of it, you might fall into the experiences of confusion, fear, and pain in the bardos and the lives that are ahead of you. So, without wasting any time, you must try to gain at least some spiritual knowledge, experience, and strength of opening, peace, joy, compassion, devotion, positive perception, and wisdom. These are the only source for the creation of meritorious karma and inner wisdom, which will improve this life and equip you to face the next bardos and your future lives.

You should also try to see and feel this life as a bardo experience, to see and feel that it is unreal, just like a dream fabricated by your mind. This will help you loosen the grip of your grasping and craving for this life. In this way, when the dying and after-death bardo experiences come upon you, you will be able to see them as dreams, and will find them familiar and handle them with ease. For when you recognize dreams as dreams, the impact of nightmares becomes ineffective.

According to general Mahāyāna Buddhism, after securing a precious human life, first it is important to find a reliable, virtuous teacher. After finding one, you should learn the teachings, think about them thoroughly and gain experience in them through meditation. It is important physically to renounce mundane life and to open your mind in an enlightened attitude to all with love, compassion, joy, and evenness, and to train in the six perfections: generosity, discipline, patience, diligence, contemplation, and wisdom. Jigme Lingpa aspires:[22]

> In the bardo of life, may I obtain a spiritual life,
> Please the Lama,
> Rely on the wisdoms of learning, thinking, and meditation,
> And train in renunciation, enlightened mind, and the six
>   perfections.

THE BARDO OF DYING

The bardo of dying starts from the beginning of the process of death and ends at the arising of the bardo of ultimate nature.

If you are highly realized, without going into the experiences of the bardo of dying, through meditative power you can unite your intrinsic awareness, which is the nature of your mind, with the union of the ultimate sphere and wisdom, which is Buddhahood. If you have accomplished this union, through the meditation of the transference of consciousness ('Pho Ba) you can transfer your consciousness into a celestial pure land of the Buddhas and take rebirth there.

Otherwise you will go through the experiences of the bardos, and that could include the following process. When the dying process begins, the five vital energies (air)[23] of your body become disarrayed, and you go through two stages of dissolution. The first stage is the dissolution of the energies of the physical elements and the impairment of the functions of the sense faculties. The second stage is the dissolution of mental concepts and emotions.

For the dissolution of the physical elements, first, the earth element dissolves into the water element.[24] At this time you feel the loss of the earth energy or connection to the earth element in your body, which is solid, strong, and supporting. You feel yourself dissolving into or moving toward water energy. This is accompanied by a sensation of falling, that the ground underneath has opened up, and you cannot get up or stand, you lose your balance and become pale. That is why dying people often beg, "Please pull me up. I feel that I'm sinking." It may feel as if you are sinking and cloudy, and you may witness miragelike appearances.

Second, the water element dissolves into the fire element. At this point you feel the loss of the energy of or connection to the water element, which is wet and sustaining. You feel very thirsty. Saliva drips. Tears drop and then dry up. That is why the dying often ask, "Please give me water. I am thirsty." You may feel suffocated and irritated and witness smokelike appearances.

Third, the fire element dissolves into the air element. At this point you feel the loss of the energy of or connection to the fire element, which is warm, maturing, and burning, and you lose your body heat. The heat withdraws from the extremities toward your heart. You cannot see objects, and everything looks full of red sparks against a dark background.

Fourth, the air element dissolves into consciousness. At this time you feel the loss of energy of or connection to the air element, which is mobile and light. You struggle for your breath and your eyes roll up. Breathing generally ends with three long breaths, and on the third breath you exhale for the last time and cannot inhale again; that is the end of breathing for this life. At this time you may see illusions in the form of various fearful or joyous visions and may witness flamelike appearances.

If your karma for living has not yet been exhausted and you are going through the dying process because of circumstantial reasons (rKyen) then, even having reached this stage, it is possible to be revived through medical or spiritual means. But if you have gone beyond this stage, you cannot be revived. (There are, however, extraordinary circumstances in which people have gone much further than this point and have come back to life.)

For the second stage, the dissolution of mental concepts and emotions, when your breathing has stopped and your mind, the consciousness, has lost its connection with the energies of the physical elements, the collective energies of channels (Tib. *rTsa*, Skt. *nāḍi*), energies (*rLung*, *prāṇa*), and essence (*Thig Le*, *bindu*) in the gross body will also be dispersed. As a result, three kinds of mental dissolutions or withdrawals will take place in three stages: subtle, more subtle, and most subtle. These dissolutions prompt three mental experiences, which in the texts are termed appearances, increase, and attainment.

First, consciousness dissolves into appearances (*sNang Ba*).[25] At this time you perceive everything as white. It is not like daylight, luminous, or bright white, but just as if everything is whiteness or whitish, like moonlight in a cloudless sky. At that time thoughts of hatred or aggression cease.

Second, appearances dissolve into increase (*mCh'ed Pa*). At this time you perceive everything as redness or reddish,[26] like the light of the setting sun in a cloudless sky. At this time thoughts of greed or attachment cease.

Finally, increase dissolves into attainment (*Thob Pa*), and everything becomes blackness, like the cloudless sky of a dark autumn night. Here, thoughts of confusion cease.

Then the experience of the state of attainment leads you into a state of unconsciousness,[27] the universal ground.[28]

If you are realized, you will not fall into unconsciousness, and the experience of blackness of the attainment stage can dissolve into or arise as primordial luminosity (*gZhi gNas Kyi'od gSal*), which we will discuss later.

How should these dissolution stages be dealt with by common people? First, you must realize that you are in the process of dying. You should try to take the experiences of dissolution as peacefully as possible. You should try to remember that all the bardo appearances and experiences are the fabrications of your own mind, like dreams. You should not be attached to them, get irritated by them, or be afraid of them. With peace and naturalness, you should watch or be one with the true nature of your own mind, calmly and clearly, instead of running after and grasping at thoughts and experiences.

You should remember your spiritual sources, such as Buddhas, masters, teachings, and experiences, and use those experiences and memories as your spiritual support. Try to remember your own spiritual meditation and all your spiritual experiences and energies, and unite with them. Feel that the Buddhas, teachers, and deities are present with you all the time and that they are protecting and guiding you. From them, let the light of peace, openness, strength, and joy come to you, fill you, and transform you into the body of peace, openness, strength, and joy. Then try to relax in that spiritual body throughout the bardo process.

One of the most important points to remember is not to be attached to, irritated by, or scared by any happenings in the bardo, but to see everything as an illustration of spiritual views and a source of spiritual experiences. Use any spiritual approach and experience with which you are acquainted in your lifetime, for those are the ones that will be easier and more effective for you.

Guru Rinpoche advises us to practice and pray not to get attached to anything at the time of death, to remember our meditation, and to merge our ultimate nature of mind with the ultimate sphere:[29]

> When the bardo of dying is dawning upon me,
> Abandoning attachment and grasping at everything,

I will focus on the clear instructions without wavering,
And transfer my unborn intrinsic awareness (true nature of
the mind) into the space of the ultimate sphere.

The bardo of dying is also one of the important times for
using the phowa practice ("transference of consciousness" to
pure lands). If you are a phowa meditator, you can do it for
yourself by yourself. Otherwise, someone else can effectuate
phowa for you. If someone else is performing phowa for a
dying person, the performer should be careful about doing it,
waiting until the dying person has completed the first stage
of dissolutions—the dissolutions of physical elements—as
the dying person might still be resisting death, and there
might be hope that she or he will come back. In that case
the performance of phowa might increase the chances of the
person's dying.

In phowa practice, with compassion, faith, devotion, calm-
ness, and one-pointed mind, visualize yourself as a divine
form, such as Vajrayoginī (or as your ordinary form) in the
center of the beautiful and joyous Blissful Buddha Land
(Sukhāvatī). Visualize Amitābha, the Buddha of Infinite
Light, above your head. Jigme Lingpa writes:

All my perceptions spontaneously arise as the totally pure
Buddha Land,
The fully arrayed Blissful Buddha Land.
In the center of it, I visualize myself as Vajrayoginī,
With one head and two arms, transparently red. I hold a
curved blade [symbolizing wisdom] and a skull
[bliss].
My legs are in the advancing posture and my three eyes are
glancing upward into the sky.

In the center (of my body) is the central channel,
Of the thickness of a bamboo arrow shaft,
Empty, clear, hollow, and luminous.
The upper end of the central channel is open at the cranial
     aperture,
And its lower end reaches the navel.
On the knot at the heart
In the center of a green sphere of air [energy]
Is my awareness [mind] in the form of a red letter HRĪH
At the length of a forearm [two feet] above my head
I visualize Amitābha Buddha [the Buddha of Infinite Light]
Adorned with most excellent signs and marks.
I pray to him with strong devotion.[30]

Then with the energy of total devotion, pray many times
to Amitābha Buddha and other Buddhas, Bodhisattvas, and
enlightened masters. At the end, with one-pointed concentration, again and again shouting PHAT or HIK, visualize and feel
that your mind, which is in the form of a HRĪH letter, is shot
upward by the force of devotion and by the force of air [en-
ergy], again and again, through the central channel and
merges into the heart, the center of the form of Amitābha
Buddha, like water poured into water. Believe, feel, and remain in the experience of being one—oneness with the
Buddha.

You can perform phowa for yourself, someone else can do
it for you, or both of you can perform it for you. But as I
said before, we should have good training on it in advance,
otherwise when the time of great pressure arrives, if you look
for an unfamiliar approach it might even be hard to remember
the practice.

Bear in mind also that realizing oneself as the Buddha,

realizing oneness with the mind of the Buddha, or realizing
the true nature of mind, as taught in different trainings, are
absolute phowa trainings, the method of transferring one's
mind to the Buddha lands.

THE BARDO OF ULTIMATE NATURE

The luminosity of the basis or the luminous primordial
wisdom of the basis arises[31] after the cessation of the outer
breathing, but while the inner breathing has not yet ceased,
as a little heat is still present at the heart. If you realize the
wisdom of the basis and maintain it, you will be liberated
from the three bonds of saṃsāra, namely the bond of physical
body, the bond of phenomenal appearances, and the bond of
conceptual mind. Because of our past karmic effects, we have
been born with this gross body and have thereby trapped ourselves in the bond of the physical body. Because of our past
habits, we have been enslaved by the objects that we perceive
and have thereby trapped ourselves in the bond of phenomenal appearances. Because of our mental consciousnesses, we
have embroiled ourselves in dualistic and emotional thoughts
and have thereby trapped ourselves in the bond of conceptual
mind. The intrinsic awareness of your mind exits through the
cranial aperture and unites with the ultimate sphere. This is
the attainment of the union of enlightened wisdom and the
primordially pure ultimate sphere. Then no succeeding stage
of bardo will arise for you.

In the bardo of ultimate nature, first the state of attainment dissolves into luminosity (*'od gSal*),[32] which is clarity
and openness, like the pure sky of an early autumn morning.

It is called "the luminosity of the basis" (gZhi gNas Kyi 'od gSal), and it is the luminosity of Dharmakāya, the primordial purity. As every being possesses Buddha nature or is Buddha in his or her true nature, when all the concepts and emotions are dissolved (such as at this time), the primordial purity and luminosity shine forth for every being. Even a small insect will have the experience of primordial purity and luminosity at the time of death. For realized and experienced people, this period presents the opportunity for them to recognize it and become enlightened. For unrealized people, although they will experience it, they may not even notice it, and its arising will not make any difference to them.

Then the luminosity dissolves into union (Zung 'Jug). It is the union of openness (emptiness) and appearances (light). In this, the images of the wrathful deities will appear. We hear the roar of loud sounds, like thunder. Although these luminous appearances are the natural power arisen from the natural purity and the openness of our own mind—in the form of oneness and enlightenment—and the sounds are the natural expression of our own natural mind, unrealized people may faint out of fear. The whole universe appears as a world of radiating lights, with the beautiful light images of the peaceful deities in infinite circles of five-colored lights. Chains of light with numerous sparks of light come from the heart of the deities and reach our hearts. Finally we feel that they have all merged into us.

Then union dissolves into wisdom (Ye Shes). In this, we first see that from our hearts a very thin beam of light extends deep into the sky. Then we will see in the sky broad beams of light—blue, white, yellow, and red—one above the other. Each beam is adorned with a circle of light of corresponding color, the size of a mirror,[33] which is again decorated with five circles of light, the size of peas. These are the wisdom lights of the wisdom of the ultimate sphere, mirror-like wisdom, wisdom of equanimity, and discriminative wisdom. Above that, we will see a parasol of five-colored lights of the five wisdoms, like a parasol of peacock feathers.

Then the wisdom dissolves into the state of the spontaneously accomplished knowledge holder (*Lhun Grub Rig 'Dzin*). In this, we will see that the four beams of light merge into the parasol-like five lights above. Then the following symbolic images appear as a luminous reflection in a mirror. We feel that we are seeing the appearances of the Dharmakāya, the primordial purity, symbolized by the cloudless pure sky above in space. Below that, we see the pure lands of the Sambhogakāya, the spontaneous accomplishment, symbolized by images of wrathful deities and peaceful deities. Below that, we see the pure lands of the Nirmānakāya, the natural presence, in various manifestations. At the bottom of these, we see the world of beings of the impure six realms. At this time we may also experience many Buddha virtues present in our minds, such as the five foreknowledges.

Most beings will have all these experiences, but unless we are realized, they could just be like a flash; we might not even notice them, and they would not be of much benefit to us. But if, when we experience the luminosity of the basis and the luminous appearances we recognize them as they are— openly and in oneness without discrimination, designations, or grasping—then we will be liberated into Buddhahood, and all the appearances will be liberated as the natural power of

Buddhahood. If not, then we will again trip off to the next stage of bardo.

The most important meditation throughout the experiences of all the bardos, and especially for the bardo of ultimate nature, is to recognize the true nature of the luminosity of the basis and its appearance, the intrinsic lights.

When we see lights or various forms and sounds, if we could recognize them as the energies of our own enlightened mind, they would arise as the spontaneously present five wisdoms and the Buddha maṇḍalas, inseparable from the enlightened mind itself. But if we see the light forms and sounds as objects separate from the mind itself, by grasping at a self with dualistic concepts, they arise as various phenomena of gross concepts, emotional afflictions, and the world of the five physical elements.

In addition to recognizing the nature of the light, forms, and sounds, it is also important to recognize the intrinsic awareness, the nature of our own mind as it is, as if we were meeting an old intimate friend again. For then we will realize the true nature of everything. Then we will transcend the concepts of existing and not existing and will attain Buddhahood, the ever-liberated state. Guru Rinpoche advises us to practice and pray as follows:

> When the bardo of ultimate nature is dawning upon me,
> Abandoning all fear and terror,
> I will recognize all the happenings as self-appearing
>   intrinsic awareness (the energies of the true nature of
>   the mind) itself,
> And I will realize it as the mere (imagined) appearances of
>   the bardo.[34]

Jigme Lingpa writes:

> If you analyze the bardo of ultimate nature,
> There are many aspects to be analyzed.
> But, instead, if you just analyze the analyzer itself,
> It exists nowhere.
> Then liberate the concept of not existing also.
> This is the ever-liberated state.[35]

Longchen Rabjam writes:

> A yogī who is attaining liberation in this very life,
> Dissolves the earth element into water, water into fire, fire
>   into air, air into consciousness, and consciousness into
>   luminescence;
> Then, uniting with (the union of) wisdom and the ultimate
>   sphere
> S/he secures permanence in the state of primordial
>   (Buddhahood).
> For the benefit of others, like a dream, wisdom with two
>   Buddha bodies
> Appears to sentient beings as the Buddha qualities that
>   serve them.[36]

You may have heard and read books on near death experiences. They are amazing! The Tibetan tradition of bardo is at least a thousand years old, and near-death experiences are a new topic, but many aspects are the same in both literatures; they speak in an almost identical language. However, the bardo teachings go much deeper. They show the causes and results of various stages of the bardo and get to the bottom of them, instead of merely giving an initial idea. In particular, the bardo teachings guide us in how to prepare for and deal with circumstances in order to improve our bardo experiences and future lives.

In the bardo of dying and the bardo of ultimate nature we witness various kinds of lights and phenomenal appearances. But for many, and especially for realized people, they are not in a subject–object mode of perception. Realized beings see and feel them as oneness. You can see or feel hundreds of things together simultaneously. You can see or feel everything, not necessarily through the eyes, but with totalness, as if it all is before you. All is joy, bliss, oneness, and openness—no discrimination, limits, conflicts, or pain. The higher your realization is, the more you can see thousands of things simultaneously. On the other hand, many people in such circumstances experience only complete pain, fear, and suffering.

When I said "light," you probably thought about beams of light or sunlightlike phenomena coming from somewhere. But in true realization you are not realizing those lights as objects—the objects of the eye consciousness and so forth. You are realizing the light as a clarity and luminosity, which is also peace, joy, bliss, openness, oneness, and all-knowing wisdom. And you are the light and the light is you, oneness. This is the union of openness nature (emptiness) and the spontaneously arising wisdom and appearances (intrinsic light). This principal is the very basis from which esoteric Buddhism speaks of nonduality, natual light, clarity, spontaneous arising, spontaneously present, simultaneous awareness, self-arisen, unborn, and fully enlightened.

In the bardo your mind has disconnected from your physical energies, and the structure of the physical body does not control or influence your mental movements. If you have made a good spiritual preparation in your lifetime, then in the bardo the power and impact of your spiritual realization will be more effective in improving the course of your life than it is now. Your mind will be more powerful and open to moving toward whatever goal you will focus on, as it is totally together.

Even if you have not realized the true nature of bardo experiences, if you could just think with a devotional mind, "They are Buddha nature and Buddha manifestations," or in simple words, think of them as positive phenomena, then they will cause peace, joy, and relaxation in you. As a result, you will gain in spiritual strength and wisdom. You will be able to handle the bardo process and will be led to a better rebirth.

At least you should try to avoid being scared, confused, or attached to any experiences or appearances by thinking, "They are all not real. They are mere fabrications of my mind." Then try to remember your spiritual supports, such as masters, teachings and, above all, your meditative experiences, with faith, trust, devotion, and joy. Again, this will enable you to handle the bardo process and will lead you to a better rebirth.

Generally, for common people, the experiences of both the bardo of dying and the bardo of ultimate nature can last from a fraction of a second to many minutes, but they might feel them to be much longer. The perception and experience of time is not necessarily measured according to one conceptual system, namely the concepts we have at present.

THE BARDO OF BECOMING

In the popular sense, among common Tibetans, this is "the bardo." This is also the bardo that will have the longest duration among the latter three bardos, since for many the second and third bardo experiences can last only briefly.

If you are a highly or even moderately realized person, you will have attained enlightenment in the bardo of life or at least in the bardo of ultimate nature, and will not go through the bardo of becoming. If you are a person of a little realization, you can go through the bardo of becoming very briefly, but with no experience of suffering; then, by remembering your meditative realizations, you will be reborn in a manifested pure land (*Rang bZhin sPrul sKu'i Zhing*). There you will receive the blessings of the five Buddha families and attain Buddhahood. If you are an unrealized person and your consciousness is not transferred to a pure land by any other means, such as phowa, you will move to the next bardo, the bardo of becoming.

Common people in the second and third bardos might have experienced falling into unconsciousness (instead of experiencing the luminosity of the basis, as it is) and become terrified by the appearances of the sounds, lights, rays, and images of the deities. You might not even have dared to see or feel your own true nature and the appearances of your true nature, but instead you would have struggled with them as objects—objects in the form of conflicting forces.

Then from the force of not realizing (*Ma Rig Pa*) the ultimate nature, the luminosity of the basis, you feel the arising of the energies of air, fire, water, and earth elements in yourself, and they are followed by thoughts of confusion, desire, and aggression. Your consciousness, or mind, will exit from your gross body through one of the nine doors. (The best door to exit through is the cranial aperture or fontanel at the top of the head.) By the joining together of those energies and your consciousness, you will mentally feel that you have a body with all the sense faculties. Some scriptures even talk of having a subtle body (or soft light body), but most agree that it is a mental or imagined body, without any real form. Nevertheless, you will feel that you have a body with some light of its own, and you will not feel the sunlight or moonlight.

Thereafter, you may go through the following experiences. You will have no stability or solidness in your life and mind, and everything will change from moment to moment, according to the changes of your thoughts and the influences of your karmic forces. You will reach any person or place that comes into your mind, unless it is beyond your karmic range. If you think "New York," you will be there instantly, without spending any time or effort in traveling there. It is hard to stay in one place and to focus on any thought, as you are always moving, floating, and being driven about. You are constantly running, flying, and moving, like a feather in a storm, with no stability. Your mind will be much sharper than an ordinary person's and will have some sort of clairvoyance, knowing other people's thoughts; but you will have less reasoning or analytic power, because of the lack of mental stability. Your mind may go through many changes of happiness and suffering, hope and fear, peace and pain in every single moment. Sometimes you imagine danger from the elements, as if you are buried under houses, caves, or collapsed earth, falling and sinking in water, burning in a fire of wood or houses, and being blown about in stormy air.

When the dead see their dead bodies, some get attached to

them, while others dislike them. Yet others do not recognize
their corpse and mysteriously see it as a different form, such
as the dead body of an animal.

You could be seeking food all the time, but be unable to
enjoy any food ujnless it is dedicated to you. Mostly you will
just be able to enjoy the smell of that food.[37] You will feel
lonely and insecure and will always be looking for shelter and
stability. As you are tired of being swept about by karmic,
mental, and emotional storms, you are always eager to gain
shelter or to find a birth, with little care about what kind of
situation you are going to be trapped in. Every week you
might experience the process of death all over again and
again, especially if it was a tragic death.

Also, at the beginning, you may not realize that you actually have died for a long time, as you have little reasoning
power. You might go to friends, but they will ignore you. You
might go to the dining table, but no one will give you a chair
or serve you food.

The duration of this bardo is generally from about a week
to seven weeks, but it could be shorter or in some rare cases
even longer. During the first half, you will feel that you have
the body of and connections to your previous life, and then
during the second half, you will feel that you have the body
and experiences of the coming birth.

Around the middle of the stay in this bardo, many experience going to the court[38] of the Lord of Death, the King of
the Law (gShin rJe Ch'os rGyal), where the place of your rebirth will be decided by checking the records of your past
virtuous and unvirtuous karma. These people witness defend-
ers and prosecutors pleading for or against their virtues and

demeritorious deeds, supporting their arguments with various proofs measured by pebbles, scales, and mirrors.

In addition, from around the middle of this bardo you will start seeing the lights of different colors, the energies of your karma and emotions, which indicate your rebirth realm. If you are going to take rebirth in the god realm you will see a soft white light. Likewise, you will see soft red for the demigod realm, soft blue for the human realm, soft green for the animal realm, soft yellow for the hungry-ghost realm, and a smoky light for the hell realm.

You might also see the realm of your birth in symbolic terms, which may include the following. If you are going to take rebirth in the god realm, you might feel as if you are going into a mansion. Likewise, you may go into a wheel of light or of war for the demigod realm, empty caves or huts for the animal realm, a forest, logs, or black blankets for the hungry-ghost realm, and a dark pit or a metal town for the hell realm. For the human realm you could feel as if you are going into a lake with swans, horses, or cows, or into a mist, houses, cities, or a crowd of people. When the time of rebirth arrives, you will see your parents engaged in intercourse, and you may feel jealousy toward your father and desire toward your mother, if you are going to become a male; or you may feel the reverse if you are going to be born as a female. That emotional feeling will trigger you to enter into the womb of conception. For egg birth, moisture birth, and also miraculous birth, your birth will usually be triggered by the force of the emotions of hatred or desire.

How should we handle the bardo of becoming? First it is

important to realize that you have died. If you do not have a reflection in mirrors, footprints on sand or snow, a shadow beside your body, and if people are not responding to you, then you are in the bardo. Try not to get sad and shocked. But try to concentrate on any of the following three important points.

First, realize that you are at the most important juncture of all of your future lives and cannot waste a moment. Second, feel joy about whatever spiritual path you have pursued in your lifetime, as that will be the great source of light, joy, and peace of today. Third, remember any one of the following three practices, according to your experiences in the past, and then stay with that practice without distractions. (If you are a highly realized person you would have already been enlightened.)

1. If you are a person who has some esoteric meditative experience, you should see those lights as bright wisdom lights, or turn them into bright lights of wisdom. Also, you can see the Buddhas of the five Buddha families, as mentioned in *Thötröl*,³⁹ and attain enlightenment. If you try to see with faith, you will see them as such, as all are creations of the mind in the bardo.

So remember your devotion to the Buddhas, masters, and meditation. Realize all those experiences as oneness, and that all the forms and sounds are the manifest power of that oneness. Be one with them, without grasping or struggling through a subjective and objective standpoint. Then remain relaxed in that realized state. Merge into it again and again.

2. If you are not a realized or experienced meditator, but

a spiritual person, first you should try to calm your mind, be stable and focused on your spiritual supports, instead of being driven everywhere, as bardo beings always are.

In Tibetan tantric Buddhism, there are many rites a Lama will perform for the deceased. Through the power of prayers, merit making, devotion, and contemplation, the Lama brings the mind of the deceased person to an image (or an object) and stabilizes him or her with it. Then the Lama gives teachings and bestows the empowerments in order to lead the mind of the deceased person to Buddhahood, or at least to a good rebirth. If the Lama's meditative rites are powerful, and if there is proper virtuous karma in the deceased person, the rites will be most effective.

Remember and remain in whatever faith, meditation, or spiritual thoughts and feelings you are familiar with. If you could remember and invoke the compassion and powers of the Buddhas, Bodhisattvas, saints, sages, spiritual masters, and meditation, your spiritual experiences will be powerful and beneficial at this lonely crossing. Whatever spiritual thoughts, memories, or experiences you have, they will generate the force of peace, joy, devotion, compassion, pure perception, and wisdom (which is the realization of the ultimate nature and its luminous appearances) in you. That force will cause you to be led to enlightenment or to a better rebirth (just as negative emotions cause birth in a lower mundane realm). That force could divert the path of your rebirth in inferior realms, even if it has been chosen. Whatever spiritual experiences and strength you have had in your lifetime, they will certainly bear their fruits at this time of need.

3. If you have no spiritual experience, when you go

through all those happenings, try not to become angry, upset, and afraid, but see them as mere fabrications of your mind, like a dream. No one is putting up all these bardo arrangements for your arrival; they are just illusions imagined by your own mind and mental emotions. Try to be open, positive, stable, and peaceful, instead of having a grasping concept, a negative perception, rushing and struggling with emotions of hatred, desire, or confusion. Feel compassion for others who are also driven about in this unknown bardo. If you can create or regain and maintain such a positive state of mind and spiritual energy, it will bring stability to your mind, release the negative energies or karma in you, and a spiritual peace and light can blossom in you, bearing the fruits of rebirth in a happy realm.

You should also try to reverse the process of taking inferior births, if you face any of them. When you see the signs of inferior birth, the soft lights and signs, or the place (or the parents) of birth in an inferior birth, the most important thing is not to get into emotional thoughts of grasping, craving, attachment, hatred, jealousy, fear, confusion, and so on. Instead, see all with a spiritual mind, a mind of peace, oneness, and openness. See them with peace by realizing them as the fabrications of your own mind, or see them as the images of male and female Buddhas. Pray to the Buddhas and spiritual masters for their blessing and guidance.

Your friends can help by performing spiritual practices, such as phowa practice, making merit, purification of demeritorious deeds, invoking the blessings of the Buddhas, saying prayers, chanting mantras, giving charity, making offerings, saving lives, making Buddha images, writing Dharma scriptures, building spiritual monuments, refraining from demer- itorious deeds, and then dedicating all the merit of these ac- tions to you and to all mother beings for their happiness and enlightenment. Whatever merit they will make and dedicate to you will benefit you, as you are inspiring them to make and dedicate them to you and to all mother beings with love, openness, and beneficial minds. It is important for your friends not to think and, especially, not to say or do things that could trigger any negative thoughts, feelings, or emo- tions in your mind, but to think and, especially, say or do things that will inspire peace, joy, and strength in you.

In this life, the mind is relatively stable because it has sta- tioned itself in this earthy, physical structure. It is therefore easier to gain spiritual views and habits through meditation. But it is also harder to make a big change or improvement precisely because the mind is trapped and programmed in the system of your rigid, earthy body.

In the bardo, however, the mind is rapidly changing in a powerful transitional junction without the conditions of the physical body. It is thus easier to change or improve your future journey. But it is also harder to find a new unfamiliar path and focus on it, since your bodiless mind floats rapidly and constantly rushes about at high speed.

So, if you could focus your mind on gaining spiritual views and experiences in this lifetime, while you still have a stable basis, in the bardo the habits of those experiences will easily affect your journey into a future life, ensuring a future of great peace, joy, and wisdom.

Today, fortunately, you are alive and I am alive. We have the opportunity to prepare for our bardos and our next lives.

If we have experienced peace, joy, strength, and wisdom, then when the day of death comes to us, we all will be able to welcome it, thinking "Oh, wonderful, I am ready for it!" The mind of bardo is much clearer and more powerful, and its experiences are much sharper than today's mind, which is programmed in this particular system of human perceptions and trapped in the structure of the body of flesh and blood. So if we have gained some Dharma experience in our lifetime, in the bardo we will be enjoying the fruits of great peace and light, and rejoicing and celebrating for what we achieved when we were alive in this world.

If there is peace, openness, and wisdom in our minds, all our mental states and the phenomena around us can arise as positive appearances. The five emotions of our minds arise as the five wisdoms, and the five physical elements as the five intrinsic lights, the Buddhas and Buddha lands, the natural energy of wisdom. Or, at least, images of the Buddhas, Bodhi-sattvas, saints, sages, Lamas, Ḍākinīs, and Ḍākas will lead us through the clear sky to the most peaceful and joyful Buddha lands with a great display of magical offerings, peaceful music, and joyful dances, filling the whole atmosphere. Now we will be acquiring the power of bringing that peace, light, and joy to all our mother beings.[40]

PART TWO

Meditation on Ngöndro: The Essential Training

◦ 7 ◦

THE NYINGMA SCHOOL OF TIBETAN BUDDHISM

THE OLDEST, MOTHER SCHOOL of the four major Buddhist schools of Tibet is the Nyingma, "the Old One." While Buddhism reached Tibet in the seventh century during the reign of Srongtsen Gampo, the thirty-third king of the Chögyal dynasty, scholars agree that Buddhism was formally established there by the late eighth century. This definitive founding of Buddhism in Tibet was accomplished by the great adept Guru Padmasambhava and the celebrated scholar Shāntarakṣhita under the patronage of Thrisong Detsen, the thirty-seventh king of the Chögyal dynasty. Thereafter, until the eleventh century, when other schools emerged by bringing newly translated teachings and lineages to Tibet from India, there was only one Buddhist school; and that school became known as the Nyingma from the eleventh century. Nyingma is a flourishing school today. But since the eleventh century, the prominent place among religious institutions has been taken successively by other schools.

This chapter is based on KZ, KZZ, SG, DD, KNR, and other sources.

CONTRIBUTION OF NYINGMA TO TIBETAN HISTORY AND CULTURE

The main distinction between the Nyingma and the other schools is not a result of the emergence of the sūtras, the common Buddhist teachings, nor of the outer tantras, the common esoteric teachings, but of the inner tantras, the higher categories of tantras. The Nyingma follows Ngag Nyingma (*sNgags rNying Ma*), "the old tantras," translated into Tibetan in the early translation period (seventh–eleventh centuries) by many great translators such as Vairochana, Kawa Paltseg, Chog-ro Lu'i Gyaltsen and Zhang Yeshe De of the eighth–ninth centuries till Smṛitijñāna in the eleventh century. The other three schools follow Ngag Sarma (*sNgags gSar Ma*), "the new tantras," translated into Tibetan during the later translation period, which begins with the great translator Rinchen Zangpo (958–1055) in the eleventh century.

At different stages, each of the four major schools became the state church: Nyingma from the seventh through eleventh centuries and then Sakya, Kagyu, and Gelug thereafter, until recent times. These four major schools developed with the support of various powerful patrons: Nyingma under the Chögyal dynasty of Tibet; Sakya, Kagyu, and Gelug with the support of Mongol, Chinese, and Tibetan rulers.

During the early period of the Nyingma, amazing changes of a social, political, educational, and spiritual order took place in Tibetan civilization. Tibetologists rarely take note of the extent of the contributions made in this early period of the Nyingma. Before Buddhism arrived, Tibetans were well

known for their warriorship, being a constant threat to neigh-
boring countries. They followed their pre-Buddhist native belief, known as Bön, mainly worshipping nature and performing sacrifices. But as Buddhism emerged and gained strength,
Tibetans slowly were drawn to the wisdom of the Buddhist
life, deeply valuing the coexistence of all beings and adopting
the attitude of peace and harmony with nature. Tibet became
a source of learning and a zone of peace for central Asia. A
script and grammar for the Tibetan language was introduced
by Thönmi Sambhoṭa in the seventh century, and Buddhist
scriptures began to be translated into Tibetan.

Tibet, a land populated by violent people, controlled by
evil ministers, and haunted by negative spirit-energies, was
pacified and transformed through the wisdom and enlightened power of Guru Padmasambhava and other Buddhist
sages into a civilized and spiritual society. Tibet's first Buddhist university, Samye, was inaugurated in the late eighth
century. Sāntarakṣhita ordained seven men as monks, "the
seven men of trial" (Sad Mi Mi bDun). Thereafter, hundreds
of others took orders, leading to the formation of one of the
greatest monastic communities in the world. Guru Padmasambhava and other masters initiated "the twenty-five: the
king and subjects" (rJe 'Bangs Nyer lNga) and hundreds of others into tantra. Even today, Tibet is known as a land of mysti-
cism, miracles, and enlightenment. During the reign of Thri
Ralpachen, the fortieth king of the Chögyal dynasty, the
translators compiled a Sanskrit-Tibetan lexicon of Buddhist
terminology entitled Chetrag Togpar Chedpa Chenmo (Tib. Bye
Brag rTogs Par Byed Pa, Skt. Mahāvyutpatti). The king decreed
that all the translations should uniformly employ standard-

ized terms to ensure consistency. Because of this policy, even today there is no difficulty in reading ninth century translations or in restoring Tibetan translations into Sanskrit. Complete uniformity in the translation of an entire literary corpus, the vast body of scriptures and commentaries of Buddhist India, is an achievement unique to Tibetan civilization. And this was a contribution of the Nyingma to the intellectual history of Tibet.

In the early period of its history, the Nyingma played an indispensable role in strengthening the secular power of the central rulers and in consolidating the whole of Tibet as one nation. At that time Tibet was free, and Tibetans stood on their own feet, enjoying prosperity based on their own resources and dealing with foreign countries from their own strength. During this period the Nyingmas established two clerical systems: the saffron-robed monks (*Rab Byung Ngur sMrig Gi sDe*), who dwelled in the monasteries, and the white-robed long-haired ones (*Gos dKar lChang Lo'i sDe*), who were lay tantric priests living in temples and villages. The introduction of the system of white-robed clergy brought the benefit of the teachings to men and women's homes, preserving the Dharma at the grass-roots level. In contrast, during the later period of the Dharma in Tibet, other schools concentrated the learning and practice of Buddhism more among the monks in the monasteries in order to preserve the purity of the tradition.

Unfortunately, Lang Darma, the forty-first and last king of the Chögyal dynasty, destroyed Buddhism, the monasteries, and the monastic tradition in central Tibet. It took almost a century to bring the Dharma back to the center. Some

prominent scholars escaped to Eastern Tibet and later
brought back many teachings, including Shāntarakṣhita's Vinaya ordination lineage, called Medul (sMad 'Dul), which is
still the main monastic lineage of both Nyingma and Gelug
schools. Many tantric masters and their teachings survived
because they blended in with the village people. In addition,
many teachings and lineages of tantra were saved by Nubchen
Sangye Yeshe, who frightened the king with a display of his
mystical power. But the most effective way of preserving the
teachings through the vicissitudes of time has proven to be
the system of Terma (gTer Ma), the concealment of Dharma
Treasures through the enlightened power of tantric masters.
The method of transmission and preservation was bestowed
on the Nyingma by its founder, Guru Padmasambhava.

UNIQUE NYINGMA LINEAGE TEACHINGS

Nyingma, the Old Tantric School, classifies the entire
Buddhist teachings into nine yānas (Theg Pa dGu). Of the
nine, the three sūtric yānas—Shrāvakayāna, Pratyekabuddha-
yāna, and Mahāyāna—are common to all the schools, but the
interpretation of them varies somewhat from school to
school. The teachings of the three outer tantras (Phyi rGyud
sDe gSum) also are more or less similar to the first three of
the four tantric divisions (rGyud sDe bZhi) of the New Tantra.
But the scriptures and the sources of the three inner tantras
(Nang rGyud sDe gSum)—Mahāyoga, Anuyoga, and Atiyoga—
are different from the three subdivisions of Anuttaratantra
(rNal 'Byor Bla Med rGyud): father, mother, and nondual tantras of the New Tantra. According to the Nyingma, the teach-

ings of the three inner tantras are revealed by various Buddhas, such as Vajrasattva and Vajrapāṇi in Sambhogakāya
form, to great Buddhist adepts, such as King Ja, the Five
Excellent Beings, and Prahevajra, at various times. Those
teachings came through three modes of transmission: enlightened mind (*dGongs brGyud*), symbolic (*brDa brGyud*), and
verbal transmissions (*sNyan brGyud*), whereas according to
the New Tantra, the teachings of Anuttaratantra were taught
by Shākyamuni Buddha in his very lifetime.

In Nyingma, the preeminent tantras are *Gyuthrul Drawa
Sangwa Nyingpo* (*sGyu 'Phrul Drva Ba gSang Ba sNying Po*),
Drubpa Kagye (*sGrub Pa bKa' brGyad*), *Do Gongpa Dupa* (*mDo
dGongs Pa 'Dus Pa*), and Dzogpa Chenpo scriptures. The
teachings of these tantras manifest themselves in two major
categories: (1) Many of the Nyingma tantras that are transmitted through unabbreviated lineages are known as Kama
(*bKa' Ma*), Canonical Tantras. All the texts belonging to this
category, those that have survived, are present in the collec-
tions of the *Nyingma Gyubum* (*rNying Ma rGyud 'Bum*) and
Kama. (2) Thousands of volumes of tantric teachings are preserved and transmitted through a short or abbreviated lineage
known as the lineage of Terma, Concealed and Discovered
Dharma Treasures.[41] These are teachings transmitted and
concealed in the enlightened nature of the minds of his realized disciples by Guru Padmasambhava in the ninth century.
They are still being discovered today by hundreds of Tertöns
(*gTer sTon*), the Dharma Treasure Discoverers, who are the
reincarnations of those disciples of Guru Padmasambhava.
Some of those major Terma texts are extant and found in

the collection of *The Precious Treasury of Termas* (*Rin Ch'en gTer mDzod*).

Each of the three inner tantras emphasizes a different meditative aspect: Mahāyoga stresses meditative training to develop one's physical form, verbal expression, and thoughts as the vajra body, speech, and mind of the Buddhas. Anuyoga seeks to perfect the luminous primordial wisdom of bliss, clarity, and freedom from concepts by exerting the channels, energies, and essence of one's vajra body. In Atiyoga (Tib. *rDzogs Pa Ch'en Po*, Skt. *Mahāsandhi*), by distinguishing the intrinsic awareness (*Rig Pa*), the Buddha essence, from the mind, one remains in the openness of self-arisen intrinsic awareness itself, without mental fabrications and elaborations.

After studying the teachings and analyzing them thoroughly, Atiyoga followers practice the stages of various preliminary trainings gradually. When one is ready for Dzogpa Chenpo, the master introduces her or him to the intrinsic awareness, the absolute nature of the mind. After realizing the true nature, one meditates on it until every situation becomes one taste in the realized state, and one merges all into the universal truth. If one has perfected the realization, every expression of life becomes the power of intrinsic awareness (*Rig rTsal*). Jigme Tenpa'i Nyima (1865–1926) summarizes Dzogpa Chenpo meditation:

> In Dzogpa Chenpo, from the beginning one employs the intrinsic awareness as the path or maintains only the intrinsic awareness. One does not employ concepts since concepts

are mind. One meditates (on the intrinsic awareness after) distinguishing the mind from intrinsic awareness.[42]

Perfection of Dzogpa Chenpo realization is the attainment of the fully enlightened state, Buddhahood. Before witnesses, many Dzogpa Chenpo masters up to the middle of this century have achieved Jalu (*'Ja' Lus*), the Rainbow Body, at the time of their death. In Jalu they dissolve their minds and even their gross bodies in the midst of lights, into ultimate nature, emptiness, without any remainder (with the exception of the nails and hair). Some Dzogpa Chenpo masters achieve Phowa Chenpo (*'Pho Ba Ch'en Po*), the Great Transformation, wherein they transform their mortal bodies into the subtle light bodies in order to serve others.

LONGCHEN NYINGTHIG LINEAGE

Longchen Nyingthig is the cycle of Terma teachings discovered by Kunkhyen Jigme Lingpa (1729–1798) as a Mind Ter. There are many important monasteries, nunneries, and hermitages in all the three provinces of Tibet, Bhutan, and Sikkim that uphold the Longchen Nyingthig tradition.

In Central Tibet there were two nunneries that became significant centers for the Longchen Nyingthig tradition because of their historical importance. They were Tsering Jong, which was built by Jigme Lingpa himself as a monastic hermitage and later became a nunnery, and Shugsesb nunnery near Kang-ri Thōkar, where Longchen Rabjam spent the greater part of his life and wrote most of his celebrated works, and where the Shugseb Lochen (1841?–1940) lived and taught for many decades.

In Kham, at Dzogchen monastery and especially at its famous Shrīsiṃha College, Longchen Nyingthig was one of the major practices. Also there were many great monasteries, simple but unique in dedicating themselves exclusively to teaching and practising the true Dharma with little or no bureaucratic structure, no collection of titles or material wealth, such as the monastic seats of Jigme Gyalwe Nyuku and Paltrul Rinpoche in Dzachukha valley, the hermitages of Nyoshul Lungtog, Adzom Drugpa, Yukhog Chatralwa, Lama Munsel, and Khenpo Chokyab.

In Amdo, Dodrupchen monastery was the most important monastery for Longchen Nyingthig, as it exclusively followed that tradition. It was the seat of the incarnations of the first Dodrupchen Rinpoche, who was the root doctrine-holder of the Longchen Nyingthig lineage, and it was a great center for learning and training. In the Rekong area, there are several large religious centers (*dGon Pa*) of tantric priests (*sNgags Pa*) that follow the Longchen Nyingthig lineage propagated by the first Dodrupchen Rinpoche and his disciples. Some of the big monasteries enrolled up to 1,900 priests.

The Longchen Nyingthig teachings became so popular that many important Lamas, priests, and members of Nyingma monasteries, who belonged to other subschools and followed different liturgical Terma traditions, practiced Longchen Nyingthig in addition to their own liturgies. Thus Longchen Nyingthig became the most popular, widespread tradition of Ter teachings throughout the Nyingma world of Tibet, where meditators practiced it exclusively or combined it with other lineages. Examples of individual masters who practiced Longchen Nyingthig in conjunction with other liturgies were Khenpo Ngagchung (1879–1941) of Kathog monastery, the second Penor Rinpoche (1887–1932) of Palyul monastery, and Kongtrul Rinpoche (1901–1959) of Zhechen monastery.

There are many reasons for the prominence of Longchen Nyingthig. First, its literature is rich with scholarship and condenses the entire vast teachings of Nyingma tantras into clear, profound, and short texts. The liturgies and commentaries of Longchen Nyingthig are the teachings of the Dharmakāya, which came through the Vidyādharas of the past, as they are based on the original tantras word by word, meaning by meaning, category by category. At the same time, they are the Termas taught and concealed by Guru Rinpoche and discovered by Jigme Lingpa.

Second, Longchen Nyingthig teachings are very poetic and beautiful, so much so that some scholars even had trouble accepting them as Termas and thought that they had to have been composed. Termas are usually worded very naturally, without employing many stylistic ornaments such as metaphors, similes, synonyms, or poetic phraseology. But, of course, there is no doubt that Longchen Nyingthig teachings are Termas that are so beautiful, condensed, wonderful, and profound in composition and meaning and so closely based upon the original tantras.

Third, a great number of celebrated masters of recent centuries taught, practiced, and accomplished the highest meditative attainments through Longchen Nyingthig practice. These are the reasons that it became a great inspiration to many great teachers and students of the Nyingma.

Longchen Nyingthig followers did not, however, create any

huge structure of monastic community since their goal was to simplify life and bring humbleness to the heart of the heart, without burning up the energies of precious lives by laboring upon external physical structures and wasting lives in the efforts of organizing.

What is the meaning of Longchen Nyingthig? *Nyingthig* means "innermost essence" or "heart essence." In the Nyingma all Buddhist teachings are categorized into nine yānas. The highest of them is Dzogpa Chenpo (Mahāsandhi) or Atiyoga, which is itself divided into three divisions— Semde (mind division), Longde (the division on sphere), and Mengagde (the division of instructions). Me-ngagde is further classified into four cycles—outer, inner, secret, and innermost secret cycles. Nyingthig is the teaching that condenses all the three divisions, but it mainly embodies the instructions of Me-ngagde and especially of the innermost secret cycle of Dzogpa Chenpo. Thus Nyingthig comes from the highest cycle of Dzogpa Chenpo. Jigme Lingpa's teachings consist of outer and inner tantras as well as sūtric teachings, but they all lead one to the path and goal of Dzogpa Chenpo, or they directly relate to it. That is why, for example, *Rigdzin Dupa* is categorized as Mahā of Ati and *Yumka Dechen Gyalmo* as Anu of Ati, and so on.

Longchen means "great expanse" or "great ultimate sphere." There are two main reasons for calling this cycle of teachings *Longchen*. First, the teachings of Longchen Nyingthig are an exposition of the essence of the ultimate sphere, which is the great expanse and universal nature, and also it is the teaching originating from the ultimate sphere.

Second, *Longchen* comes from the name Longchen Rabjam,

the greatest scholar and realized master of the Nyingma tradition. Jigme Lingpa, the revealer of Longchen Nyingthig, had three pure visions of Longchen Rabjam through which Jigme Lingpa reached the highest stages of realization. These were followed by another pure vision in which Jigme Lingpa went to Boudhanath stūpa in Nepal and received the symbolic scripts (*brDa Yig*) of Longchen Nyingthig from a Ḍākinī. He ate those symbolic scripts, and that caused the discovery of the Longchen Nyingthig as a Mind Ter, but not an Earth Ter.

So, the significance of the title, *The Innermost Essence of the Great Ultimate Sphere,* lies in the fact that it is the innermost secret teachings of Dzogpa Chenpo on the most profound, great ultimate sphere, which were concealed and entrusted by Guru Padmasambhava to King Thrisong Detsen, and were later discovered by Jigme Lingpa, a reincarnation of the king, when they were awakened in him by the blessings of Longchen Rabjam.

THE TERMA TRADITION OF
THE NYINGMA SCHOOL

> People who have well-being of mind, even if the Bud-
> dha is not present, will receive Dharma from the midst
> of the sky, walls, and trees. For those Bodhisattvas
> whose minds are pure, teachings and instructions will
> appear just by the wishes in their minds.
>
> —BUDDHA[43]

IN A GREAT NUMBER of spiritual traditions of the world
there are many instances of the discovery of teachings and
objects through mystical power. Similarly, in various traditions and lineages of Buddhism, in India as well as Tibet,
numerous mystical discoveries of teachings and objects have
taken place.

In the Nyingma school of Tibetan Buddhism the tradition
of concealment and revelation of teachings and materials of
religious value through the mystical power of enlightened beings is most prevalent by far. This tradition of mystical discovery is known in Tibetan as Ter (*gTer*, "Treasures"), Terma

---

This article was published in *The Tibet Journal*, Dharamsala, India, Winter
1990.

(gTer Ma, "Treasured Ones"), or Terchö (gTer Ch'os, "Dharma Treasures" or "Treasured Teachings").

Ter do not belong to the category of revelations through psychic power (rTsa Khams) or through the beings of the spirit world (Mi Ma Yin). Psychic discoveries take place through the power of a mind, which is a gifted but conceptual cognition. Further, most spirits have more physical power and knowledge than ordinary human beings, but their spiritual wisdom and true virtues are limited. The discoveries of Terma take place from the omnipresent enlightened nature of the mind through the spontaneously arisen wisdom power of the enlightened nature itself, whereas other discoveries are through dualistic concepts and supernatural deeds.

In Mahāyāna Buddhism in general and especially in tantra, the true nature of the universe is viewed as ultimate peace, emptiness, openness, the enlightened or awakened state, bliss, oneness, freedom from dualistic concepts, and the wisdom of knowing all simultaneously, and that is known as the state of the fully enlightened nature or the Buddha. Mahāyānists, including tantric practitioners, believe that the true nature of the mind of beings is as pure as Buddha, but that it has been obscured by wrong views, emotions, and habits. We are distracted by dualistic phenomena and thus are trapped in the unending turmoil of the mundane world. The *Hevajratantra* says:

> Beings are Buddha in their nature
> But their nature is obscured by adventitious defilements.
> When the defilements are cleansed, they themselves are the
>   very Buddha.[44]

If you attain freedom from the mind of grasping at the selfless phenomena as self and transcend dualistic perception through spiritual trainings, then the whole universe before you merges into the oneness of great peace. And that is the attainment of Buddhahood, the absolute nature. If you attain Buddhahood, then every activity becomes spontaneously arisen Buddha action. All things appear and are seen through the omniscient Buddha wisdom as they are, simultaneously without discriminations, limitations, and dualities. You see all through the all-knowing wisdom of Buddha nature, not through the dualistic conceptual mind.

According to Buddhist tantras, in order to bring an ordinary person to the realization of the enlightened nature, it is very important for the person to receive the transmission of the power or blessing of the realization (*rTogs Pa'i Byin rLabs*) from a realized master. Then, such a lineage of transmission moves through various stages and times as the link to the realization, the true awakened nature, and as the means of communicating the teachings.

I am writing this article based on the interpretation of the Ter tradition by the third Dodrupchen Rinpoche, Jigme Tenpa'i Nyima (1865–1926).[45]

The main source of the Terma tradition of the Nyingma school is Guru Padmasambhava. He was one of the greatest tantric masters and saints of Buddhist history. In the eighth century, at the invitation of King Thrisong Detsen of Tibet, he came to Tibet from India and fulfilled three major missions. First, through the display of spiritual power, he pacified the human and nonhuman forces who were obstructing the founding of Dharma in Tibet. Second, he brought Buddhism in general and especially the transmission of the teachings and blessing powers of tantra for his many Tibetan disciples and their followers. Third, through his enlightened power he concealed numerous teachings and transmissions, as well as religious objects, as Ter for the benefit of future followers.

While transmitting esoteric teachings to his realized disciples in Tibet, Guru Padmasambhava concealed (*sBas*) many teachings with the blessings of his enlightened mind stream in the nature of the intrinsic awareness (*Rig Pa*) of the minds of his disciples through the power of "mind-mandate transmission" (*gTad rGya*); thereby the master and disciple became united as one in the teachings and realization. Here, the master has concealed the teachings and blessings, the esoteric attainments, as Ter in the pure nature of the minds of his disciples through his enlightened power, and he has made aspirations that the Ter may be discovered for the sake of beings when the appropriate time comes. By the power of this method, which is called the mind-mandate transmission, the actual discoveries of the teachings take place. The mind-mandate transmission is the heart core of the Ter tradition of Guru Padmasambhava.

Then, in the succeeding centuries, when the time for benefiting beings with a particular teaching arrived, the reincarnations of the realized disciples of Guru Padmasambhava discovered those teachings that had been transmitted and concealed in them by the master in their past lives, through the power of the enlightened aspirations of the master and disciples and the good karma of beings. There are thousands of images, symbolic scripts, complete texts, medicinal material, and ritual tools concealed by Guru Padmasambhava and discovered as Ter substances (*gTer rDzas*), but the main Ter is the teachings and the blessings transmitted through the minds of the disciples.

TRANSMISSION OF TER

The transmission of Ter has been channeled through six kinds or stages of lineages (*brGyud Pa Drug*). Of the six lineages, three are identical to the lineage of general tantric transmissions in Nyingma scriptures. They are the lineage of transmission from "enlightened mind to enlightened mind among the Buddhas" (*rGyal Ba dGongs brGyud*), the lineage of transmission through mere "indications among the knowledge holders" (*Rig 'Dzin brDa brGyud*), and the lineage of "oral transmission among ordinary beings" (*Gang Zag sNyan brGyud*).

The next three lineages are unique to the Ter transmission, and the accomplishment of Ter discoveries are based on those three transmissions. The first is the "transmission of aspirational empowerment" (*sMon Lam dBang bsKur*) or the mind-mandate transmission whereby, through his concentration of enlightened power, Guru Padmasambhava transmits and conceals the esoteric attainments and the teachings in the field of intrinsic awareness, the enlightened nature of the disciple's mind. This is the main aspect of the transmission. The second is the "transmission through prophetic authorization" (*Lung bsTan bKa' Babs*), in which the master inspires the disciple and gives prophecies concerning his becoming a Tertön in the future. It is not just a foretelling of the future; rather, by his enlightened power, he makes happen that which he prophesies. The third is the "entrustment to the Ḍākinīs" (*mKha' 'Gro gTad rGya*), in which the master entrusts the Ter, the Tertön (*gTer sTon*, Ter Discoverer), the teachers, and the followers of the tradition to the protection of the Ḍākinīs and Dharma protectors. In the case of an Earth Ter, the master entrusts the objects, such as the caskets containing the yellow scrolls with symbolic scripts, to the Ḍākinīs and Dharma protectors to keep them and hand them over to the Tertön when the time comes. Thus, every Ter teaching is transmitted through the six types of transmission.

TWO MAJOR CATEGORIES OF TER

While Ter can be divided into eighteen categories and so on, there are two major categories of Ter based on their way of discovery. They are Earth Ter (*Sa gTer*) and Mind Ter (*dGongs gTer*). The discovery of Earth Ter involves earthly materials such as symbolic scripts (*brDa Yig*) written on a scroll of paper known as a yellow scroll (*Shog Ser*) and so on. These are to assist the discovery of the concealment or to awaken the memory of the Ter enshrined in the enlightened nature of the mind of the Tertön. However, people usually conceive of Mind Ter being transmitted through mind, but that Earth Ter is something that Tertöns discover from earthly objects, such as rocks, lakes, and so on. Actually the symbolic script merely becomes the key, but is neither the real Ter of teachings nor the transmission of the attainment, which comes only from the Tertön's mind.

EARTH TER

There are different ways of concealing the Ters, but mostly they involve three stages. First, Guru Padmasambhava transmitted his esoteric teachings and attainments to his disciples and concealed them in their minds' absolute nature. Ordinary mind is changing because of concepts and emotions, but the true nature is changeless and preserves the teachings intact within itself. That is the place where the actual concealment of Ter takes place. The third Dodrupchen wrote:

> The ultimate place, the sacred treasure where the wisdom blessing of the vajra speech is preserved without deterioration through the power of the mind-mandate transmission made by Guru Rinpoche (Padmasambhava), is the sphere of changeless intrinsic nature of the mind of the Tertön.[46]

Second, with his consort Yeshe Tsogyal, Guru Padmasambhava put the teachings into symbolic or coded scripts in various languages, mostly what is called Ḍākinī language, and wrote them on yellow scrolls or on various objects such as images and ritual objects. Because of the power of the aspirational transmission of Guru Padmasambhava, the symbolic script will have the power to awaken the transmission when the Tertön reads it. Then the Tertön puts the yellow scrolls in a casket and conceals the casket (gTer sGrom) in a place of Ter concealment (gTer gNas), such as in rocks, mountains, lakes, temples, images, and the sky through his or her mystical power, and it becomes invisible until the time of discovery.

Third, Guru Padmasambhava inspires his disciples to be

Tertöns and gives prophetic blessings concerning when and how each one will become a Tertön. This is not a mere prediction of the future, but a blessing that makes the prophesied events happen because of the power of the truth of the master's words.

It is said that there will be one hundred major Tertöns and a thousand minor Tertöns. Starting with Sangye Lama (eleventh century), a great number of Tertöns appeared in Tibet, and thousands of volumes of teachings and a vast number of religious artifacts were discovered as Ter. Even today, since the beginning of the 1980s, the discoveries of Ter have resumed in Tibet. Tertöns are the reincarnations of the disciples of Guru Padmasambhava, and from him they have received the mind-mandate transmission of the teachings and have accomplished high attainments. With the exception of a few Tertöns, most of them have been tantric practitioners living at home with families. They transmute their everyday life into the training of the union of bliss and emptiness without discriminations and propagate the teachings they have discovered.

Some of the great Tertöns are Nyang Nyima Özer (1124–1192), Guru Chöwang (1212–1270), Ogyen Lingpa (1323–?), Rigdzin Gödem (1337–1408), Sangye Lingpa (1340–1396), Dorje Lingpa (1346–1405), Ratna Lingpa (1403–1478), Pema Lingpa (1450–?), Rigdzin Jatsön Nyingpo (1585–1656), Minling Terdag Lingpa (1646–1714), Rigdzin Jigme Lingpa (1729–1798), and Khyentse Wangpo (1820–1892).

Most of the Tertöns, before discovering any Ter, seem to be ordinary people. They do not necessarily appear as scholars, meditators, or Tulkus. However, due to their inner spiritual attainments and the transmissions they have received in their past lives, they suddenly start discovering mystical Ters at the appropriate time, without the need of any apparent training. At the beginning, skeptics often raise doubts about these discoveries from such unexpected people. In some cases, a Tertön's natural directness and honesty may appear as unconventional or even impolite to those who hold conservative values. But gradually, if they are true Ter discoveries, they gain the recognition of higher spiritual authorities and the respect of the people, whom they benefit. It is important to understand this cultural context, otherwise a great Tertön might be mistaken for a charlatan. For example, it is unfortunate that a Western author recently disparaged a great Tertön of the Nyingma tradition by citing criticism of the Tertön by some of his unqualified contemporary detractors and by portraying the Tertön's expressions of humility and confidence in realization as contradictions, even though these are characteristics of the writings of many Buddhist sages.

The following is a description of the common process of Earth Ter discovery; however, it is certainly not the only one, for Ters have been discovered in many other ways. First, the Tertön receives the prophetic guide (*Kha Byang*) in pure visions, directly, or in indications from Guru Padmasambhava, Ḍākinīs, or deities. Then he or she performs the Ter preparatory practices (*gTer sGrub*), doing meditations or rituals as instructed in the prophetic guide.

When the time comes, the Tertön goes to the concealment place, either alone or with selected followers, such as his or her consort and heart disciples or just onlookers. Many Ter discoveries take place in secret (*gSang gTer*) and many in public (*Khrom gTer*). There, while performing the feast-offering ceremony (*Tshogs*), the discovery takes place in different ways. It may be that the Ter descends from the concealment place into the hands of the Tertön at the end of a rainbow beam; or the Tertön climbs up a rock, which in ordinary circumstances is too steep to climb, opens a door in the rock, and climbs down with the casket; or the Tertön disappears and then reappears with the Ter; or the Tertön uses a tool such as a chisel to dig into the rock, and after hard digging takes out the Ter; or the Tertön jumps into a lake and brings out the Ter. Sometimes the Tertön discovers the Ter from images, temples, or from the sky. Sometimes Tertöns discover Ters concealed at far distances through their meditative power, without needing to go there, because the Ter protectors bring the Ters to them.

Among the discovered Ters there are also images, religious objects, and ritual tools, but the important ones are the symbolic letters written on yellow scrolls. Most of the scrolls are kept in the sealed Ter caskets made of precious materials, stone, wood, and so on.

Again by the performance of more Ter preparatory practices, the Ter casket spontaneously opens, and in it the Tertön discovers the yellow scroll. It is called "yellow scroll" because most of them are of yellowish or golden color, but in fact they could be of any color, length, or design. On these yellow scrolls the Tertöns find symbolic script in any of the various human and nonhuman scripts and languages, such as those of India, Tibet, and the Ḍākinī land.

Symbolic scripts are in various characters, and they are

categorized into three groups: "Just visible" (sNang Tsam) is one syllable or more, but not necessarily a word. "Just a basis" (rTen Tsam) is a phrase or a few phrases, a sentence or a few sentences related to the teachings of the text, such as a brief outline of the text, a part of the text, the title of the text, or an event linked to the concealment. Sometimes it is a piece of writing unrelated to the subject. "Complete text" (mThar Ch'ag) is a discovery of the whole text.

The Tertön sees, contemplates, or unites his naked wisdom, which is self-arisen from his innate luminous nature, with the symbolic scripts and thereby awakens the power of Guru Padmasambhava's vajra speech wisdom, which is concealed in him. He decodes the words in the symbolic scripts (brDa bKrol) and discovers the meaning, the Ter, from them. The discovery of Ter is the arising of the Dharma treasures of the ultimate sphere (Tib. Ch'os dByings, Skt. dharmadhātu) as the power of the intrinsic awareness (Rig rTsal) or the arising of the power of the intrinsic awareness as the teachings.[47] If you do not have the realization of the intrinsic awareness of Dzogpa Chenpo, which pervades the ultimate sphere, you cannot discover a Ter of Guru Padmasambhava, which comes through mind-mandate transmission.

So the symbolic scripts become the key to awaken the memories of the teachings and attainments from the expanse of the intrinsic nature of the Tertön's mind. Then, after more Ter preparatory practices, when the Tertön sees the signs of the appropriate time, he transcribes the teachings. Thereafter the Tertön transmits the teachings to the followers and entrusts them to the chief recipient of the Ter, called the doctrine holder (Ch'os bDag). Doctrine holders are usually people who also have received the transmission of the teaching from Guru Padmasambhava and have taken responsibility for the propagation of the teachings.

MIND TER

The methods of concealment, transmission, and discovery are similar to those of Earth Ter, except that they do not rely on any external earthly source, such as yellow scrolls, as the key to discovery. In many instances of Mind Ter, seeing or hearing symbolic words or sounds in visions causes the discovery of the Ter, but usually the discovery does not rely on any external sources, and there is no involvement of earthly objects as the means of discovering the Ter. A Mind Tertön discovers the Ter by awakening the mind-mandated transmission spontaneously from the expanse of the intrinsic awareness of his mind, when the circumstances have matured and the time has come.

There is a third category of discovered teachings known as Pure Vision (*Dag sNang*). Pure-vision teachings are not Terma. They are merely teachings given by Buddhas, deities, and teachers in visions. For this discovery the discoverer does not need to be such a highly realized person, and there is no mind-mandated transmission. However, there are cases in which Ter teachings have been discovered or designated as pure-vision teachings, and when that is the case they are in fact Ter teachings.

In the Nyingma literature there are thousands of volumes of Ter texts discovered by hundreds of Tertöns, starting in the eleventh century and continuing to this day. The majority of texts concern sādhana, ritual, prayer, and various esoteric performances (*Las*). There are a great number of texts on philosophy, meditation, and the result of Buddhist practice in general and especially of the tantric tradition. Also, there are numerous texts on medicine, astrology, history, and biography.

It is astonishing to realize the scope and impact of the spiritual treasures conferred by Guru Padmasambhava in order to improve the value of the social, literary, and spiritual life of Tibetan society and the offspring of its tradition, over the course of a millennium without cessation. And it is shocking to see that even many Tibetans have little awareness of the significance of this tradition. According to Tibetan historians, Buddhism may have never been able to be established in Tibet without the blessings of Guru Padmasambhava. In Tibet there is hardly a single significant mountain, lake, or valley that was not blessed by him individually by visiting, meditating, displaying miracles, and concealing Ters in them. Even many physical marks such as imprints, spontaneously arisen images, or caves of meditation are still visible. The Ter tradition includes some of the most striking evidence of the great imprint left in Tibet for the welfare of the world through the enlightened activities of Guru Padmasambhava. At the time of his departure from Tibet, he expressed his kindness and his promise to the Tibetans in the following words:

> When you face the bad times of the dark age,
> Every day and night I will come to Tibet.
> I will come to you riding the rays of the sun,
> And on every tenth day of the waxing moon
> I will come to you in person.[48]

○ 9 ○

THE EMPOWERMENTS
AND PRECEPTS OF
ESOTERIC TRAINING

EMPOWERMENTS

EMPOWERMENT OR WANG (Tib. *dBang,* Skt. *abhiṣheka*) is the initiation that transmits or awakens the esoteric (tantric) wisdom, the power or realization in the mind of the disciple. Precepts (Tib. *Dam Tshig,* Skt. *samaya*) are the trainings for observing the disciplines of the esoteric practice (tantra). Receiving empowerment and observing precepts are prerequisites of tantric Buddhist training, which includes the Ngöndro practice. Receiving empowerment and observing precepts are the esoteric causation, the forces that sow the seeds of the realization of fully enlightened Buddhahood. They form the esoteric path upon which we progress toward the accomplishment of the union of bliss and emptiness.

A talk given at Mahasiddha Temple, Hawley, Mass., on September 20, 1987. This chapter is based on NS, LST, DD, DN, SGG, KZZ, TRD-II 200a/4–264b/6, and NCC, and all these texts and commentaries in turn are based on original tantras.

They are the esoteric fruition of, or the confidence of securing, the awakened Buddha essence and Buddha qualities.

People may have a feeling that the concepts of empowerment and samaya are very different from common (sūtric) Buddhist disciplines, but they are not. In common Buddhist teachings we talk about disciplines and karma. What is karma? It is a chain or process of causation. Also, we talk about interdependent causation, the process by which everything functions through causes and conditions. Empowerment and precepts are based on the same principle. When you receive the transmission of esoteric power and realization through an empowerment, which acts as the cause, and if you preserve that transmission by maintaining precepts, the disciplines, you will reach its goal as the fruition. So it is a karmic causation. It is not something based on a different principle, but it has a different quality. In ordinary Buddhism, karma and interdependent causation, the process of spiritual practice and result, is like the process of growing a tree. The tree has lineage, it has causation, it grows through a process; but its functioning is less powerful, its growth is slower, it has less potential, and is also less risky. But empowerment and precepts are like electricity. The process is fast; it has more power, energy, speed, and can also be more risky.

The word for empowerment has also been translated as "initiation." Receiving the empowerment is the taking of the esoteric, or tantric, transmission of Buddhism from a vajra master, and it is the entering into the esoteric path of training. It is also the awakening of wisdom and wisdom power that every individual inherits, like the switch that turns on the light. In order to complete the esoteric path and to perfect the awakened wisdom, it is essential to maintain the continuity of the transmitted power by observing the precepts.

A highly intelligent person with full potential is initiated into the esoteric training of Buddhism by receiving the empowerments. The initiate then maintains and perfects the esoteric training by the total dedication of his or her life, mind, and perceptions through the most skillful spiritual path of observing the precepts. According to Tibetan Buddhism, that is the most skillful and swift means to attain Buddhahood.

Tantric training is a practice of transformation. Here it is important to understand the meaning of transformation. It is not, especially in the inner tantras, like transforming iron into gold or bad into good; it is the transformation of phenomenal existence into its true nature, as it is. When you receive empowerments and observe the precepts, what will be transformed? The obscurations of perceptions and emotional afflictions will be cleansed, and the wisdom of your realized mind will shine forth by realizing what you actually are. Through receiving empowerments we realize the Buddha essence, which is called primordial wisdom, the meaning of the empowerment in us.

Through observing the precepts, we realize and maintain the Buddha essence and we attain the Buddha qualities, which are present in ourselves from the beginning. It is not as though we are getting the Buddha essence and Buddha qualities from external sources; rather, our own nature and qualities present within ourselves, from primordial time, are being purified and refined.

QUALITIES OF THE TANTRIC TEACHER

The tantric teacher is like the father in tantric training. The teacher should be a fully qualified master, not just an

ordinary preacher or scholar. Mere performance of a ceremony or giving talks will not suffice. This might work just as
a show or performance, but it would be just like a reflection.
The teacher should embody the following qualities:

1. He or she should be one who has received the complete
empowerment. If he is giving the empowerment of a particular text, he himself should have previously received the empowerment of this particular text. Unless he has received the
empowerments for this text, he cannot perform them, though
he may be a great master. Even if he has received empowerments of a higher tantra and the text is one of a lower tantra,
still he cannot perform the empowerment if he has not received the transmission of this particular text.

2. He should also be someone who has taken the precepts
and is observing them. Even if he has received the empowerment but is not observing the precepts he is not qualified.

3. He should have the knowledge of the unique traditions
of the particular lineage. Even though he may be preserving
the precepts, if he does not know the unique traditions
(*Phyag-bZhes*) of the lineage, he is not qualified.

4. He should be skilled in performing the rituals of the
empowerment. Even though he has knowledge of the unique
tradition and has received the empowerment, if he is not
skilled in performing the empowerment ceremony, he is not
qualified.

5. He should have perfected or completed the mantra recitations of the sādhana of the particular text. For example, if
the teacher is performing the *Rigdzin Dupa* empowerment he
should have completed the recitations, repeating the mantras
13,000,000 times in strict retreat. Different texts have different systems for specifying the number of required recita-

tions to complete in retreat. But there is an exception. In many cases it is difficult to fulfill this requirement. For example, the *Rinchen Terdzö* collection has hundreds of texts and sādhanas; it would be very difficult to find someone who has completed the recitations of all of them. It would take almost half a lifetime to finish the recitations of all of these texts. So it is generally accepted that if a teacher has completed the recitations of a major root tantra, for example the *Guhyagarbha-māyājāla-tantra,* he will be able to perform the empowerment for the others.

6. He should be someone who is unstained by any kind of breaking of the precepts. If he himself has committed any root or gross infractions then, like water from a broken pitcher, what kind of wisdom power can he transmit to others?

THE NATURE OF THE MAṆḌALA

The maṇḍala, or altar, is like the mother in the transmission of empowerment and tantric trainings. For the transmission of the empowerment, there must be the maṇḍala, representing the assembly of the deity, filled with various important symbolic substances of empowerment. Before giving the empowerment, the master performs the sādhana of the deity by himself, without the presence of any disciple, in order to prepare himself and the symbolic maṇḍala as the wisdom deities, maṇḍalas, and empowerment substances. In that performance, which is called the preparation of the empowerment (*dBang sGrub*), the fully qualified tantric master consecrates the symbolic maṇḍala as the actual maṇḍala of the deity. In each empowerment there are many different empowerment substances (*dBang rDzas*), and each symbolic substance has a different meaning and power bestowed by the teacher. There are four major maṇḍalas for empowerments of the inner tantras: the Vase, Secret, Wisdom, and Verbal empowerments.

(I) The maṇḍala of the Vase Empowerment (*Bum dBang*) is the body maṇḍala. For the Vase Empowerment we generally use a vase. However, in its true sense, the vase represents the whole maṇḍala of the deity. It is the empowerment of the body or physical realm of the deities, and so it represents the whole physical aspect of the maṇḍala, including the deities, mansions, and pure land. Body has three categories:[49] The excellent maṇḍala of the vase initiation is the body maṇḍala—one's mental and physical aspects are the wisdom bodies, the maṇḍalas of the deities in their true nature. The middle-level maṇḍala of the vase initiation is a painted maṇḍala. The lesser maṇḍala of the vase initiation is a sand maṇḍala. (2) The maṇḍala of the Secret Empowerment (*gSang dBang*) is relative bodhichitta, the essential fluid. (3) The maṇḍala of the Wisdom Empowerment (*Sher dBang*) is the consort and her secret lotus. (4) The maṇḍala of the Verbal Empowerment (*Tshig dBang*) is the absolute wisdom, the enlightened mind, which is the ultimate meaning or goal of the empowerment.

QUALITIES OF THE DISCIPLE

The tantric disciple is like the child of the father/master and mother/maṇḍala in tantric trainings. There are five essential qualities of a tantric trainee.

I. One must have confidence, trust, or faith. If you do not

have faith or trust, you are not a vessel able to receive any kind of blessing. You are not a container for the esoteric attainments.

2. One must have diligence. If you do not have diligence, then even if you have received the empowerments you will not be able to preserve the transmitted power and strive toward the goal.

3. One must persevere in meditation. Even if you are diligent, if you do not meditate then you will not progress or obtain many benefits.

4. One must perform sādhana, the esoteric rites and meditations of the development stage and the perfection stage, to achieve the result. Without meditation on the sādhanas there are no means to achieve the attainments.

5. One must keep the precepts, the disciplines that maintain and advance the transmitted esoteric wisdom, in order to reach the fruition.

CATEGORIZATION OF EMPOWERMENTS

Empowerments are categorized as the empowerment of cause, the empowerment of path, and the empowerment of result. But there are two different ways of designating what is the empowerment of cause, path, and result. Although there are two ways of categorizing these, it is not the case that one must be right or better and the other wrong, since they are different. This is a way of classifying with respect to different aspects. For instance, you may categorize people as tall or short and also as older or younger. These two ways of classification are not contradictory, but are based on different criteria.

(1) The presence of the Buddha essence and Buddha qualities in us is the empowerment of cause. The Buddha essence is not something that is external or that the teacher gives you. Rather, the teacher helps you through the empowerment to realize or to awaken the wisdom that you already have and always have possessed. (2) The aspect of the ritual performance of the transmission of the empowerment by the teacher and the contemplation on the process of that transmission by the disciple is the empowerment of the path. (3) Having received the transmission and followed the path, one matures as the four Buddha bodies and five Buddha wisdoms. This is the empowerment of result.

The second system of categorization is as follows. (1) The empowerments given to disciples who have not been initiated before are classified as empowerments of cause. (2) The empowerments given to disciples for developing their maturation or restoring the broken precepts are classified as empowerments of path. When you have not received an empowerment before, but are receiving it for the first time, this would be the empowerment of cause, because the empowerment becomes a cause, the start of your esoteric training. For example, if you had never received the *Rigdzin Dupa* empowerment and you received it today, this would be the empowerment of cause. But then when you receive it repeatedly to help you to mature your realization and experiences and to restore your broken precepts, it becomes the empowerment of path. (3) The empowerments given to disciples who are ready to achieve the final attainment and which cause the disciple to attain the final goal are classified as empowerments of result because they bring the final result. If you are fully enlightened, you do not need the empowerment. But until you become fully enlightened, you will need the empowerment in order to help you to initiate or upgrade your spiritual realization. This classification of empowerments depends on the receiver, rather than on the empowerment itself or the teacher.

EFFECTS OF EMPOWERMENT

The question of what kinds of benefits we will get if we receive an empowerment often arises for us. There are three main benefits listed in the texts. (1) The supreme effect of the empowerment causes you to realize primordial wisdom, the meaning of the empowerment. If you are a gifted person and all conditions are perfect, then during the empowerment you will realize primordial wisdom, the meaning or true goal of the empowerment, the actual goal of spiritual practice. (2) The middle-level effect of the empowerment causes you to develop experiences of bliss, clarity, and no thought. (3) The lesser effect of the empowerment causes the arising of confidence in seeing your own three doors (body, speech, and mind) as the body, speech, and mind of the deities.

These are the three categories of effects given in the texts, but they all seem too elevated or too hard for many of us to achieve in the empowerments. My personal feeling is that when we receive an empowerment, even if we do not have any of these three types of experience, as long as we have a peaceful, blissful, or devotional mind that opens, relaxes, pacifies, and calms us down, this will become a transmission of the blessings of the teacher and the deities, and it will establish a connection with the particular esoteric practice. So we should feel fortunate. Also, when we receive transmission from an authentic teacher, at least we are receiving permission to study and practice the particular teaching. We may not be receiving even the lesser effects, but we should still be proud of our good fortune.

The Two Causes and Four Conditions of Empowerment

The empowerments are comprised of two aspects: the first are the two causes and the second are the four conditions. The gathering together of these two causes and four conditions completes the requirements for an empowerment.

The two causes are as follows:

1. The similar (common or mutual) cause (*mTshung lDan Gyi rGyu*) is the presence of one's natural essence as the Buddha essence, free from elaborations from primordial time. It is also the presence of the qualities of the five aggregates, five elements, and five emotions as the five male and five female Buddhas and the five primordial wisdoms in their true nature.

2. The cooperative cause (*Lhan Chig Byed Pa'i rGyu*) is the blessed substances of the empowerment, such as the vase, images, crown, and so forth.

The four conditions consist of the following:

1. The causal condition (*rGyu'i rKyen*), which is the receptive disciple who has faith, three types of diligence (in acting for self, others, and both), and maintains the precepts.

2. The empowering condition (*bDag Po'i rKyen*), which is the fully qualified teacher who is learned in the five aspects of tantra: (a) suchness of self—the realization of emptiness, (b) suchness of deities—the realization of the three doors as

the three vajras, (c) suchness of tantra—the perfection of the two stages, the stages of development and perfection, as well as the four actions: peaceful, increasing, powerful, and wrathful, (d) suchness of recitation—the completion of the recitation of mantra, and (e) suchness of projection and withdrawal of lights of blessings during meditation.

3. The observed objective condition (*dMigs rKyen*), which is the realized teacher's wisdom (knowledge) of the rituals, deities, and mantras, and the contemplation of the empowerments.

4. The immediately preceding condition (*De Ma Thag rKyen*), which is the preceding empowerment as it opens the opportunity for the succeeding empowerment.

THE ACTUAL EMPOWERMENT

In general there is a preliminary, main, and concluding section in each empowerment. The preliminary section has two aspects: the outer and inner enterings. The main section has two aspects: the five common empowerments of the five Buddha families and the four uncommon empowerments. And then there are the concluding empowerments. All empowerments of inner tantras will not necessarily contain all these aspects, and some may have more, but they will be present in most elaborate empowerments.

PRELIMINARY SECTION

1. The outer entering begins with entering the door of the shrine room and rinsing the mouth with sanctified water for purification, and ends with the casting of flowers into the maṇḍala to determine your Buddha family.

2. The inner entering begins with the returning of the flowers, the crown deity, to you by the master, which is symbolized by the throwing of rice by the Lama, and ends with the showing of the maṇḍala.

MAIN SECTION

If it is an empowerment of Kriyāyoga, it is mainly a vase and crown empowerment. If it is an empowerment of Charyā-yoga, it has the five empowerments of the five Buddha families. If it is an empowerment of Yogatantra, it contains the five empowerments of the five Buddha families, the empowerments of deities, and the empowerments of the activities of the master.

For the inner tantras, Mahāyoga, Anuyoga, and Atiyoga, in addition to containing the five empowerments of the five Buddha families and so on, it contains the four uncommon empowerments. All the inner tantras contain the four uncommon empowerments.

Then what is special about Atiyoga? For Dzogpa Chenpo the special emphasis is on the fourth uncommon empowerment, the verbal empowerment. Many of us have received the *Nyingthig Yazhi* (*sNying Thig Ya bZhi*) empowerments. It has a detailed Atiyoga empowerment with its four aspects: the elaborate, simple, very simple, and utterly simple empowerments. The fourth uncommon empowerment introduces you directly to the intrinsic awareness, the Buddha essence. In Mahāyoga and Anuyoga tantras, the fourth uncommon empowerment introduces you to the great bliss, the meaning of the innate wisdom, which is produced as the result of the third empowerment, in which one has realized the symbolic innate wisdom (*dPe'i Ye Shes*) through the path of skillful means by relying on mudrā. During this fourth empowerment, through dependence upon the experiences of the third empowerment, one realizes directly the meaning innate wisdom (*Don Gyi Ye Shes*). So the fourth empowerment of the Mahāyoga and Anuyoga tantras is different from the fourth empowerment of Atiyoga.

The Five Common Empowerments of the Five Buddha Families

By the five common empowerments of the five Buddha families one receives the power of transforming one's ordinary qualities into Buddha qualities.

1. By the Vase Empowerment one transforms the aggregate of consciousness into Akṣhobhya Buddha, the element of space into his consort, and the emotion of anger into the wisdom of dharmadhātu.

2. By the Crown Empowerment one transforms the aggregate of feeling into Ratnasambhava Buddha, the element of water into his consort, and the emotion of pride into the wisdom of evenness.

3. By the Vajra Empowerment one transforms the aggregate of concept into Amitābha Buddha, the element of air into his consort, and the emotion of desire into the discriminative wisdom.

4. By the Bell Empowerment one transforms the aggregate of formation into Amoghasiddhi Buddha, the element of fire into his consort, and the emotion of envy into the all-accomplishing wisdom.

5. By the Name Empowerment one transforms the aggregate of form into Vairochana Buddha, the element of earth into his consort, and the emotion of ignorance into the mirrorlike wisdom.

The Four Uncommon Empowerments

1. By the Vase Empowerment one receives the blessing of the vajra body of the Buddha, purifies the karma of one's body and the obscurations of one's channels, and attains or establishes the basis of attaining the perfection of the path of accumulation, the state of Vidyādhara with residues, and Nirmāṇakāya.

2. By the Secret Empowerment one receives the blessing of the vajra speech of the Buddha, purifies the karma of one's speech and the obscurations of one's air or energy, and attains or establishes the basis of attaining the perfection of the path of application, the state of Vidyādhara of control over life, and Sambhogakāya.

3. By the Wisdom Empowerment one receives the blessing of the vajra mind of the Buddha, purifies the karma of one's mind and the obscurations of one's essence, and attains or establishes the basis of attaining the perfection of the path of insight, the state of Vidyādhara of great sign, and Dharmakāya.

4. By the Verbal Empowerment one receives the blessing of the vajra wisdom of the Buddha, purifies the karma of universal ground and the obscurations of one's intellect, and attains or establishes the basis of attaining the perfection of the nine stages of the meditation path, the state of Vidyādhara of spontaneous accomplishment, and Svabhāvikakāya.

PRECEPTS

After receiving an empowerment from a tantric master, one maintains the realization by means of spiritual or esoteric views, experiences, realizations, and life in accord with the teaching. This is the observing of precepts (samaya). It is the continuation of one's esoteric and innermost spiritual attainments, which are received during the empowerment.

THREE DIVISIONS OF PRECEPTS

In Buddhism there are three principal divisions of disciplines or precepts (sDom Pa). First are the Vinaya precepts, the disciplines of Buddhist monks and lay devotees. The Vinaya disciplines are mainly a physical discipline. Second are the Bodhisattva precepts. This training is based on having and preserving an aspiration and dedication to serve all beings without any self interest. So the Bodhisattva precepts are mainly mental. Third are the tantric precepts. They are based on primordial wisdom. When receiving empowerment, one should understand and realize the meaning of the empowerment, the wisdom, and then maintain that wisdom by maintaining pure precepts. So to maintain primordial wisdom is the tantric precept. Thus the Vinaya precepts are mainly based on physical behavior, the Bodhisattva precepts are based on mental attitude, and the tantric precepts are based on primordial wisdom, pure perception.

TIME OF TAKING THE PRECEPTS

There are differences in when you receive the various precepts. In the Vinaya or Bodhisattva training, the texts and the disciplines explained in them are studied first, and then one decides whether or not to undertake them. But in tantra, first the empowerment is received, and then study is undertaken. Traditionally one does not see, read, or hear anything about tantra until one has received the transmission by being initiated into it. Here, one may have doubts: "How can I receive tantric precepts without knowing about them?" That's the whole point! Tantra is only for exceptional people who are ready for it and are without doubt. It is not meant for the unknowing or unready. In tantra, after you receive empowerment you have to preserve the precepts. It has strong potential for benefiting as well as harming. For receiving the empowerment, the student must be an especially gifted person, the teacher a realized person, and the maṇḍala blessed as wisdom substance. When the combination of these three qualities is present, there is no need to go through the process of learning first and then deciding whether or not to proceed. To be ready means to be receptive to tantra.

PRECEPTS COMMON TO BOTH OLD AND NEW TANTRIC TRADITIONS

There are many categories of precepts. Within the inner tantras, common to both the old and new tantras, there are fourteen root infractions (or root downfalls, *rTsa lTung*) and eight gross infractions (or auxiliary downfalls, *sBom Po*).

THE FOURTEEN ROOT INFRACTIONS[50]

After entering into the inner tantric trainings, we should refrain from committing any of the following fourteen root infractions:

1. To have contempt for the teacher from whom you have received transmissions of tantra.
2. To transgress the precepts of the Buddha.
3. To get angry at your vajra sisters and brothers.
4. To wish to hurt any being or to forsake love for any being.

5. To abandon the Bodhichitta, the mind of beneficial thoughts for others.

6. To deride other religions, such as Hīnayāna, Mahāyāna, Hindu, Christian, or any religious traditions.

7. To give secrets of tantric teachings to people who are not matured. If someone is ready, then you should give the secret teachings; but if someone is not ready and you give the teachings, it will be harmful to yourself as well as to the other person, as he or she will misunderstand and abuse it.

8. To afflict one's own five aggregates, which are the Buddha families. One should not abuse one's own body but take care of it.

9. To have doubt about the primordially pure nature, as well as to have doubt about the basis, path, and result.

10. Not to perform exorcism toward negative forces due to perverted compassion. You can perform exorcism to help people. As you know, in a previous life the Buddha killed someone for the sake of saving many lives, and it caused the multiplication of his merit. This was not demonstrated as esoteric practice, but rather as exoteric practice. But in order to perform exorcism, you should be someone who has power and high attainment, not an ordinary person.

11. To conceptualize the dharmadhātu, the ultimate sphere, which is free from conceptions.

12. To hurt the minds of faithful people, which means hurting the feelings of faith among faithful people.

13. To not enjoy the substances of precepts. This means to refuse to take the substances of precepts, such as the five nectars, the feast substances, and other esoteric substances, without discrimination.

14. To deride or have contempt for women, who are the wisdom nature.

THE EIGHT GROSS INFRACTIONS

After entering into inner tantras, we should refrain from committing any of the following eight gross infractions:⁵¹

1. To have a consort who is ordinary, not initiated in the esoteric path.
2. To receive the nectars from an improper source, an uninitiated consort of tantra.
3. Not to conceal the secret symbols of tantra from improper vessels, uninitiated people.
4. To make physical and vocal disturbances in esoteric assemblies such as feast ceremonies.
5. Not to tell the truth or not to teach someone who is a proper vessel, but to tell that person something else. For example, if someone who is a proper vessel for Atiyoga is given a teaching of the sūtras.
6. To remain in a group that lacks respect for the view and practices of tantra for more than seven days. The important point is that you should always check and evaluate what is most beneficial.
7. To pretend or boast that you are a Vajradhara (esoteric master) of tantra with pride, although you have no such knowledge.
8. To give secret teachings to someone who has previously received secret teachings but currently has no faith.

THE UNCOMMON PRECEPTS OF DZOGPA CHENPO⁵²

For those who are initiated into Dzogpa Chenpo training, it is essential to observe the following general and special precepts in order to maintain and perfect their meditation and realization.

GENERAL PRECEPTS OF DZOGPA CHENPO⁵²

The general category has twenty-eight precepts, and they are divided into two groups. The first group is the twenty-seven precepts of the outer, inner, and secret aspects of the body, speech, and mind of the root master or Lama. The whole universe is one in the maṇḍala of the esoteric master. Each outer, inner, and secret aspect is further divided into outer, inner, and secret aspects. The last precept, number twenty-eight, is designated as the collection of branch precepts.

First, the twenty-seven root precepts (*rTsa lTung*):

A. Precepts of the Body of the Root Master
1. The secret of the outer is to refrain from killing.
2. The inner of the outer is to refrain from sexual misconduct.
3. The outer of the outer is to refrain from stealing.
4. The outer of the inner is to refrain from having contempt for one's parents, brothers, and sisters.
5. The inner of the inner is to refrain from having contempt for Dharma symbols.
6. The secret of the inner is to refrain from abusing one's own body, which is the maṇḍala of the deities.
7. The secret of the secret is to refrain from even stepping on the shadow of the master.
8. The inner of the secret is to refrain from harassing the consort of the teacher or one's vajra brothers or sisters, even in play.
9. The outer of the secret is to refrain from beating one's vajra brothers or sisters.
B. Precepts of the Speech of the Root Master
10. The outer of the outer is to refrain from lying.
11. The inner of the outer is to refrain from divisive speech.
12. The secret of the outer is to refrain from harsh speech.

13. The outer of the inner is to refrain from being disrespectful toward people who teach Dharma.

14. The inner of the inner is to refrain from being disrespectful toward people who are pondering the Dharma.

15. The secret of the inner is to refrain from being disrespectful toward people who are meditating on the absolute nature.

16. The inner of the secret is to refrain from deriding the consort of the teacher.

17. The outer of the secret is to refrain from deriding one's vajra brothers and sisters.

18. The secret of the secret is to refrain from deriding the teacher.

C. Precepts of the Mind of the Root Master

19. The outer of the outer is to refrain from covetousness.

20. The inner of the outer is to refrain from malice.

21. The secret of the outer is to refrain from wrong views.

22. The outer of the inner is to refrain from perverted activities.

23. The inner of the inner is to refrain from excitation and torpor in meditation.

24. The secret of the inner is to refrain from perverted views.

25. The outer of the secret is to refrain from not thinking of the master and his or her consort for one whole day and night.

26. The inner of the secret is to refrain from not thinking about one's yidam for one whole day and night.

27. The secret of the secret is to refrain from not thinking of the view, meditation, and action for one whole day and night.

Second, the twenty-five branch precepts (*Yan Lag*):

A. The Five Precepts in Which One Should Employ Extraordinary Skillful Means
   1. Elimination [liberation] or exorcism. The main purpose of this performance is to eliminate the grasping at self and ignorance from one's own mind stream through realization and elimination of them from others' mind streams through compassionate activities.
   2. Union. This has two aspects: relative and absolute. The relative aspect is physical union, which brings about bliss, the symbolic primordial wisdom. The absolute aspect is the contemplation and realization of the union of appearances and emptiness, which generates absolute great bliss directly.
   3. To take things that are not given when the purpose is greater.
   4. To lie for the sake of benefiting others.
   5. To gossip for the purpose of leading someone to the Dharma.

B. The Five Precepts of Not Abandoning: In this case we are not talking about ordinary emotions, but the energies with pure intentions.
   6. Not to abandon desire—the desire toward all mother beings with compassion.
   7. Not to abandon hatred—the hatred that eliminates wrong views.
   8. Not to abandon ignorance—the ignorance that has no discriminating thoughts because of the realization of the equanimity of saṃsāra and nirvāṇa.
   9. Not to abandon pride—the pride that has confidence in the view of equality.
   10. Not to abandon jealousy—the jealousy that will not

admit dualistic views and activities into the sphere of the ultimate nature. If you are jealous, you will not want to let someone in through the door. In the same way, jealousy is not to let duality into the sphere of the ultimate nature.

C. The Five Precepts of Accepting: This signifies the acceptance of anything without discrimination.

11. Accepting feces (purīsha).
12. Accepting urine (mūtra).
13. Accepting blood (rakta).
14. Accepting meat (māṃsa).
15. Accepting semen (shukra).

D. The Five Precepts of Realizing the Purities

16. The five aggregates as the five Buddhas of the five Buddha families.
17. The five elements as the five female consorts of the five Buddhas.
18. The five sense objects as the five female Bodhisattvas.
19. The five faculties as the five male Bodhisattvas.
20. The five colors as the five primordial wisdoms.

E. The Five Precepts of Achieving Attainments: Through the power of having the previous five knowledges, such as realizing the five aggregates as the five Buddhas, it is to attain the state of the five Buddha families.

21. Attainment of the Buddha family.
22. Attainment of the Vajra family.
23. Attainment of the Ratna family.
24. Attainment of the Padma family.
25. Attainment of the Karma family.

SPECIAL PRECEPTS OF DZOGPA CHENPO

By realizing Dzogpa Chenpo and maintaining its realization, one preserves the special precepts—the view, meditation, and action of Dzogpa Chenpo, which is total, all-pervading, spontaneously accomplished, and free from conceptualization, experiences, discriminations, and limitations. There are four special precepts of Thregchö and Thögal in Dzogpa Chenpo.[53]

Two Precepts of Thregchö

1. Nonexistent (*Med Pa*). Dzogpa Chenpo has a standpoint devoid of rejecting and accepting. This precept refers to the realization of the nonexistence of the self that commits transgressions by having understood, experienced, or realized the intrinsic awareness of primordial purity.

2. All-pervading (*Phyal Ba*). By maintaining the essence, nature, and compassion through the four natural contemplations (*Chog bZhag bZhi*) of Thregchö, all the hundreds of thousands of precepts will be encompassed, just as hundreds of streams can be covered by one bridge.

Two Precepts of Thögal

3. Single (*gChig Pu*). By receiving the special transmission of Dzogpa Chenpo, one attains the state that encompasses all phenomena of saṃsāra and nirvāṇa as one, and that pervades all phenomenal existence through the power of the single intrinsic awareness.

4. Spontaneous accomplishment (*Lhun Grub*). If one has perfected the realization of Dzogpa Chenpo, then since one has abandoned the very basis of hurting others, one has perfected the observance of the Vinaya precepts. Since one has conceptionless compassion toward all unrealized living beings, one has generated beneficial thoughts for others and so

has perfected the Bodhisattva precepts. Since one has perfected the intrinsic awareness, one has perfected the tantric precepts. Such a person has perfected all the precepts with a single realization.

CONCLUSION

Panchen Pema Wangyal summarizes the tantric precepts in the following lines.

> In brief, if you realize your own body (i.e., body, speech, and mind) as the three vajras (the body, speech, and mind of the deities),
> Then the observance of hundreds of thousands of millions of precepts of tantra is encompassed in this realization.[54]

There are various categorizations of precepts. What I have given here are just the main precepts of tantra and Dzogpa Chenpo in particular. If you study the different tantras, each of them has its own system of precepts. But in essence, if you have and maintain pure perception, then all tantric precepts are included in it. Seeing all phenomena as the body of the Buddha, perceiving all speech as mantra, the pure speech of the Buddha, and realizing mind as the enlightened mind of the Buddha is pure perception. But perhaps this is too profound for us. Just to have respectful thoughts toward any phenomenon, whatever is in front of us, is pure perception. Having that kind of pure perception, having a positive mind, and being respectful and compassionate encapsulates the tantric precepts.

At the end of the performance of the Longchen Nyingthig empowerments, Kyabje Dodrupchen Rinpoche gave us the essence of precepts to observe. He said, "There are many pre

cepts such as the fourteen root infractions, but it is important and also manageable for you to have good relationships
between disciples and teacher, and good relationships
amongst yourselves and with people who are around you,
close to you. If you get angry then don't express it. If someone is sick or in any kind of trouble, try to be helpful."

This is a practical and common sense way of seeing, dealing with, and living by the precepts, and it is the discipline
of tantra. Last year, when we gathered together for a weekend
to meditate on compassion, most of the people liked it and
benefited by this. But there were some people who thought
compassion was not Dzogchen and that it was not "high"
enough, and that it was emotional or not a traditional way of
practicing Tibetan Buddhism. That kind of high-sounding
meditator proves how low the level of our tolerance has fallen
even toward compassion and the recitation of Avalokiteshvara's name. There is no trace of the great openness of the
Dzogpa Chenpo view. The problem is that we do not look at
ourselves, we do not see where we are standing and what our
situation is. Being respectful is pure perception, and compassion is the openness or the process of opening. Being respectful and compassionate toward the people or things around
you, with whom you are dealing in flesh and breath, is putting
spiritual training into true, living practice.

Think of the kind of attitude or feelings we have with each
individual among us. Do we feel: "I am better because I have
more money, a higher position, am more handsome, more
beautiful, or so forth. He or she is inferior to me." That is
pride. Do we feel a pain or itching in the stomach, thinking:
"He or she is higher than me." That is jealousy. But, if we

are thinking: "How wonderful that he or she is happy and making progress—much better than me. I am so happy for him or her," that is a rejoicing mind. It is proof that our Dharma practice is progressing. If, while keeping all the negative emotions in our heart, we talk about service to the whole world or to people in distant continents, then people with proper sense will perhaps laugh at us in their hearts. If we really want to help others, then first we must start with ourselves and with the people around us. You might have thought that when Rinpoche said to be respectful and kind to each other, that it was not a teaching and did not have any esoteric meaning, but just social virtue. But it has the most esoteric meaning, if we can apply it. To be kind and helpful to others embodies the Vinaya precepts, being physically disciplined. It contains the Bodhisattva precepts, having beneficial attitude to others. To be respectful embodies tantric precepts, having pure perception. So, to be kind, helpful, and respectful to others is the essence of esoteric disciplines.

RESTORING BROKEN PRECEPTS

If we have committed any infractions of precepts, then what should be done? We should repair this through purification practices, such as the Varjrasattva rites. Any kind of Ngöndro practice, going for refuge, developing Bodhichitta, or making maṇḍala offerings will be powerful in purifying negative karma; but the meditation and recitation of Vajrasattva is unique and specialized in purifying the traces of our evil karma and negative emotions, and for restoring and strengthening our precepts. For performing that purification it is necessary to complete the four powers (sTobs bZhi):

1. The power of support (*rTen Gyi sTobs*). We need some-one, an enlightened force, to rely upon. Since we have dualis-tic and judgmental minds, in order to help ourselves we need some higher authority on which to rely. We must have trust in the power of the support, in this case Vajrasattva.

2. The power of remorse (*Sun 'Byin Pa'i sTobs*). We should assault our misdeeds with strong remorse for what we have done, just as one who had consumed poison. If we do not have remorse, we will not want to purify our misdeeds because we will not feel that we have any negativities within us. For some people, if they kill an insect they will feel bad. For others, even if they kill many human beings they may only feel pride. The ability of reversing our negative life does not depend on what we did, but on how we feel about it. So remorse is very impor-tant in changing the attitude and course of life.

3. The power of commitment (*sDom Pa'i sTobs*). We should make a pledge, a promise, that we will not commit such deeds again at any cost. Generally people think, "I do not want to make any kind of commitment because making a commitment is the beginning of breaking a commitment." But if we do not make a commitment, there is nothing to break. The scriptures say that it is important to make a com-mitment, because a commitment produces a strong determi-nation and will power not to commit misdeeds again.

4. The power of antidote (*gNyen Po'i sTobs*). This is the power of the formula that purifies the impurities. In this case, it is the practice or sādhana of Vajrasattva, in which we purify the traces of bad karma, habits of negative emotions, through the blessing nectars of the united male and female of Vajra-sattva.

Support, remorse, the promise, and then the actual purification—these four aspects are very important. In general, in the Vinaya, if you break your precepts, if you commit any of the four root infractions, then you cannot restore them. The Bodhisattva precepts can be restored through the power of yourself and others. In tantra, precepts can be restored by yourself, by doing practice yourself. So broken precepts are restorable, and they will be restored by using the four powers. The pure and perfect precepts, the continuum of the esoteric wisdom and power, is the heart and body of tantric practice.

THE MEDITATION
ON NGÖNDRO

THE ESSENTIAL TRAINING OF THE
LONGCHEN NYINGTHIG TRADITION

L ONGCHEN NYINGTHIG[55] has many texts comprising the
outer, inner, and secret cycles of teachings. The Ngöndro, which concludes with the Guru Yoga practice, belongs
to the outer cycle, meaning that it utilizes more common and
ordinary practices for beginners. *Ngöndro* means "preliminary
practice," that which goes before the main training. Although
its main focus is the foundation of the training, it includes
the highest practice of unifying oneself with Buddhahood
through dissolving into ultimate nature. Ngöndro starts with
the trainings on turning the mind toward Dharma, but it

A transcription of a talk given at the Maha Siddha Nyingmapa Temple,
Hawley, Mass., on September 4, 1989. It is an explanation of the shorter
version of the Longchen Nyingthig Ngöndro by Jigme Lingpa, restructured by the fourth Kyabje Dodrupchen Rinpoche as the daily practice
for the students of the Maha Siddha Nyingmapa Center. This article is
mainly based on NL, KDN, KZ, NLS, TS, KZZ, and KT.

ends with the unification of one's mind with the enlightened wisdom of the Buddha, Guru Rinpoche. Therefore, I am translating *Ngöndro* as "the essential practice." If Ngöndro is practiced properly and earnestly, it includes a complete path that leads to the highest goal—enlightenment. So the result is up to us; it depends on how we can understand, assimilate, and practice. If we have the capacity, Guru Yoga will lead us from the beginning to the highest Buddha realization.

The Ngöndro text of Longchen Nyingthig was revealed by Jigme Lingpa and compiled as *Namkhyen Lamzang* (*rNam mKhyen Lam bZang, The Excellent Path of Omniscience*) by the first Dodrupchen Rinpoche (1745–1821). The text we are using here is the shorter form of *Namkhyen Lamzang*, restructured in 1973 by the fourth Dodrupchen Rinpoche (b. 1927), so that it would be fit for the busy lives of his Western students.

PRAYERS TO THE LINEAGE MASTERS

The prayer to the Buddha, at the beginning of the text, through the four verses on turning the mind to Dharma and most of the prayers of dedication at the end are not part of the original Ngöndro text of Longchen Nyingthig, but were included by the fourth Dodrupchen Rinpoche in this new compilation.

First, there is the prayer and mantra of Shākyamuni Buddha, the historical Buddha, followed by the *Vajra Seven-Line Prayer,* the most popular and powerful prayer to Guru Padmasambhava.[56]

It is followed by the prayers to the lineage teachers starting with Samantabhadra, the Dharmakāya; Vajrasattva, the Sambhogakāya; Garab Dorje, the Nirmāṇakāya, and many of the major masters through whom the transmission of Nyingthig teachings came to us.

Next is the prayer to Longchen Rabjam, who practiced, taught, and wrote in hermitages hidden in the forests. He lived as a humble hermit even though he was one of the greatest scholars and adepts of Tibet, comparable to the six ornaments and two supreme ones of ancient Indian Buddhist scholarship. Although there are different ways of listing the masters of ancient India, according to many the two supreme ones are Nāgārjuna and Asaṅga, and the six ornaments are Āryadeva, Vasubandhu, Guṇaprabha, Shākyaprabha, Dignāga, and Dharmakīrti, who lived in the first through the eight centuries.

This is followed by prayers to Jigme Lingpa and the first Dodrupchen Rinpoche. Jigme Lingpa was one of the greatest writers, masters, and propagators of the Dzogpa Chenpo teachings of the Nyingma school, and he is the one who revealed the Longchen Nyingthig teachings as a Mind Ter. Jigme Lingpa entrusted the Longchen Nyingthig teachings to the first Dodrupchen and recognized him as the root doctrine-holder or the main disciple to receive and propagate these teachings. Generally, every Tertön has a principal disciple to whom he or she entrusts his or her teachings. For us, Dodrupchen has the greatest importance, not only because he is the most important master after Jigme Lingpa in the lineage, but also because our particular transmission comes from him, and his fourth incarnation is our own root teacher.

Next is the prayer to the root teachers (*rTsa Ba'i Bla Ma*). There are many different ways of designating who qualifies as the root teacher. In the highest meaning, "root teacher" means the master who introduces us to our true natural mind, Buddhahood. According to general tantric views, the root teacher is the spiritual teacher or teachers from whom we have received all the three transmissions: empowerment (*dBang*), word transmission (*Lung*), and meaning explanations (*Khrid*). But if we are not at that level, then he or she could be the teacher from whom we receive the highest spiritual teachings or for whom we have the strongest devotion and trust.

We may have one, many, or one main and several other root teachers. However, there is a story about this, concerning two Lamas. One went to receive teachings from every teacher he could find; the other received teachings from only three teachers throughout his entire life. A student asked a master which way was better—to have many teachers or just a few? The master replied that if you are a beginner and have many emotions and a judgmental mind, it is better to have fewer teachers, because it is easier to maintain good relations with a small number of teachers in whom you believe and trust and to focus on practicing their teachings. However, if you have strong devotion and pure perception then it is better to receive teachings from every teacher you can find, since you will not have any problems handling a large number of teachers or maintaining your samaya,[57] the esoteric relationship, and will therefore be able to benefit from as many people as those you go to for teachings.

From another perspective, however, we should respect as a teacher anyone who bestows on us four-line Dharma teachings, without grading them or thinking, "This is my best teacher" and "This is my second class teacher." Rather, try to respect them all as teachers because as tantric practitioners, we try to maintain pure perception of everybody and everything.

Whenever we start our practice, first we pray and invoke the blessings of the lineage teachers so that our actual practice may become inspiring, powerful, and successful. That is why these prayers to the lineage masters are given at the beginning of the practice.

THE FOUR PRELIMINARY PRACTICES

These verses are not from the original Ngöndro practice of Longchen Nyingthig, which contains prayers that are much longer. Because the original is too long for us to practice, Rinpoche arranged these four four-line prayers using words from the scriptures.

DIFFICULTIES OF OBTAINING A PRECIOUS HUMAN LIFE

We might think, "It is important to practice Dharma in order to have spiritual experience and inner peace, but I will pursue that path in future lives." But the Buddha said that it is not easy to obtain a precious human life with the freedom and endowments that we now have, because we need to have much good karma, causes, conditions, and circumstances to obtain it. So we must practice in this very lifetime while we do have this precious human life. Shāntideva said:

> It is exceedingly difficult to obtain a human life with the freedoms and endowments.
> When you have got the chance to fulfill the goal of life,

If you do not take advantage of it,
How can you get this opportunity again?[58]

IMPERMANENCE

We might think, "It is right; I have to practice Dharma in this lifetime because human life is precious and hard to obtain. But first I should make some money, travel, wait until my children grow up, or wait until another day for whatever reason." Of this the Buddha said that life is impermanent. It is as impermanent as the clouds of autumn; they appear in the sky one moment and disappear the next.

There is a very beautiful parable by Gongthang Tempe Drönme. One day a man fell off a cliff. Halfway down the steep, rocky slope there was a tuft of grass growing, which the man was able to grasp to stop his fall. He hung onto the grass with all his might, for if he were to let go, he would die. Then, as he clung to it, a white mouse came and started to nibble on a bit of the grass. Later, a black mouse arrived and ate a bit more of the grass. Gradually, the mice kept nibbling at the grass that the man was clutching—first the white mouse, then the black, then the white again—until finally, when one of the mice gnawed through the last blade of grass, the man slipped off the rock and fell down the cliff to his death. In this parable, the white mouse represents day, the black one night. The man is really dying from the beginning and is just temporarily hanging on. Day comes and exhausts itself; then night comes and exhausts itself. Then, at last, death arrives. In the same way, we too are just waiting or hanging on until death comes, since that is our ultimate destiny. We are here not to live, but to die. But even so, we do not really think or care about it.

Like a shooting arrow, the speed of life is moving very fast toward its target, which is death. We do not even realize this truth. While it is not obvious that there are such things as karma, rebirth, and realization because we cannot readily see or know them, the certainty of death is right in front of our eyes, yet it is still shocking for us to realize it. The Buddha said:

> The three worlds are impermanent, like the clouds of autumn.
> The births and deaths of beings are like watching a dance.
> The speed of human lives is like lightning in the sky.
> It passes swiftly as a stream down a steep mountain.[59]

If we watch a dance, first we can see the dancers' faces, next their backs, and then their faces again. In the same way, today we die, tomorrow we take rebirth, and the next day we die again. Our lives are moving so fast that we are not able to postpone even a single moment as we go straight from birth to death, without realizing it. If we think we will wait until tomorrow to practice we are fooling ourselves, since we are just hanging on a cliff. So we must start our practice today, and not even today, but right now.

KARMA: CAUSE AND EFFECT

The meaning of karma has been greatly misunderstood in the West. Many uninformed Westerners think that karma is some form of a curse or the effects of a curse experienced by the people in the East. But it is the law of interdependent causation. Every happening of everybody's life and of the whole world develops, functions, and ceases because of causes and conditions. Our spiritual experiences and growth are also

caused and driven by causation. It is really just a description
of how phenomena come into being, like the process whereby
a flower comes from a seed: first you see the seed, then the
shoot, then the buds, until the flower finally blossoms. Then
the flower produces seeds, which take the process back to the
beginning again. If we have an open and peaceful mind and
are a positive person, we will have a positive life, peaceful
feelings and experiences.

It is important to believe in karma, for if we really believe
in it, we will never engage in negative acts that we can avoid
because they will just foster negative results, and we do not
want to be victimized by our own doing. We engage in nega-
tivity only because we do not believe in karma—that doing
something bad will produce bad results.

Especially at the time of death, nothing else will follow us.
Money, power, friends, and family will not come with us. We
will not have the opportunity to take even our most cherished
body with us. Only the karma, the virtuous and unvirtuous
traces and energies we have created in our mind, will accom-
pany us, lead us, and push us through our bardo stages.[60] The
effects or energies of whatever karmic tendencies we have will
arise as or create the phenomena of our next lives. So every
experience of our enjoyment and suffering is dependent on
and the product of our own creation, the karma of the past.
So understanding karma from the depth of the heart is essential in order to inspire our minds to develop good karma by
doing such things as Dharma practices. The Buddha said:

> If, when his time comes, even a king should die,
> His wealth and his friends and relatives shall not follow
>   him.

Wherever men go, wherever they remain,
Karma, like a shadow, will follow them.

THE SUFFERING CHARACTER OF SAṂSĀRA

People also have trouble understanding what is meant by "suffering." Some even claim that they do not experience suffering as they are not going through any severe pain. However, according to Buddhism, there is nothing in this world that is not suffering. To be sure, suffering is relative. But even if we think we are happy and free from suffering at this very moment, our so-called happiness is intolerable pain in comparison to the higher states of happiness of the Buddha state. From that perspective, our happiness is not true happiness.

There are three kinds of suffering: suffering of suffering (or ordinary suffering), suffering of change (or suffering caused by changes), and all-pervasive suffering.

The first suffering is what we usually call suffering. It is the experience we feel when we have a specific problem, like being sick, losing money, or feeling the pain of the death of a close person.

The second kind of suffering is produced by so-called happy experiences, which then bring about unhappy results due to the impermanence of saṃsāric phenomena. For example, although we are enjoying eating good food, the enjoyment might change into the pain of digesting it. Similarly, today we are enjoying earning a lot of money, but it might cause us to worry about protecting, preserving, or investing it. Someone could be excited today with his or her lover, but one day might be in pain because of separation.

Third, all compounded things are subject to change and decay, and they are all created by the cause of suffering—dualistic concepts and emotional afflictions. So there is nothing in the world that is not permeated by suffering. For example, imagine that you have a light body, such as that described in the god realm. You fly through space whenever you move or travel. There is no darkness around you and no need of the light of the sun or moon, as your own body light illuminates the area around you. There is no physical pain and pressure, since your body is immaterial, intangible, indestructible, and untouchable. You enjoy it for years. Then one day your body suddenly changes into a flesh, bone, and blood body wrapped in a bag of skin and filled with all kinds of filth. You can not move except by measuring the ground with the two bone poles of the legs, step by step. You do not see anything if there is no light from other sources. You will easily be crushed down, smashed flat, pierced through, broken into parts, or cut into pieces—never to heal or walk again—if you are not careful about watching, avoiding, and negotiating with everything all the time. This would be an intolerable suffering.

Although we do not know or feel that we are suffering because we are used to what we have and have no sense of any other spectrum of life, all mundane phenomena are permeated by suffering in comparison to the true joy of Buddhahood. Compared to the Buddha wisdom of openness, oneness, and omniscience, and the Buddha body of wisdom light itself arisen as the light body—what suffering bodies have we become trapped in, not even knowing or accepting this!

It is essential to understand our own situation when we

start to move on the path of the spiritual journey. That is why Buddha taught Buddhism as being based on the four noble truths, starting with the truth of suffering. Some non-Buddhists think that Buddhism is pessimistic. The notion that there is nothing but suffering in this life does not mean that human beings are inherently full of suffering. In fact, the essence of Buddhism is that human beings are pure, enlightened, and perfect, but because of grasping at self and intellectual and emotional afflictions, their true nature and qualities are obscured, and they fall into the nightmare of illusory, suffering experiences. In fact, to reach this ultimate state of mind and to dispel the delusions of suffering, the practice is to generate joy, peace, positive view, and equanimity as the path. So Buddhism actually holds a very realistic and positive view. The Buddha said:

> Due to ignorance, craving, and becoming
> In the worlds of men, gods, and the three inferior spheres,
> The five realms revolve foolishly,
> Like the turning of a potter's wheel.[61]

Thinking about the difficulty of obtaining the precious human life, impermanence, karma, and suffering turns our minds toward Dharma and creates the urge toward a spiritual goal. That is why these verses are the instructions on turning our minds toward Dharma practice.

THE FOUR ESSENTIAL TRAININGS
GOING FOR REFUGE

Going for refuge is making a commitment. After the fourfold practice has turned our minds to practice, we are ready to make a commitment to the path, the spiritual training, and to the goal, the attainment of enlightenment. Going for refuge is the laying of the foundation, the initiation of commitment. Traditionally it starts with a ceremony of going for refuge; but the most important thing is the development of faith and trust in the objects of refuge. If we have that kind of strong urge and trust in the path and the goal that is taught in Buddhism, the vow of going for refuge is born in us.

We must think about taking refuge in a common-sense way. If we make a commitment or determination, we will succeed faster and more easily. But if we are hesitant, doubting, or unsure about whether or not to commit ourselves, we will become increasingly lazy and will not find it easy to succeed. For example, if you would like to walk to Charlemont but are hesitant, you might take a couple of steps forward but then a couple of steps backward and might never get there until you made a firm decision. In the same way, if we develop a determination to rely on the Buddha, Dharma, and Saṅgha, to make them the support and means of our lives, we will succeed much faster than we would otherwise.

First, we should visualize and see in front of us a huge, rich, and beautiful refuge tree[62] with five branches, filling the whole atmosphere. In the central branch of the tree is Guru Rinpoche,[63] with deities, Ḍākinīs, and Dharmapālas. On the front branch are the Buddhas of the past, present, and future. On the right branch are the Bodhisattvas. On the back branch is the Dharma, symbolized by volumes of texts emanating the sounds of Dharma. On the left branch are the sages of Hīna-

yāna, the Shrāvakas. In the sky above are all the lineage teachers, from the Dharmakāya to our root teachers.

On the ground, along with ourselves, visualize that the
whole earth is filled with human beings, animals, and all kinds
of beings, everyone facing the refuge tree. They are all one in
the warm heart of devotion to the refuges, blossoming faces
celebrating joy, with wide-open eyes of concentration, all
looking at the refuges. All are saying the same prayer in one
voice, filling the whole atmosphere with the pure sound of
boundless peace and devotion. The visualization for going
for refuge is the same as those we do for developing Bodhichitta and offering the maṇḍala later.

Then, in front of the refuge tree as the object, witness,
and support of refuge meditation, we take the vow of going
for refuge by repeating the four-line verses, again and again.

> The three absolute Jewels, the three bliss-gone Roots,
> The true nature of the channels, energies and essence;
> The maṇḍala of the essence (emptiness), nature (clarity),
>   and compassion (all-pervading power) of enlightened
>   mind,
> To these I go for refuge until the enlightened essence is
>   attained.

In the training of taking the refuge vow, there are many
levels of going for refuge. The first, outer level is going for
refuge in the the three Jewels—Buddha, Dharma, and Saṅgha.
We go for refuge in the Buddha as the guide who teaches us
and shows us the path of enlightenment, in the Dharma as
the path through which we proceed to Buddhahood by practicing, and in the Saṅgha as the companions supporting us
on the path.

We are taking the three Jewels as the refuge, not because merely relying on them will ease our problems, but because we are taking them as the support or key for developing in ourselves spiritual thoughts and experiences, such as devotion, peace, and positive perception. If spiritual experiences are developed in us through the support of spiritual objects, we will be released from suffering and its cause, and we will attain enlightenment. So the Buddha said, "I have shown you the path to enlightenment, but now it is up to you to follow it."

The second level is going for refuge in the three Roots. They are the Guru (the male principle), Ḍākinī (the female principle), and Tutelary deity, or Yidam (union principle)— the three main deity trainings of tantra. By dedicating oneself to the Guru, by having the Ḍākinī as the support, and by relying on the Tutelary deities as the source of power, we develop and perfect pure perception, which is the basis of tantric practice. Pure perception or transformation involves seeing all forms as Buddha, hearing all sounds and expressions as Dharma, and realizing or experiencing all thoughts as Buddha wisdom.

The third level is going for refuge in the nature of the channels, energies, and essence of the vajra body. This is refuge at the secret level of tantra, which centers on the physical qualities of the body and uses them as important means for practice. Here, we are going for refuge by relying on the physical channels, the cause of accomplishment of the Buddha body as the Nirmāṇakāya; purifying the energies, the source of accomplishment of Buddha speech as the Sambhogakāya; and perfecting the essence, the source of accomplishment of

Buddha mind as the Dharmakāya. Especially in Anuyoga, as in the practice of *Yumka Dechen Gyalmo*, the main emphasis is more on the vajra body than on the pure perception of outer phenomena of appearances and sounds.

The final level is taking refuge in the maṇḍala of the essence, nature, and compassion (or power) of the enlightened mind according to Dzogpa Chenpo. In Dzogpa Chenpo the intrinsic nature of the mind, the Buddha mind, is explained as having three qualities. Its essence is emptiness (openness), its nature (or appearance) is limitless clarity, and its compassion (power) is all-pervasive (omnipresence). So we are going for refuge in the threefold quality of the enlightened mind of the refuges and of ourselves.

Taking refuge does not mean that we take these objects as superior, but that we rely on them and strive to become one with them. We take refuge in them until we attain enlightenment; and when we become enlightened, we will become one with them, with the Buddha qualities, and so will not need to rely on them as something else any longer.

At the end[64] we visualize beams of light emanating from the refuges and touching us. By the mere touch of the lights, like iron being pulled toward a magnet, we unite with and dissolve into the refuges as water dissolves into water. Then the refuges dissolve from the outside inward, into Guru Rinpoche. Guru Rinpoche also dissolves into emptiness. Then relax in contemplation, free from conceptions.

DEVELOPING BODHICHITTA

Again, we visualize the refuge tree as in the training on going for refuge. Looking at the refuges in front, with one-

pointed trust and total devotion develop the enlightened
mind (or mind of enlightenment, Bodhichitta) by repeating
the verses:

> Ho! Deceived by myriad perceptions, like the reflection of
> the moon in water,
> Beings are wandering through the cyclic chain of lives.
> In order for them to be at ease in the luminescent sphere of
> self-awareness,
> I shall develop the enlightened mind by contemplating on
> the four boundless attitudes.

We can develop the enlightened mind by creating the attitude of taking responsibility for helping all mother beings
without any discrimination or selfish motivation. Enlightened mind[65] can be developed through the inspirational force
of the four boundless attitudes. These are loving kindness—a
strong attitude of wishing to have happiness for all beings,
compassion—a strong attitude of wishing that suffering does
not come to any being, joy over the happiness of others, and
evenness (or equalness) toward all beings, with no distinctions of friends, enemies, and so on.

(There are many degrees of enlightened mind. If we have a
wonderful compassionate mind, although it may not necessarily be the enlightened mind that Buddhas have, it is nevertheless an enlightened mind or a mind with a great light and
wisdom. So, in a sense, if we compare it to ordinary mind, we
can call it enlightened mind.)

In developing and maintaining such a mind, there are two
aspects: the aspirational enlightened mind and the practice of
the enlightened mind. The aspirational enlightened mind is
to have an attitude of taking responsibility for helping all

mother beings without any distinction between friends and enemies or any expectation of reward. If we have this kind of attitude, then whatever we do will become the practice of the enlightened mind. By the same token, whatever we do with a bad mind will be detrimental.

For example, if I am an angry person, whatever I say will be hurtful and harsh. If I have a bad attitude, whatever I do physically will be rough and hurtful. But if I have aspirational enlightened mind, even if I am behaving in an apparently strange way I will be benefiting others. It is like when good mothers discipline their children; they may seem stern, but they are actually benefiting them.

Shāntideva says that the aspect of aspirational enlightened mind is like wishing and preparing to go to a place, while the practice of enlightened mind is the actual going. To be specific, for the practice of enlightened mind, there are major trainings, known as the six perfections: generosity (or openness), discipline (or moral conduct), patience, diligence (or effort), contemplation (or absorption), and wisdom (or realization). At the same time, every practice and every good action inherently encompasses all six perfections. For example, saying a prayer requires the generosity of giving time, energy, and effort, and so it is the practice of generosity. It also requires discipline to sit down and say the prayer instead of wandering around. It requires overcoming other temptations, like wanting to go outside on a nice day, sun bathe, or even stop in the middle because of pain in the legs. Thus, saying prayers requires tolerance, patience, diligence, and endurance. Further, one-pointed concentration on saying the prayer is contemplation, and realization of the meaning of it is wisdom. As *Kunzang Lame Zhalung*[66] explains, there are three wisdoms: that created by study, that created by thinking or research, and that developed through meditation. So whatever results or experiences we attain are a form of wisdom. If we are good practitioners, the wisdom we attain is the realization of emptiness (openness) or the true nature of the mind. In our case, however, we should say that whatever result we attain through practice is wisdom—even if it is the result of just giving one mouthful of food to a needy person. Such an action contains all six perfections. So, in a sense, the six perfections encompass all Buddhist practices and are at the same time encompassed within every little act of practice. The six perfections are not something you should do somewhere else or separately. They are part of everyday spiritual life, and the Ngöndro practice is a great example.

We must start from somewhere in generating enlightened mind. It is not easy simply to have beneficial thoughts for all beings without discrimination. We need to start from the point of developing compassion by thinking of someone who is close to us and who is suffering. Maybe a friend, a relative, or an animal who is sick, dying, or whatever. Think about that person and develop compassion by wanting that person not to suffer. Generate a very strong feeling, even to the point of having tears come to your eyes. Then expand that feeling and gradually let it encompass other people. In the saṃsāric world there is no one who is free from suffering, so we should try to develop this feeling toward everybody. Then, if we develop a strong feeling of compassion, it will be easy for us eventually to take responsibility for serving all mother beings. It will not be hard if we start from somewhere, even with an animal or a person who is suffering in pain, wars, or earthquakes.

Generally, it is said that taking refuge is the entrance to Buddhism, after which we can say we are a Buddhist. Developing the enlightened mind makes us a follower of Mahāyāna Buddhism.

At the end of the development of enlightened mind, think that the refuges, starting from the periphery, dissolve[67] inwardly, and all dissolve into Guru Rinpoche. Then Guru Rinpoche dissolves into us, and we believe that we have received the enlightened mind of the refuges.

PURIFICATION: VAJRASATTVA RECITATION

It is important to purify negative karma and emotional afflictions in order to restore and strengthen samaya,[68] the connection to the inner esoteric power. Here, the Vajrasattva recitation is placed in the preliminary trainings, but it is a very powerful tantric training on its own.

In order to make the Vajrasattva purification effective, it is essential to employ all the four powers (*sTobs bZhi*) in the purification. They are the power of support, Vajrasattva as the spiritual force to rely on for the purification; the power of remorse, feeling strong remorse for the misdeeds we have committed, which are comparable to our having consumed poison; the power of commitment, a strong promise not to repeat the misdeeds again; and the power of antidote, the formula of Vajrasattva meditation as the means of purification.

Visualization is very important for the Vajrasattva purification. In Buddhism we do not worship idols or images and do not believe that they can change our lives or purify our bad karma. However, we do visualizations to which we pray, and we do put up statues to which we make offerings. The reason is that the main focus of Buddhism is to purify our own minds and develop pure perception, compassion, and devotion as mental attitudes. Putting up statues is a means of generating these mental qualities since simply looking at peaceful, compassionate images brings peace and tranquility to the mind. They are a source and a tool to invoke and strengthen spiritual experiences in us. Similarly making offerings to statues helps to generate and develop virtuous thoughts, such as generosity. So also visualizing and concentrating on an image is a most powerful means of training in contemplation and mindfulness. When we have very little control over our minds, the visualization may be here one moment and gone the next. But the efforts of trying to visualize and focus on this will slowly calm our minds and generate a contemplative strength. At the same time, visualizing and focusing on a loving, majestic, peaceful face, surrounded by many signs and symbols of Buddha qualities, inspires our mind and evokes spiritual experiences in us. But if we cannot visualize, we should just feel the presence of Vajrasattva, pray to him, and think that we are receiving blessing nectars from him.

First, we visualize Vajrasattva above our heads, facing the same direction that we are facing. He is white and radiant, like a snow or crystal mountain touched by hundreds of thousands of rays of the sun simultaneously. He is fully adorned with beautiful and majestic Sambhogakāya attire and ornaments. In his right hand he holds a vajra at his heart, symbolizing the union of emptiness and awareness. In his left hand he holds a bell resting on his left hip, symbolizing the union of emptiness and appearances. He is in union with his vajra consort, the female form of Vajrasattva. She is white, in Sambhogakāya attire and ornaments. She holds a curved vajra blade in her right hand and a skull brimming with nectar in her left hand. Although male and female Vajrasattvas are visualized in two forms, in reality they are one. Their union symbolizes the oneness of female and male qualities: emptiness and bliss, emptiness and clarity, wisdom and skillful means, the ultimate sphere and intrinsic awareness, and object and subject.

On a moon disc the size of a flattened mustard seed at the heart of Vajrasattva,[69] is a white HŪM letter, surrounded by the hundred-syllable mantra, like a rosary of white letters as fine as though written with a single hair. As much as we recite the hundred-syllable mantra, that much the compassionate mind of Vajrasattva is invoked. As the result, from the rosary of a hundred syllables drips an unending stream of nectar, as if frozen milk is being melted by fire. Nectars of bliss and light then descend from the point of the union of the male and female forms of Vajrasattva and enter the cranial aperture at the top of our heads. The nectar fills our head, throat, heart, abdomen, and whole body. As it descends, feel that all our defilements, emotions, and sicknesses are all washed away, just as water washes a dirty bottle. All our negativities are cleansed and washed away in the form of dirt, blood, silt, dregs, and so on, and these fall into the open mouths of the lord of death and all our karmic debtors waiting under the earth. They are satisfied, and our karmic debts are paid. Then, as our body becomes cleansed, a white nectar fills it from the bottom up, just as a bottle is filled with milk. Feel the joy, bliss, and peace—the blessing nectar of Vajrasattva. Then do this visualization again, feeling the purification and filling up with blessing.

Then we pray to Vajrasattva for purification by confessing and acknowledging our transgressions of the sacred obligations of body, speech, and mind—the root and branch defilements (or root downfalls and auxiliary faults)—and ask for purification of our stains and obscurations. Think that by hearing our prayers, Vajrasattva is pleased. Smiling, he says, "All your wrongdoings and defilements are cleansed." Taking his words as the power of truth, we believe that all our defilements and breaches of samaya are totally purified, and we feel relieved. Having given the word of forgiveness, he melts into light, which then dissolves into us. Now we become Vajrasattva, the male and female form and quality of Vajrasattva. Then, at our (Vajrasattva's) hearts, we visualize the mantra OM VA JRA SA TTVA HŪM on a moon disc. Blue[70] HŪM is in the center, white OM in the front, yellow VAJRA at the right, red SA at the back, and green TTVA at the left. From these letters at our hearts beams of light are projected and spread throughout the whole universe, which becomes transformed into the pure land of Vajrasattva, whereupon all the beings in the world become Buddhas and Bodhisattvas. The world is not just rough, gross, and ugly, but a land of light, joy, and peace of the Vajrasattva pure land. Then recite the five-syllable Vajrasattva mantra as many times as possible and think again and again about the transformation of the world. Repeat the mantra many times.

Then stop and contemplate silently, during which time you

dissolve the pure land from the outside inward. Gradually, all dissolves into us (Vajrasattva), and then we dissolve into the five letters of the mantra at our hearts. Then the outer letters dissolve into the central HŪM letter. The HŪM letter dissolves from the bottom upward into emptiness. Then we remain in the state of emptiness (openness).

MANDALA OFFERING

Visualize the refuge tree as the object of the mandala offering. Then visualize the whole universe according to ancient Indian cosmology for the mandala of the actual offering. In the center is Mount Meru, the center pole, surrounded by four continents, with the sun and moon, filled with all the riches of the world. Then see the visualized world not in gross, earthly form, but of the nature of the Buddha's pure land, with peace, joy, lights, and wisdom, and offer it to the refuges with joy, openness, and celebration.

To summarize, once we have turned our minds toward practice with the four preliminary trainings, we go for refuge and make a commitment, develop enlightened mind, purify ourselves, and then offer the mandala of the universe to the refuges. Turning the mind is like coming from the street and looking at the temple, wishing to come toward it. Refuge is like entering the temple. Now that we are in the temple, we need to undertake the basic work of settling in, which is developing enlightened mind. But we also need to clean the temple, which is Vajrasattva meditation. Then we need to furnish or enrich the cleaned temple, which is the mandala offering—the practice of generosity and the others of the six perfections that create the two accumulations of merit and wisdom.

THE MAIN PRACTICE: GURU YOGA

All the practices up to Guru Yoga, the unification with Guru Rinpoche, are preparatory essential practices, except Vajrasattva, which is also an esoteric training. Guru Yoga is the main or actual practice of Ngöndro, and it can bring us to the realization of the intrinsic nature of our own mind as taught in the Dzogpa Chenpo teachings, and to the attainment of Buddhahood.

In Guru Yoga training, when we say "E MA HO" we should see that the whole universe becomes emptiness, the totally open ultimate sphere. From that space, which is like clear, empty openness, arises the spontaneously present pure land of Guru Rinpoche.

Although the appearances of the world will not cease, the concept of grasping at self or perceiving them as real—as objects separate from us—will ease or cease. The reason we practice pure perception is to change our way of seeing, handling, and feeling. Trainings such as the visualization of seeing everything as a Buddha land will change our way of relating to objects and to ourselves. Just as when we are angry or frustrated, all the objects we perceive give rise to anger and frustration, regardless of how beautiful or precious they are, so too if our mind is pure and realized, the objects we perceive will be seen as a pure land.

This is why we should see the entire world as Zangdog Palri (Copper-Colored Mountain), the pure land of Guru Rinpoche. We should visualize ourselves as Vajrayoginī or Yeshe Tsogyal,[71] Guru Rinpoche's vajra consort. Above us in the sky, Guru Rinpoche[72] is sitting on a moon and sun seat above a huge blossoming lotus with thousands of petals. He is youthful, compassionate, cheerful, beautiful, and majestic. If our minds are in need of inspiration, we should visualize him as huge, filling the entire sky before us. If our minds are distracted and wild, it is best to concentrate on a small visualization of him, even as small as the size of our thumb. Otherwise, we could visualize him as large, filling the whole space in front of us, or as life-size.

When we open our minds in devotion to Guru Rinpoche, he is always there to bless us. He never goes away, as he is the manifestation of Buddhahood, our own pure nature. He himself has said:

> For men and women who have trust in me,
> I, Padmasambhava, have never gone anywhere, but am
>   standing at their door.
> There is no birth or death in my life.
> In front of every person there is a Padmasambhava.

If we see, feel, or behave in a negative way, it is we who are distancing ourselves from Guru Rinpoche because we are concealing our own true nature and obscuring our true qualities from shining forth. It is not he who leaves us, as he is our own true nature.

We visualize ourselves as Vajrayoginī in order to see ourselves with pure perception, not as ordinary beings but as an enlightened figure. Also, because she is Guru Rinpoche's vajra consort, there is a special interdependent causation between us and Guru Rinpoche, and there will be swifter blessing results. This visualization as Vajrayoginī is a skillful means of bringing about the union of bliss and emptiness. Even if you cannot visualize Guru Rinpoche or yourself as Vajrayogiṇī, feel the presence of Guru Rinpoche and feel that you are Vajrayogiṇī. The important thing is the feeling of his presence and compassion and energy. He looks and listens to us, all mother beings, just as a mother looks and listens to her children. He has the wisdom of knowing all the details of the whole universe simultaneously, the power to purify our defilements, and the power to grant all the common and uncommon attainments simultaneously, if we are ready and open for this. So with devotion and belief from the depth of the heart we pray with one-pointed minds, just as a baby relies for all its sustenance on its mother. Then we receive blessings in the form of blissful, warm lights and believe that we have received Guru Rinpoche's blessings, that all impurities in us are purified, and that all our wishes have been fulfilled. The whole universe is filled with blessing energies of peace, prosperity, and enlightenment. It is through our own faith that Guru Rinpoche's power will be able to reach us and that all these positive energies will multiply. But if our minds are closed, it is not possible for anyone to help us help ourselves. So the focus should be on opening our own minds and hearts in spiritual experiences and developing trust in them. Of course we should trust in the proper way, with the proper goal, using a proper form and support. If we do so, then because of our own conviction, trust, and positive energy, we will be able to receive the blessings and attainments. So the important thing is pure perception and faith in Guru Rinpoche, seeing him as the embodiment of all the Buddhas, bodhisattvas, saints, and sages—as the source of peace, power, strength, and compassion. It is important to have faith that we have been purified and have received the blessings. All spiritual blessings and attainments come through and from the mind. If our minds resist, block, or reject and do not trust, then we will obtain very little or nothing. So we should try to open our minds for our own sakes and to have trust for our own sakes.

THE VAJRA SEVEN-LINE PRAYER

This prayer has many meanings, and it provides many levels of practice.[73] We recite this prayer to invite Guru Rinpoche and all the deities, to invoke their compassionate minds, to receive their blessing, to see ourselves as inseparable from them, and to unite ourselves with their enlightened nature.

THE SEVEN ASPECTS OF DEVOTIONAL PRACTICE

After having visualized Guru Rinpoche with hosts of divinities and invited them with the chanting of *The Vajra Seven-Line Prayer*, now we pay homage to him by doing prostrations as if, having invited important guests, we will greet them and treat them with celebration.

We can visualize ourselves in an infinite number of manifestations—as infinite as the number of atoms in the universe. We visualize an infinite number of Buddhas with their pure lands on each of the atoms of the universe. We pay homage to them by doing physical prostrations, paying vocal homage, and generating mental devotion.

Second, we make the offerings, which have two aspects— actual, arranged offerings and visualized offerings. If you arrange any real offerings, that is wonderful. But if you do not, visualize and think that the whole atmosphere in front of your perception—the whole universe—is filled with wonderful, beautiful things, sources of joy, peace, and wisdom, and offer them to Guru Rinpoche and the others.

Third, we confess and purify all our physical, vocal, and mental obscurations fabricated by delusory mind in the luminescent Dharmakāya, ultimate peace and openness, which is the ultimate state of mind and the true nature of the universe, free from concepts and self.

Fourth, we rejoice and celebrate by generating great joy and total happiness because of all the happiness, prosperity, and enlightenment of others, without any jealousy or hesitation.

Fifth, we request the Buddhas and spiritual masters to turn the Dharma wheel of teachings to fulfill the needs of beings according to their abilities.

Sixth, we pray to the holy ones, the Buddha and his manifestations, to remain present without going into nirvāṇa in order to be the source of benefit for mother beings.

Seventh, we dedicate or give away all the merit we have accumulated to all mother beings so that the merit may become the cause of their happiness and achievement of Buddhahood.

DEVOTIONAL PRAYERS

These prayers are to open our minds and hearts in the warmth of devotion and to invoke the compassionate mind of Guru Rinpoche and all the enlightened ones. These prayers are very powerful, inspiring, and wonderful. In Paltrul Rinpoche's biography it is written that when the third Dodrupchen used to study with him, he used to hear Paltrul Rinpoche's voice through the walls chanting these lines constantly. So it seems that they might have been his main prayers and practice. Let our minds be inspired by these lines and use them as a powerful invocation of Guru Rinpoche.

MANTRA OF GURU RINPOCHE

Recite or chant and repeat the siddhi mantra[74] as prayer, homage, breath, thought, and meditation. Say the mantra prayer just like the cry of a baby in need of the care of her or his mother, Guru Rinpoche. Say the mantra prayer as a song of celebration and proclamation of the joy of being in the presence and warmth of Guru Rinpoche and being in spiritual union with him.

Think that by chanting the mantra Guru Rinpoche's compassionate mind is inspired, and in answer he sends beams of light of different colors. Just by their touching us, feel peace, warmth, bliss, and spaciousness in every part and aspect of our bodies and perceptions. All our intellectual and emotional obscurations are purified, and we are filled with the enlightened experiences of Guru Rinpoche's mind. Lights fill our whole bodies with peace, bliss, warmth, and joy. Then our body transforms into a body of light, the blessings of Guru Rinpoche. The whole world is filled with the blessing lights of peace, joy, tranquility, and bliss.

Repeat the visualization, generating faith, receiving blessings in the form of lights, the purification of the entire world, and the attainment of enlightened experiences by all beings again and again.

FOUR EMPOWERMENTS

At the end, we receive the four empowerments from Guru Rinpoche[75] in the form of lights. These light blessings are the body blessing of Guru Rinpoche to our bodies, the speech blessing to our speech, the mind blessing to our minds (or thoughts), and the vajra-wisdom blessing to our universal basis. The blessing lights purify all the defilements and endow us with the vajra qualities and mind of Guru Rinpoche.

UNIFICATION

The final stage of Guru Yoga practice is the dissolution or unification. Meditation on dissolution is not only the most important step leading to Dzogpa Chenpo realization, but according to Gyalse Zhenphen Thaye and other masters, it is a swift and powerful means to perfect the Dzogpa Chenpo realization.[76]

First, see that Guru Rinpoche's face has blossomed with a great smile and that his eyes are moved with compassionate love. As the result, a brilliant red light with warmth extends to us from Guru Rinpoche. By the mere touch of the blessing light we feel bliss in our minds and bodies. The light causes us to melt into a red light sphere of great bliss, the size of a pea, which is the indivisibility of the mind and energy. Like a spark, it shoots up and merges into Guru Rinpoche's heart, and we become inseparable from his enlightened mind, like a drop of water merging into the ocean.

Then with the force of devotion and trust, feel and believe that our minds have become one with the mind of Guru Rinpoche, and relax in the natural state of mind without any thoughts. Here, we could meditate on Dzogpa Chenpo according to whatever instructions and training experiences we have received in the past. As Dzogpa Chenpo meditation has to be followed strictly according to our individual nature and experiences, and because each individual is different, it is not helpful to try to explain how to meditate in a few words.

Devotion is very important in this training. If we have a very strong belief, we will have a great deal of energy, so that as we dissolve ourselves into Guru Rinpoche we may have a wonderful experience, such as a feeling of freedom, openness, bliss, and freshness, like a person who is released after having been trapped in a house for a long time.

CONCLUSION

The Ngöndro meditation concludes with the dedication of merit and making of aspirations. As followers of the Bodhisattva path of Mahāyāna Buddhism, we have started the Ngöndro meditation with the development of Bodhichitta, the intention of doing the practice for the benefit of all mother beings. Now we conclude it by dedicating or offering all the merit we have earned in the past, the merit we will earn in the future, and especially the merit we have accumulated by our present Ngöndro meditation to each and all mother beings. We do so without any selfish interests and without any expectation of reward.

Giving our hard-earned merit away to all impartially with love and generosity has three major results. Instead of decreasing our merit, dedicating it actually multiplies it enormously. Dedicated merit causes benefits for all beings who are open to its effects. By dedicating our merit, we preserve it from possible destruction by our negative emotional forces and evil deeds. Also, we can offer our merit to the Buddhas. By doing so, it will be increased and, more importantly, protected from destruction.

With our dedicated merit as the seed, we should make pure aspirations that this will bear fruit of all kinds of joy and enlightenment for all mother beings and ourselves without selfishness. The outcome of our merit depends upon the aspirations we make. The more vast and broad our aspirations and the more frequently we repeat them, the more our merit will increase. The third Dodrupchen advised, "Don't be humble in making aspirations." The most important and grand public ceremony in Tibet used to be the Mönlam (aspiration) ceremony in Lhasa. During this ceremony, thousands of monks would recite various aspirational prayers and meditate on them for weeks. Powerful dedications and aspirations turn even the most simple merit into a seed of vast fruits of joy, peace, and wisdom for great numbers of beings.

◦ 11 ◦

THE MEANING OF *THE VAJRA SEVEN-LINE PRAYER* TO GURU RINPOCHE

THIS CHAPTER is a summary of a commentary on *The Vajra Seven-Line Prayer*, entitled *Padma Karpo (The White Lotus)*, written by Mipham Namgyal (1846–1912), a celebrated scholar of the Nyingma Buddhist tradition of Tibet. The original Tibetan text of Mipham's commentary is very profound and difficult to understand or to translate, and I have summarized the basic points of his text in this chapter.

The Vajra Seven-Line Prayer is the most sacred and important prayer in the Nyingma tradition. This short prayer contains the outer, inner, and innermost teachings of the esoteric trainings of Buddhism. By practicing *The Vajra Seven-Line Prayer* according to any one of these trainings, the result of that particular training will be attained.

In this summary there are five levels of interpretation. They are (1) the general or common meaning; the path of

Published by Buddhayana. First edition, 1979; second edition, 1989.

the hidden meaning (*sBas Don*), consisting of the next three levels; (2) the meaning according to the path of liberation (*Grol Lam*); (3) the meaning according to the perfection stage (*rDzog Rim*); (4) meaning according to the Nyingthig of Dzogpa Chenpo: the direct realization of the spontaneous presence (*Lhun Grub Thod rGal*); and (5) the meaning according to the accomplishment of the result. From among these levels of meaning it is proper for a person reciting the vajra prayer to learn and practice the particular level that is suitable to his or her capacity.

I have arranged this summary merely with the hope of being able to indicate that this brief prayer contains different levels of meaning and training, as many followers of the Nyingma teachings who are acquainted with *The Vajra Seven-Line Prayer* are often unaware of its deeper meanings. But in order to comprehend the complete meaning of the prayer, I urge the readers to read the original text of Mipham Rinpoche.

In Tibet, the Nyingmas recite *The Vajra Seven-Line Prayer* to Guru Rinpoche three times before reciting any other prayers, doing any meditation, or performing any ceremony. Many devotees repeat it hundreds of thousands of times, reciting it during all their waking hours, making it as their main prayer, breathing, life, and contemplation.

STRUCTURE OF THE TEXT

Because of the complex organization of the text a number of headings, subheadings, italics, and brackets have been supplied, and a note of explanation may therefore be of benefit to the reader.

Mipham's commentary has divided each level of interpretation of *The Vajra Seven-Line Prayer* into an introduction, the utterance of the seed syllable, the object of the prayer, the prayer, the mantra for invoking blessings, and (for the first level of interpretation only) the contents of the prayer.

On the basis of each level of interpretation given by Mipham's commentary I have extracted a root meaning for *The Vajra Seven-Line Prayer,* and the reader will find that, for each level of interpretation, the root meaning is given first, followed by Mipham's commentary (with its subdivisions).

With respect to format, there are three different uses of italics. First, throughout the body of the text, italics are sometimes used for unfamiliar Tibetan words (given in phonetic forms), followed either by an English equivalent or, occasionally a Sanskrit equivalent (indicated by the abbreviation Skt.) in parentheses. Second, English words in italics, appearing in the commentary, are used to indicate that they are the translated words of *The Vajra Seven-Line Prayer* itself. The reader is encouraged, when reading the commentary, to refer back to the root-meaning section to see how the italicized words comprise a coherent root meaning. Third, beginning with the hidden meaning (second) level of interpretation onward, the esoteric meanings in the root-meaning sections are followed by the corresponding phrases of *The Vajra Seven-Line Prayer,* which are given in parentheses in italicized Tibetan phonetic form.

Throughout the text, square brackets are sometimes used to indicate words added so as to make the meaning clear. Finally, in order to keep the number of footnotes to a mini-

mum, key Tibetan terms are put in parentheses in a translit-
erated form.

There are differences in spelling at two places in the Tibetan of *The Vajra Seven-Line Prayer*. For the last syllable of line
6, I have used *kyee* (*Kyis*) according to Mipham's commentary,
where some texts use *kyi* (*Kyi*). For the third syllable of the
seventh line, I have used *lab* (*brLab*) as in the Longchen
Nyingthig texts, as it is the version commonly recited, although Mipham and some others have used *lob* (*rLobs*).

HISTORY OF
THE VAJRA SEVEN-LINE PRAYER

It is said that these lines are the prayers of invitation of
Guru Rinpoche (Padmasambhava) to the assembly of feast
offerings[77] by the Dorje Khadromas (Skt. Vajra Ḍākinīs).

Once there came to the monastery of Nālandā heretical
teachers, learned in languages and logic, who reviled the
Dharma. The Buddhist scholars were unable to refute them.
Then most of the scholars had the same dream. In it, Ḍākinī
Zhiwa Chog (Supreme Peace) prophesied as follows:

"You will not be able to defeat the heretics. If you do not
invite here my elder brother, Dorje Thöthreng Tsal (Vajra
Skull-Garland Power, Guru Rinpoche), who lives at the Dark
Cemetery, the Dharma will be destroyed."

"How can we invite him when it is so difficult to go
there?" asked the scholars.

The Khadroma said: "Set up a great offering on the roof
of the monastery, with music and incense, and with one voice

recite the vajra prayer." And she gave them *The Vajra Seven-Line Prayer.* The scholars prayed accordingly, and in an instant Guru Rinpoche came miraculously from the sky. He presided over the Buddhist scholars and defeated the heretical teachers by means of textual reference and intellectual reasoning. When he was threatened by the magical powers of the heretics, he opened the casket given him by the Lion-Faced Ḍākinī, and he found in it the mantra of "fourteen letters."[78] By reciting it, he eliminated the evil ones among the heretics with a rain of lightning bolts. He caused the remaining ones to enter the Dharma. It is said that the prayer originated from that incident.

Later on, when Guru Rinpoche came to Tibet in the eighth century, he gave it to the king and his subjects. Intending it for future disciples capable of training, he concealed it in many Ters.[79] Later, *The Vajra Seven-Line Prayer* was revealed in the Ters of most of the one hundred great Tertöns of the last ten centuries of the Nyingma lineage, again and again, as the heart of the prayers, teachings, and meditation.

THE COMMON MEANING

Root Meaning

> HŪM—invokes the mind of Guru Rinpoche.
> 1. In the northwest of the country of Oḍḍiyāṇa
> 2. Born on the pistil of a lotus:
> 3. Endowed with the most marvelous attainment;
> 4. Renowned as the Lotus-Born (Padmasambhava);
> 5. Surrounded by a retinue of many Khadros[80]

6. Following you I practice:

7. Please come forth to bestow blessings.

Master (GURU) Padmasambhava (PEMA), please bestow (HŪM) attainments (SIDDHI) [upon us].

Commentary

INTRODUCTION

This is the level of practicing *The Vajra Seven-Line Prayer* in relation to the way of Guru Rinpoche's appearance in this earthly world as a manifested form (Skt. Nirmāṇakāya).

In actuality, Guru Rinpoche is not separate from Samantabhadra (Universally Excellent), who is fully liberated from the beginning as the self-arisen Dharmakāya (the ultimate state). Without moving from the sphere of the Dharmakāya, he is spontaneously accomplished in the Sambhogakāya (the enjoyment body in pure forms), which has five absolute qualities.[81] He is also the self-arising manifestation in various displays of Nirmāṇakāya (the manifested body in impure forms), the self-reflection of compassion. This is the actual way in which Guru Rinpoche dwells and appears. It is the display of the Buddhas, and they alone can perceive all aspects of his display.

Eight (or twelve) years after the mahāparinirvāṇa of Shākyamuni Buddha, Guru Rinpoche appeared on a lotus in Dhanakosha lake of Oḍḍiyāna for the ordinary beings of this world who have good karma. He followed different esoteric disciplines and accomplished various attainments, such as the light body of great transformation (*'Ja' Lus 'Pho Ba Ch'en Po*). He served devotees of India, Oḍḍiyāna, and Tibet through multiple manifestation, such as the eight forms of the Guru (*Guru mTshan brGyad*). This level of interpretation is the way that we, the common disciples, pray to Guru Rinpoche, an extraordinary object of devotion.

THE UTTERANCE OF THE SEED SYLLABLE

The prayer begins with the invocation of the enlightened mind of Guru Rinpoche by the utterance of the syllable HŪM, the self-arisen seed syllable of the mind of all the Buddhas.

THE OBJECT OF THE PRAYER

Line 1. In the west of the Jambu continent, at the *northwest* of *Oḍḍiyāna, the land of* the Khadros (Ḍākas and Ḍākinīs) in the Dhanakosha lake, filled with water of eight pure qualities.

Line 2. On the stem ornamented by the *pistil,* leaves, and petals of a *lotus,* Guru Rinpoche was born.

All the qualities and blessings of the three secrets (body, speech, and mind) of all the Buddhas came together in the form of the syllable HRĪH, and it dissolved into the heart of Amitābha Buddha. From his heart, a light of five colors spread out and came down on the pistil of the lotus. They transformed into the form of Guru Rinpoche, and he took birth in the manner of the lotus-born [miraculous birth].

Line 3. He spontaneously accomplished the twofold benefit (of self and others), and he exhibited *marvelous* forms, such as the eight manifestations of the Guru. He *achieved the extraordinary attainment* of the Vajradhara state, not just ordinary attainment.

Line 4. His name is *renowned as the Lotus-Born* (Padmasambhava).

Line 5. And he is *surrounded by retinues of manifold Khadros* (Ḍākas and Ḍākinīs).

THE PRAYER

Line 6. One should pray with the three kinds of faith,[82] thinking, "O Protector, I will *follow after you,* and I will *practice accordingly.*"

Line 7. "In order to protect beings like myself, who are sunk in the ocean of the three sufferings, you, the omniscient, compassionate, and powerful one, *please come* to this place for the *blessing* of our body, speech, and mind with your body, speech, and mind, as iron is transmuted into gold."

THE MANTRA FOR INVOKING BLESSINGS

GURU means master or spiritual guide, one who is prosperous with excellent qualities; to whom no one is superior.

PADMA is the first part of Guru Rinpoche's name.

SIDDHI is what we want to accomplish—the common and uncommon attainments.

HŪM means the supplication to bestow the siddhis (attainments).

So, *O Guru Padma, bestow the siddhi.*

THE CONTENTS OF THE PRAYER
THE OBJECTS OF THE PRAYER

Line 1. The place of birth.

Line 2. The way of taking birth.

Line 3. The greatness of his qualities.

Line 4. The name of Guru Rinpoche in particular.

Line 5. Retinues.

THE PRAYER

Line 6. Praying with the aspiration of achieving inseparability from Guru Rinpoche or developing confidence in him.

Line 7. Accomplishment of the inseparability of Guru Rinpoche from oneself.

THE MANTRA FOR INVOKING BLESSING

THE PATH OF THE HIDDEN MEANING

THE PATH OF LIBERATION

Root Meaning

HŪM—awakens the self-arisen wisdom, the ultimate nature.

1. The Mind[83] (*ogyen yul*) is the freedom (*tsam*) [from the extremes] of saṃsāra (*nub*) and nirvāṇa (*chang*).

2. It is the realization of the union (*dongpo*) of the primordially pure ultimate sphere (*pema*) and luminous, vajra intrinsic awareness (*kesar*) and (*la*) . . .

3. It is the Great Perfection, the marvelous (*yatsen*). It is the attainment (*nye*) of the supreme siddhi (*chogki ngödrub*), the state of Vajradhara.

4. This is the wisdom of the absolute nature, renowned as (*zhesu trag*) the ultimate basis (*jungne*) of the Buddhas (*pema*).

5. This wisdom is with (*kor*) its numerous manifestative

powers (*mangpo*) emanating (*dro*) in the ultimate sphere (*kha*) as attributes (*khortu*).

6. I firmly develop confidence (*dag drub kyee*) in the nature of the nondual primordial wisdom (*khye kyi je su*).

7. In order to (*chir*) purify all the attachments to appearances as the primordial wisdom (*chinkyee lob*), may I realize (*shegsu sol*) the ultimate nature.

The primordial wisdom is emptiness in its essence (Dharmakāya) (GURU), clarity in nature (Sambhogakāya) (PADMA, and all pervasive in compassion [power] (Nirmāṇakāya) (SIDDHI) with fivefold wisdom (HŪM).

Commentary

THE UTTERANCE OF THE SEED SYLLABLE

The prayer begins with the utterance of the seed syllable of the mind, HŪM, which awakens the self-arisen primordial wisdom, the true nature of saṃsāra and nirvāṇa.

THE OBJECT OF THE PRAYER

Line 1. The country of *Oḍḍiyāna* is a special source of tantra. In terms of the actual path, one's own *Mind* is the special source of tantra, so that is what *Oḍḍiyāna* means.

The *Mind* or the ultimate nature of the mind is the *freedom* from sinking in *saṃsāra* and rising to *nirvāṇa*, as it is neither remaining in nor partial to the two extremes—saṃsāra and nirvāṇa.

Line 2. Pema, the lotus, signifies the *ultimate sphere* (Dharmadhātu), the nature that is to be realized. It does not dwell anywhere and is pure from the beginning, just as a lotus is unstained by any impurity.

"Kesar," the pistil, signifies the *luminous, vajra intrinsic awareness* (*Rig Pa'i rDo rJe*), which is the means of realizing the nature. The spontaneously accomplished, self-radiant intrinsic awareness, primordial wisdom, is blossoming with clarity; so it resembles the pistil of a lotus.

As the stem (*Dongpo*) holds the pistil and the petals of a lotus together, the self-arisen, great blissful primordial wisdom dwells as the *union* of the ultimate sphere (*dByings*) and primordial wisdom (*Ye Shes*), and it is the ultimate nature of the mind or the innate luminosity of the mind.

Line 3. Mind is the spontaneously born, luminous Great Perfection (Dzogpa Chenpo), the primordial wisdom of the absolute nature, the meaning of the fourth empowerment, which is *marvelous.* It is present spontaneously as the basis of the Mind of all the Buddhas, the *attainment of the supreme siddhi,* the state of Vajradhara.

Line 4. Mind is the basis of all the *Buddhas* of the three times, who have blossomed forth like lotuses, the ultimate nature; so it is *renowned as the basis of* Pema, the *Buddhas.* This is the recognition of *Pema Jungne* as the absolute Buddha.

Line 5. In that primordial wisdom there are inconceivable qualities of attainment which, if divided into their varieties, include the five types of primordial wisdom (*Ye Shes lNga*).[84] So, in the uncovered space of the *ultimate sphere, numerous manifestative powers* of the intrinsic-awareness primordial wisdom are *emanating as* its *attributes* ceaselessly.

THE PRAYER

Line 6. To realize the nature of nondual *primordial wisdom* (*Ye Shes*) and to perfect it through contemplation with unchanging *confidence*, which is great wisdom (*Shes Rab*), is expressed as "I will follow after you, and I will practice."

Line 7. If one has become experienced in and has ascertained this ultimate nature (*gNas Lugs*) by *realizing* the view (*lTa Ba*) and perfecting that realization through meditation, one will transform all the attachments to impure appearance into the pure essence[85] of *primordial wisdom* (*Ye Shes*).

Or, if one could not attain primordial wisdom, then in order to receive the blessing of the path in one's own mind, one aspires as follows: "May I *realize*[86] the ultimate nature (*Ch'os Nyid*) by dissolving subjective-objective duality into it, as waves of water into water, through the *blessing* powers of the instructions of the Lama and through study and reflection."

MANTRA FOR INVOKING BLESSINGS

The primordial wisdom is the emptiness essence (*Ngo Bo sTong Pa*), the Dharmakāya, and since it is not inferior to any conceivable characteristic, it is the supreme one, the GURU.

The primordial wisdom's nature is luminescence (*Rang bZhin gSal Ba*). It is spontaneously accomplished Sambhogakāya, with a ceaseless display of power. Yet it is not separate from the ultimate sphere. So it is PADMA, the lotus, which means not stained by relative characteristics.

The inseparability of that essence and nature[87] is the universal compassion, which arises in the saṃsāric and nirvāṇic display (*Rol Pa*), fulfilling the wishes of all the endless beings, which is SIDDHI or attainment.

HŪṂ signifies the self-arisen primordial wisdom, the seed syllable of mind, possessor of five primordial wisdoms.

THE PATH OF SKILLFUL MEANS (*Thabs Lam*)
ACCORDING TO THE PERFECTION STAGE

Root Meaning

HŪM—awakens the self-arisen innate wisdom.

1. At the center (*tsam*) of the roma (*nub*) and the kyangma (*chang*) channels of the vajra body (*ogyen yul*),

2. At (*la*) the eight-petaled chakra of the heart (*pema*) in the "essence" (*Thig Le*) (*kesar*), in the uma, the central channel (*dongpo*),

3. Dwells (*nye*) the marvelous (*yatsen*), great blissful, stainless primordial-wisdom mind—the changeless luminous essence, the attainment of supreme siddhi (*chogki ngödrub*).

4. It is renowned (*zhesu trag*) as the spontaneously present, absolute Padmasambhava (*pema jungne*).

5. This primordial-wisdom essence is with (*kor*) many (*mangpo*) kinds of energy (*rLung*) and essence (*Thig Le*), which are manifesting in the empty sphere (*khadro*) of the channels as animations (*khortu*).

6. According to the skillful nature of the vajra body (*khye-kyi jesu*), I will train in the primordial wisdom (*dag drub kyee*) through the stages of esoteric training.

7. In order to (*chir*) transform all existents into the sphere of great bliss (*chinkyee lab*), may I attain the great bliss of the vajra body (*shegsu sol*).

The supreme primordial wisdom (GURU) and the un-stained and self-arisen great bliss (PADMA) bring the ultimate, great primordial wisdom (SIDDHI), the holy Mind of the Buddhas (HŪM).

Commentary

INTRODUCTION

For those who are unable to realize the absolute primordial wisdom (*Don Gyi Ye Shes*) through the trainings elucidated in the path of liberation, it could be achieved through the most extraordinary trainings of the path of skillful means.

THE UTTERANCE OF THE SEED SYLLABLE

The HŪṂ syllable signifies the awakening of the self-arisen, innate primordial wisdom.

THE OBJECT OF THE PRAYER

Line 1. The country of Oḍḍiyāna signifies the *vajra body*, the extraordinary base of tantra.

In that vajra body, on the right side is the red *roma* (Skt. rasanā) channel in which the sun energy (*Nyi Ma'i rLung*) moves about, decreasing the essence (Tib. *Thig Le*, Skt. *bindu*). On the left side is the white *Kyangma* (Skt. *lalanā*) channel in which the moon energy (*Zla Ba'i rLung*) moves about, increasing, cleansing, cooling, and pacifying the essence.

Between these channels, at the *center* [where the primordial wisdom energy flows]:

Line 2. The lotus (*pema*) signifies the *eight-petaled Dharmachakra of the heart* (*sNying Ka Ch'os Kyi 'Khor Lo*). The pistil (*kesar*) signifies the *essence* (or semen), the vital essence of the five elements. The stem (*dongpo*) signifies the *uma* (Skt. *avadhūti*) or central channel in which the primordial wisdom energy (*Ye Shes Kyi rLung*) flows about.

Line 3. Within that cycle of channel, energy, and essence—the extraordinary vital essence (*Dvangs Ma*) of the vajra body—and originating simultaneously with them from the beginning, like camphor and the smell of camphor, dwells the luminous essence (*'od gSal Ba'i Thig Le*), which is unstained great bliss, the self-arisen primordial wisdom.

So it is very *marvelous.* This luminous essence is the inseparable union of bliss and emptiness that transcends thoughts and description, and it is the spontaneous accomplishment of the supreme siddhi, Vajradhara.

Line 4. The primordial wisdom of realizing that luminous essence is *renowned* as the *absolute,* self-arisen *Pema Jungne* (Padmasambhava).

Line 5. That primordial-wisdom luminous essence, Padmasambhava, *is with many essences* and energies (*rLung*) as its manifesting power (*rTsal*) of the great essence of primordial wisdom itself. These are *manifesting* in the *space* of the empty hollows of the central channel and smaller channels as their *animations.* If one applies the training on skillful means, the cycle of vajra body arises as the great blissful primordial wisdom of luminous essence.

THE PRAYER

Line 6. "I will follow after you, and I will practice" signifies, first, that it is the *training* on understanding and accomplishing *the nature of the vajra body;* and second, the primordial wisdom of great bliss through the profound trainings with characteristics (*mTshan bChas Kyi rNal 'Byor*) of the perfection stage (*rDzogs Rim*), which include practice on the heat yoga (*gTum Mo*), the trainings through the supports of inner or outer vajra consorts. These trainings will bring the result of admitting the karmic energies and mind into the central channel, and realizing the state of illusory body, luminous absorption, and dream yoga, because of the force of physical exercises, discipline of energies, and mental concentration on the subtle essences (*Phra Mo'i Thig Le*).

Line 7. Through the training of skillful means, one transforms all the existents into the *attainment of* the nature of the immaculate *great bliss* of the vajra body, and transforms them into the maṇḍalas of the body, speech, and mind of the Buddhas.

To attain the great bliss of the vajra body, all the habitual inclinations of the changing karmic energy—the cause of saṃsāric appearances, due to the mind defiled by thoughts with characteristics—dissolve into the central channel of changeless primordial wisdom, and are bound to the changeless great essence, the very ultimate sphere of the basis. So, *Come* (attain) to the *Dharmakāya,* the ultimate sphere of the basis.

THE MANTRA FOR INVOKING BLESSINGS

The primordial wisdom of the path, which is achieved through the extraordinary path of training, is supreme; hence GURU (master).

All the impurities, such as the five emotional afflictions, arise as supports of immaculate great bliss and self-liberation; hence PADMA (lotus).

As the final result, the great primordial wisdom will be achieved swiftly; hence SIDDHI (attainment).

In wonderment at the arising of primordial wisdom

through trainings of the path of skillful means comes the seed letter of the Minds of the Buddhas—HŪM.

ACCORDING TO THE NYINGTHIG OF DZOGPA CHENPO: THE DIRECT REALIZATION OF THE SPONTANEOUS PRESENCE

Root Meaning

HŪM—invokes the self-arisen wisdom that brings the realization of the face of the ultimate primordial wisdom.

1. The light of the heart (*ogyen yul*) and its (*kyi*) inner ultimate sphere (*nub*), outer ultimate sphere (*chang*), and the water light of the eyes (*tsam*), and

2. The light of the pure ultimate sphere and the light of emptiness thig-le (*pema*) with the vajra chains—the power of the intrinsic awareness—(*kesar*) are present for us. Upon (*la*) firmly stabilizing intrinsic awareness on them through contemplation (*dongpo*),

3. One achieves (*nye*) the marvelous (*yatsen*) first three visions (*sNang Ba*) and attains the supreme siddhi (*chogki ngö-drub*), the fourth vision.

4. This attainment is renowned (*zhesu trag*) as the attainment of the primordial Buddhahood (*pema jungne*).

5. Then the light of self-arisen wisdom emanates (*kor*) many (*mangpo*) rays and thig-les as its manifesting power (*rTsal*) (*khortu*) moving about in space (*khadro*).

6. I contemplate (*dag drub kyee*) on the natural vision of original purity (*khye kyi jesu*).

7. In order to (*chir*) attain the rainbow vajra body of great transformation (*shegsu sol*), may I purify all phenomena into the expanse of primordial wisdom (*chinkyee lab*).

This supreme (GURU), unstained (PADMA), and ultimate attainment (SIDDHI) is amazing (HŪM).

Commentary

INTRODUCTION

Natural, self-arisen primordial wisdom dwells primordially as the ultimate nature (*Ch'os Nyid*) of the mind. However, because of the impactedness of karma and emotional afflictions, the ultimate nature has been covered and its face (*Rang Zhal*) could not be observed.

THE OBJECT OF THE PRAYER

HŪM signifies the essence of spontaneously accomplished thögal, the self-arisen primordial wisdom. Thögal brings about the vision of the true face of self-arisen primordial wisdom from the state of spontaneously accomplished luminous absorption, even for us ordinary people, if we follow the instructions of this supreme yāna.

Line 1. Orgyen yul signifies the *light of the heart* (*Tsita Sha Yi sGron Ma*). The youthful body in a vase (*gZhon Nu Bum sKu*), the radiant thig-le of primordial wisdom, dwells invisibly (*Nub*) in the space of the vajra body, the *inner ultimate sphere* (*Nang Gi dByings*).

Chang is the *outer ultimate sphere*, the clearly appearing space, the cloudless sky. *Tsham*, the channel of the two outer and inner spheres, is the *water light of the eyes* (*rGyang Zhag Ch'u Yi sGron Ma*).

Line 2. Through the *water light of the eyes*, in the outer ultimate sphere, appears the pure sky—blue, clean, with nets of rainbow rays beautified by circular thig-le, like mirrors. All these are the *light of the pure ultimate sphere* (*dByings rNam Dag Gi sGron Ma*).

Then, by gaining experience at that, the *light of emptiness thig-le* (*Thig Le sTong Pa'i sGron Ma*) in red—clear, round, and clean—will arise like designs on water made by throwing a stone in a pond. These two lights (*sGron Ma*) function as the ground, a container, or a house. They are both signified by the *pema* (lotus).

Kesar (pistil) signifies the *vajra chain* (*rDo rJe Lu Gu rGyud*), which is the power of intrinsic awareness (*Rig gDangs*). It is the essence of the light of self-arisen wisdom (*Shes Rab Rang Byung Gi sGron Ma*) and the self-radiance of the actual intrinsic awareness, primordial wisdom.

Dongpo (stem) signifies *stabilization* of the ultimate sphere (*dByings*) and the intrinsic awareness (*Rig Pa*) by confining the power of intrinsic awareness (*Rig gDangs*) in the realm of the ultimate sphere and pressing the point (*gNad gZhi Ba*) through the thought-free natural mode of intrinsic awareness (*Rig Pa Rang Bab rTog Med*). By getting experience *in* (*la*) those skillful means,

Line 3. One will *achieve* the four confidences gradually and will accomplish the *marvelous* visions of the direct realization of the ultimate nature (*Ch'os Nyid mNgon gSum*), the development of experiences (*Nyams Gong 'Phel*), and the perfection of the intrinsic awareness (*Rig Pa Tshad Phebs*). After that, one will *achieve* the state of dissolution of (all dharmas into) the ultimate nature (*Ch'os Nyid Zad Pa*)—the supreme attainment, the state of Vajradhara—in this very life.

Line 4. Then one will be inseparable from the Mind of

Pema Jungne, who is the primordial Buddha (Samantabhadra). So, *"He is renowned as Pema Jungne."*

Line 5. Though not moving from the state of evenness of the light of self-arisen wisdom, there will be spontaneous *emanation* of *manifesting power* (*rTsal*) of that self-arisen wisdom, in the form of *many* clear and moving rainbow rays, thig-les, and small thig-les *in the space.*

Line 6. At that time all these developments are the mere power of intrinsic awareness. So, one *contemplates* on the luminous absorption of the four natural contemplations (*Chog bZhag bZhi*) in the unmodified *natural vision of original purity* (*Ka Dag*).

Line 7. By practicing like that, may I *purify all the phenomena* produced by the impure karmic energy *into the expanse of* indestructible *primordial wisdom to attain the rainbow vajra body of great transformation* (*'Ja' Lus 'Pho Ba Ch'en Po*).

THE MANTRA FOR INVOKING BLESSINGS

The path of innermost essence of the luminous absorption is the extraordinary training, as it meditates on the result, the Buddhahood itself, as the path of training. So, it is supreme (GURU), and immaculate (PADMA), and the ultimate attainment in this very lifetime (SIDDHI). Amazing (HŪM)!

THE ACCOMPLISHMENT OF THE RESULT

Root Meaning

HŪM—invokes the primordial wisdom.

1. The esoteric training awakens one's tantric lineage (*ogyen yul*) of the Mind that (*kyi*) transcends the juncture

(*tsam*) of sinking (*nub*) in the saṃsāra and liberating (*chang*) from it through

2. The attainment of the speech (*pema*), mind (*kesar*), and body (*dongpo*) of the Buddhas, and (*la*)

3. [The primordial wisdom of the attainment] is marvelous (*yatsen*). This is the attainment (*nye*) of the supreme accomplishment (*chogki ngödrub*), the state of Vajradhara,

4. Which is renowned (*zhesu trag*) as the self-arisen absolute Padmasambhava (*pema jungne*).

5. This wisdom is with (*kor*) infinite (*mangpo*) manifestation, boundless as space (*kha*), functioning (*dro*) as its power (*khortu*).

6. I remain (*dagdrub kyee*) in the realized state (*jesu*) of effortless nature, primordial purity (*khyekyi*).

7. In order for (*chir*) phenomenal existents to arise as the maṇḍala of the four vajras (*chinkyee lab*), may I attain (*shegsu sol*) the maṇḍala of the primordial basis.

This is the realization (HŪṂ) of the path and wisdom, which is supreme (GURU), unstained (PADMA) ultimate attainment (SIDDHI).

Commentary

INTRODUCTION

HŪṂ—the sacred primordial wisdom.

THE OBJECT OF THE PRAYER

Line 1. The country of Oḍḍiyāna (*ogyen yul*) is a source of tantras, and the definition of the word *Oḍḍiyāna* is "going by flying." In tantra, the *awakening of one's tantric lineage* (*sNgags Kyi*

Rigs Sad Pa) of one's own mind and attaining liberation from the swamp of dualistic (*gNyis sNang*) appearances of saṃsāra is very swift, like flying.

By awakening the mind, one transcends the *juncture* (*Tsam*) of saṃsāra and nirvāṇa by *liberating* (*chang*) it from *sinking* (*nub*) in the mud of saṃsāra, purifying it from all the defilements, and dissolving illusory appearances into the ultimate sphere.

Line 2. The attainment of the purity of all sound as the maṇḍala of *speech* (*Pema*), the perfection of all thoughts as the maṇḍala of mind (*kesar*), and the maturation of all appearances as the maṇḍala of body (*dongpo*)—the three secret aspects (*gSang Ba gSum*) of Buddhahood—and (*La*)

Line 3. The primordial wisdom of the attainment, which is oneness and evenness, is *marvelous* (*yatsen*).

When one realizes this, it is the attainment of the indivisibility of the basis and result, the supreme attainment (*chogki ngödrub*), the state of Vajradhara.

Line 4. This [attainment] is *renowned* (*zhesu trag*) as *the absolute Padmasambhava* (*pema jungne*),

Line 5. And its nature is that it does not stray from the primordial ground. Yet from the primordial wisdom, there *arise* (*kor*) *infinite* (*mangpo*) *functions* (*dro*) of manifestations of saṃsāra and nirvāṇa, as boundless as the sky (*kha*), *appearing as its power* (*khor*).

THE PRAYER

Line 6. If, having realized the meaning of the nature and reality of this attainment, one then remains in it without being diverted, then just as no stone can be found on an island made all of gold, so all the impure appearances will come to an end, and only primordially pure appearances will arise. One will attain liberation from all the bonds of karma and from the emotional afflictions. All good qualities will be accomplished spontaneously and effortlessly, and one will attain the Dharmakāya stage permanently. So it is the *remaining (dagdrub kyee) in the realized state (jesu) of the primordial purity (khyekyi)*.

Line 7. All phemomenal existents arise in the form of *the maṇḍala of the four vajras*[88] *(chinkyee lab chir)*, the blessings of the primordial wisdom of one's own mind. This attainment arises as the result of attaining *(shegsu sol)* the primordial basis, the ultimate truth.

THE MANTRA FOR INVOKING BLESSINGS

This is the *realization* (HŪṂ) of the path and wisdom, which is *supreme* (GURU), *unstained* (PADMA) *ultimate attainment* (SIDDHI).

CONCLUSION OF THE PRACTICES

First, the practice of *The Vajra Seven-Line Prayer* as Guru Yoga, according to the common meaning, will cause the arising of the profound primordial wisdom. By learning the crucial points of the paths of liberation, skillful means, or great perfection from a qualified Lama and practicing them diligently, one will achieve confidence in the realization, the result itself as expounded in the teachings, and will reach the state of Vidyādhara (knowledge holder).

With unshakable faith, visualize Guru Rinpoche, the embodiment of all refuges, on the crown of one's head. Pray to him strongly with *The Vajra Seven-Line Prayer*. By the nectar pouring down from the body of the Guru, all the illness, bad karma, and sufferings of one's body, speech, and mind are washed away in the form of pus, blood, insects, soot, and offal. At the end, one's own body dissolves, like salt into water, and then the liquid goes down into the mouth of Yamarāja, the Lord of Death, and other creditors of karma beneath the ground. Believe that it has satisfied all of them and that all the debts are cleared. At the end, one should regard them all as having vanished into emptiness.

Again, visualize your own body in the form of the radiant body of a divinity—whichever form you like. In the heart of the divinity, at the center of an eight-petaled lotus, the Lama comes down from the crown of your head and becomes one with the indestructible essence (bindu), the primordial wisdom. Then one should remain in the blissful primordial wisdom.

The postmeditative period should be treated as follows: all appearances viewed as a pure land and as divinities, food and drink as offerings, and the activities of sitting and walking as prostration and circumambulation. When you sleep, you should visualize the Guru in your heart. In all daily activities you should try to transform everything into virtuous practices without interval. It is important to visualize the Lama in the sky before you and to present offerings, offer praise, invoke his mind, and receive the blessings of his body, speech, and mind. This is because generally the good qualities of the higher realms of liberation, and especially the development of realization of the profound path, depend only on the entry of the blessings of the Guru into one's own mind.

In order to attain the absolute primordial wisdom in one's own mind, one must become familiar with the teachings given in the sūtras and tantras in general and, in particular, with the instruction on the direct introduction (*Ngo 'Phrod*) to the absolute primordial wisdom (*Don Gyi Ye Shes*). And, according to one's experience, realization, and ability, one should meditate on any of the paths of liberation or skillful means that is appropriate for oneself. By doing this, one will achieve the fulfillment of both the temporary and the ultimate result.

◦ 12 ◦

RECEIVING THE
FOUR EMPOWERMENTS OF
NGÖNDRO MEDITATION

THE FOUR EMPOWERMENTS or wangs are received at the
end of the Ngöndro, *The Excellent Path of Omniscience* of
the Longchen Nyingthig tradition, revealed by Rigdzin Jigme
Lingpa and compiled by the first Dodrupchen Rinpoche. The
four empowerments are received through the power of blessing lights from Guru Rinpoche. We visualize the blessing
lights being emitted from different sacred points of Guru
Rinpoche's body and then merged into the different energy
points of our own bodies. As the result, we see, feel, and
believe that we are empowered to achieve various purifications
and attainments.

In the lines related to the empowerments in *The Excellent
Path of Omniscience*, there are many technical terms, which practically cover the whole scope of tantric trainings and results,

A transcription of a talk given at Maha Siddha Nyingmapa Temple, Hawley, Mass., on December 15, 1991. This article is based mainly on SC,
NS, DD, KZ, KZZ, TS, TY, YG, and BG.

for the empowerments are the methods that initiate us into all the tantric trainings and attainments.

In the text, the subdivisions of trainings and attainments of tantra are arranged according to the sequence of the four empowerments, and it is complicated to give an explanation following that sequence. So I will discuss them by arranging them together, as the four seed syllables, four vajras, four lights, four energy centers, four karmic defilements, purification of four obscurations, four vajra blessings, four tantric practices, four stages of attainment, and the four Buddha bodies. At the beginning I am going to explain the meaning of those individual divisions, and at the end I will explain how to incorporate them as the parts of the four empowerments.

Empowerment, or initiation, is classified into three different levels, as mentioned earlier. The first is the empowerment of cause (or basis). When we receive an empowerment for the first time, the empowerment initiates or opens up our physical energy, emotional, and intellectual systems to the esoteric trainings, experiences, and attainments.

The second is the empowerment of the path. After being initiated on the esoteric path, through trainings such as Ngöndro practice and by receiving the empowerment again and again, which includes the tantric trainings discussed in the following pages, our realization and experiences progress.

The third is the empowerment of result. It is the perfection of the goal of the empowerment, the ultimate wisdom with the attainments and the bodies discussed in the following pages.

The receiving of empowerment in Ngöndro practice is mainly the empowerment of the path. But, of course, it could be the empowerment of cause if we are not really initiated or have not had any esoteric spiritual experience yet, and we are receiving it as our starting point. Also, if we have realized the ultimate wisdom, it perfects our realization. Then it is the empowerment of result.

Generally, there are three stages of our mental and spiritual condition. They are negative, positive, and perfection. Through proper view, living, and meditation we can transform our negative mundane life into a positive meritorious life, and then finally perfect our life into one of fully enlightened wisdom. Here, although our ultimate result or goal is the attainment or the perfection of the ultimate wisdom (in which the whole of phenomena is one in the enlightened nature and the whole universe is one as the manifesting power of that enlightened nature), we are not yet ready to jump from negative to perfection, as most of us are individuals with negative habits of a discriminative and emotional type. So where are we? We are in the negative turmoil of conceptual, mental, physical, and emotional battles. All of our concepts and emotions are negative. Most of our waking and sleeping time is overwhelmed with discriminations, mental afflictions, defensive and offensive actions and reactions, worries, stress, and struggles.

Now, by practice, such as receiving the four empowerments, we are trying to transform our lives of negative habits into positive spirituality. The positive experiences could be developed through being compassionate or meditating on compassion, devotion, or pure perception and so on. Ordinary compassion and so forth is not the meditation of oneness, nondual. The ultimate compassion, devotion, and purity, on the other hand, are none other than the omnipresence of the primordial wisdom, the oneness. Yet in ordinary compassion there still are the powerful view and experience that create much good karma, merit, blessings, energies, and benefits for ourselves and others. Such transformations take place by changing our lives from negative to positive, for that empowerment of the path is one of the most powerful practices.

If we have the positive force and strength with us, then the realization of perfection, which is the ultimate wisdom, will be possible, and that realization is the resultant empowerment. Perfection is becoming one with or rediscovering our own absolute nature—all-knowing, blissful, and peaceful Buddhahood. Perfection is our goal, but we should not be ambitious only about the ultimate goal and forget to work on transforming our negative life into positive, for otherwise it will not work.

ELEVEN DIVISIONS OF RECEIVING THE FOUR EMPOWERMENTS

THE THREE (OR FOUR) SYLLABLES (*Yi Ge gSum*)

In the four empowerments, we visualize a white OM letter at the forehead of Guru Rinpoche, red ĀḤ at his throat, and blue HŪṂ in his heart as the seed letters or root syllables that signify or represent his vajra body, vajra speech, vajra mind, and vajra wisdom in order to receive the empowerments.

First, I would like to say a few words about the significance of the letters or syllables. You might have learned in the tantric meditation sādhanas that the syllable always plays a significant role when you are creating or dissolving the visualizations. In tantric sādhanas (not so much in the Guru Yoga practice) that have the elaborate meditation on the development stage and perfection stage, such as *Rigdzin Dupa* and *Yumka Dechen Gyalmo,* first, in an empty openness sphere, we visualize a syllable, the seed syllable, and then the syllable changes into the image of the deity. Or sometimes we first visualize a syllable, then the syllable changes into a pure land, and then we visualize another syllable in the pure land, which turns into a lotus seat; and on that lotus we visualize another syllable, and then that turns into the deity with syllables at his energy centers. So the syllables are the seeds of visualization in the development stage and are the center of the source of power. Also, during the perfection stage, all phenomena dissolve into the deities, and the deities dissolve into the syllable, and finally the syllable dissolves into emptiness. So the syllables have a very special role in the development stage as well as in the perfection stage.

Why are the syllables so significant? When we think about or see something, a mountain for example, the process of our thoughts goes this way: "Oh, this is a mountain." Or, "This is here." Even if we do not know that it is a mountain, still we think, "Here is this," "This is a green one," or something like that. Immediately we put a label, word, or term on it. Without that labeling with some description, we cannot engage in the process of thought. Labels are the root or one of the most important aspects in the creation of mundane delusions as well as in dissolving and returning into the zero stage.

So now, when we practice, we visualize the words in the form of letters (or sometimes even in the form of symbolic implements held by the deities) for the sake of meditation. The letters in forms or characters are not the actual or original letters or words. The actual letters are the conceptual labels we put on the mental objects in order to express our concepts or to stamp the seal of our ideas. They could be thoughts like "mountain," "you," or "I," which express mundane concepts, or like OM, ĀḤ, and HŪṂ, which present the spiritual or indescribable expressions, or the ultimate meaning that goes beyond conceptual expressions.

In order to concentrate our minds on transforming negative situations into positive ones through visualizations or communications, we visualize or see the letters in forms. The actual letters or syllables are just the labeling of our minds, and that is the root, origin, and beginning of the elaboration of concepts and emotions. That is why seeing and purifying the syllables is dealing with the root, the beginning of the concepts, by using forms.

(Even in grammar, according to the Tibetan system, syllables or letters, such as "ka" and "a" are the foundation of the language. It is something that may not convey any meaning. The combination of many letters makes a noun. The combination of many nouns or words as subject, object, verb, and adjective makes a sentence. So the letters, such as "ka" and "a" are the first thing, the root of all the complexity of communication or the expression structure, and they are essential for completing a thinking process.)

Why do we visualize them in forms? There are two main purposes: for beginners like ourselves, the visual form of the original letters helps to discipline the mind to see and concentrate on the proper point. It brings us back to the beginning point of mental evolution, which could lead us to cross over to nirvāṇa.

How do we use the letters in the empowerments? In the practice of Ngöndro, white OM at the forehead of Guru Rinpoche is the seed or root letter of the vajra body of Guru Rinpoche; red ĀH in his throat is for vajra speech; blue HŪM in his heart is for vajra mind; and also a second blue HŪM in his heart is for vajra wisdom. We incorporate those letters of pure lights as the power or energy centers of Guru Rinpoche and blessing sources for our meditation.

Why does it have to be only those letters? It could be any letter or symbol instead, as every phenomenon is the expression of the ultimate nature, the blessing power of Buddhahood. However, for the training of an unrealized person, it is important to focus on a particular structure and goal, a structure of positive and spiritual expressions and energy without conventional truth.

OM, ĀH, HŪH, and HŪM are given in the scriptures as the seed symbols of the body, speech, mind, and wisdom of Buddhas. To use those as an object of meditation brings concentration and builds up discipline and positive perception in our minds, and they become a source of blessing, power, and enlightenment. For example, if a great realized master has stayed and meditated somewhere and displayed lots of miracles of realization, later we think that place has a special blessing power and energy, and we call it a pilgrimage place. So, in the same way, the OM, ĀH, HŪH, and HŪM have been blessed by hundreds of thousands of saints, sages, and Buddhas as the essence or as the seed letters, the first creating point of the enlightened vajra body, speech, mind, and wisdom. So those words have not only been designated as symbolic letters of body, speech, mind, and wisdom—as when we say "mountain," the image and idea of a mountain come to our mind—but they actually have blessing power and energy.

According to the scriptures, one blessed letter, like OM, can symbolize many meanings; for example, OM is the compound of A, O, and M, symbolizing the vajra body, speech, and mind. Also A is the primordial nature, the source of all expressions. A is the symbolic letter of the nondual, unborn, and emptiness. HŪM has five parts, which symbolize the five wisdoms and so on. There are different ways of symbolism and different ways of seeing them.

THE THREE (OR FOUR) VAJRAS

The three vajras are the blessing energy centers of Guru Rinpoche's vajra form for receiving the empowerment in our meditation. They are the forehead (between the eyebrows) of Guru Rinpoche as the focal point for vajra body, his throat for vajra speech, and his heart for vajra mind and vajra wisdom.

Why do these particular focal points represent his vajra body, vajra speech, vajra mind, and vajra wisdom? In the meditation, the body of Guru Rinpoche is his whole vajra body, from head to toes. His vajra speech is his whole energy and expression that come from or are present in all the channels of his vajra body. Vajra mind is the fully enlightened and compassionate mind, free from concepts and limitations. Vajra wisdom is the knowing of the ultimate truth as it is and conventional truth as it appears.

However, in the meditation, for the sake of concentrative

discipline, we pinpoint the forehead, throat, and heart as the focal points for his vajra body, vajra speech, vajra mind, and vajra wisdom blessing energies. If we are meditating, we need to be focused, and we must have a pinpointed place to concentrate. When we see the vajra body of Guru Rinpoche, we mainly see the youthful, powerful, and kind face. For the eyes of a spiritual mind, the most attractive or important part of the body to see is the face, and especially maybe the forehead. So the forehead becomes the focal point of the vajra body for practice. Vajra speech is more understandable for us, since we talk from the mouth or through the throat, and so that is why the mouth or the throat is the focal point for vajra speech. Vajra mind as well as vajra wisdom is more realization, feeling, experience from the depth of the heart, and the heart is the center of the whole physical structure; so the heart is designated as the focal point of vajra mind and vajra wisdom.

What are the vajra body, vajra speech, vajra mind, and vajra wisdom? They are the complete aspects of a Buddha (as well as of an ordinary being). However, here we are talking about the vajra body, vajra speech, and vajra mind, and vajra wisdom of Guru Rinpoche.

The vajra body is in two forms: Guru Rinpoche is a Buddha and in true form his vajra body presents itself as an enjoyment body (*Longs sKu*), the utmost pure body with qualities of the five certainties. But for us, who cannot see his enjoyment body, the pure form of the Buddha, we see him in the manifested body (*sPrul sKu*) as Guru Rinpoche, the form that can be perceived by any person as having various mundane characteristics. During meditation we visualize his body in radiant pure-light form, with amazing beauty, power, and energy.

The vajra speech of Guru Rinpoche is the expression of Dharma energies, qualities, and communication with sixty harmonious melodies.

The vajra mind of Guru Rinpoche is free from all dualistic concepts as well as the two obscurations—the obscuration of its primordial nature and the obscuration of adventitious defilements. So it is pure in its nature and also pure from the sudden arising of defilements.

The vajra wisdom of Guru Rinpoche is knowing the two truths—knowing the ultimate truth as it is and knowing the conventional truth, every happening in the world, spontaneously and simultaneously.

BLESSING LIGHTS ('od Zer)

It is very interesting and very important to understand what light is. For us ordinary people, "light" means something like the sunlight, the rainbow light, or the light emitted from a crystal. Those kinds of light are very beautiful and one of the most subtle forms that are visible to the eyes of flesh. But, then, according to Buddhist scriptures, at the stage of a highly realized person or in the state of Buddhahood, the mind of the Buddha, as well as the phenomena in front of the Buddha, do not function as subject and object, but are present as oneness. He sees or rather realizes and knows all and everything simultaneously, without being in subjective and objective positions, which have limits of time and restrictions of space or dimensions. All is present as rangnang (*Rang sNang*), self-appearing phenomena, or as rigtsal (*Rig rTsal*), the power of the enlightened wisdom itself. Sometimes it is also termed rang-ö, self-light or self-radiation, which means that the objective and material phenomena are not two separate arenas, but one in pure light—the radiation of the enlightened nature itself.

When we say "self-creation" or "self-radiation," we might instantly think that there is a wisdom in the center as the creator and the light over there as the creation. We immediately characterize and classify everything as it suits our usual mundane mind. But there is no such classification of creator and creation of mind and matter, and all are naturally present, like space and the openness of space. We cannot give any example of it because whatever a conceptual mind thinks or designates is in terms of dualistic and grasping concepts. And that is the very point, that the ultimate truth, Buddhahood, is described as nangtong yerme (sNang sTong dByer Med), the indivisibility of emptiness and appearances. In the union of emptiness and the self-appearing light of Buddhahood there are no dualistic concepts, no limitation, no boundaries, no restrictions, and no separation of you and me—all are in oneness: oneness of peace, joy, and light. When we say that phenomena appear as the nature of light or the self—appearing light of Buddhahood, we are not talking of ordinary light, like rainbow light or lights in the form of shining, sparkling, and flickering phenomena, but the pure light of the changeless clarity of the pure nature.

Ordinary light is not the actual goal we are pursuing. However, as a skillful means for the sake of meditation, we see Guru Rinpoche and his blessings in the form of ordinary light (the most subtle of all the visible mundane phemonena), and it helps us, for now, to see things as less rigid, less gross, unhindered, clear, open, peaceful, and calm. Then, that kind of view and feeling, created by the light, will help to lead us to the utmost pure light of the nondual presence of Buddhahood in the ultimate future. As you know, for us, due to our dualistic and rigid concepts and emotions, phenomena before our conceptual mind appear and function as gross, solid, and sharp, and as a changing and unending source of pain and excitement. When we unwind the rigid dualistic concepts and emotions and attain the fully enlightened state, all phenomena will become one in peace, openness, calm, and light, and that is the attainment of pure light or ultimate light. But in the meditation of Ngöndro, as an unenlightened person, we use the ordinary form of light as the means of training.

A Dzogpa Chenpo scripture says that for ordinary people all these solid phenomena in front of us are manifesting as composites of the five elements, but in Buddhahood they are present as the pure light in five colors, the self-appearing lights of Buddha wisdom. The five colors are the five wisdoms of Buddhahood, for there is no material that is not Buddha wisdom. But for ordinary people like ourselves, as the true nature is obscured, the five-color pure light has taken the form of the material world of solid, gross, and changing phenomena composed of five gross elements. As a result, this rigid mentality has become the source of pain and excitement because of the afflictions of craving, greed, and hatred, which are rooted in the grasping at self.

If you read some of the books on near-death experiences, you will find that not only enlightened people but even ordinary people who have had near-death experiences have experienced the pure light. (Esoteric Buddhist scriptures agree that everybody experiences a flash of the ultimate nature and pure lights at the time of death.) This was not an object over there, but was nondual; and that light was not a thing, but the feeling of peace and bliss. That light was not just the light of our ideas, but the light of feeling, the light of experiences, the light of peace and bliss. I think that what they are talking about is a glimpse of the pure light. Also, the peace and bliss is not what we ordinary people conceptualize about peace and bliss, but it is beyond description, time, and dimensions. So even the people who have near-death experience have some glimpses of pure light.

Visualizing Guru Rinpoche in his light body and receiving blessings in the form of lights is a process of bringing blessing energies into our minds so that we can purify and transform our mental view and feeling into the realization of the ultimate Buddha-wisdom, which is the union of openness and pure light. Also, of course, instead of light, we can use any means, such as nectar, fire, or air as the means of purification and perfection; but in this empowerment we use light as the means of training.

According to Khenpo Ngagchung,[89] when you receive the white light of body, visualize it as being like moonlight; when you receive the red light of speech, visualize it as being like lightning; when you receive the blue light of mind, visualize it as being like incense smoke (this is not a dark smoke, but pure, light-blue smoke); and for the wisdom blessing it is a blue HŪM letter.

THE FOUR (OR THREE) CENTERS
OF THE BODY (gNas gSum)

These are the crown of the head, throat, heart, and heart, which are the four crucial energy points of the body, where we receive the blessing lights. The reason for selecting these places was discussed earlier.

THE FOUR KARMAS (Las bZhi)

We purify the four unvirtuous karmas by means of receiving the four blessing lights from Guru Rinpoche. The four unvirtuous karmas are the unvirtuous karmas of body, speech, mind, and the universal ground.

There are numerous kinds of unvirtuous karmas committed by our body, speech, and mind, but they are identified and divided into ten unvirtuous deeds. The ten unvirtuous karmas are: the three unvirtuous karmas committed by our physical body: killing, stealing, and sexual misconduct; the four unvirtuous karmas committed by speech: lies, slander, divisive or harsh words, and chatter or gossip; and the three unvirtuous karmas committed by mind: greed, hatred, and perverted or wrong view based on ignorance.

The fourth is the karma of the universal ground. In order to explain the universal ground, we had better talk a little about all eight (or seven) consciousnesses.[90] The system of the eight consciousnesses belongs mainly to the interpretations of the Yogāchāra school of Mahāyāna Buddhism, the followers of the scriptures that belong to the third turning of the wheel of Dharma by the Buddha. However, the system of the eight consciousnesses is also a prevalent view in tantric scriptures. The eight consciousnesses are not eight different individual consciousnesses, but are eight different stages of our mental process as it develops into a full-fledged, active mind capable of formulating a karma and experiencing the results.

The universal ground is a neutral and inactive state, like sleep, or perhaps you could say an unconscious state in which there are no thoughts, as your mind is not yet exposed to any subject. However, it is the basis, foundation, or ground from which saṃsāric concepts and emotions grow, and pain and suffering are created as the result. Also, by transcending or going beyond that state, through the wisdom of realization of the true nature, one attains Buddhahood.

For saṃsāric beings, from that universal ground arise the eight consciousnesses, and karma is formulated, which fuels the cycle of births. (1) The consciousness of the universal ground is a consciousness in which the mind clearly sees (*mThong*) the vague objective field in general. Mind is exposed or open to the general objective field. But there are no thoughts that conceive (*rTog Pa*) of anything as object.

(2–6) The five consciousnesses of the senses are those in which mind becomes clearly aware (*Rig Pa*) of the five individual sense objects, which appear to it through the particular sense consciousnesses: eye consciousness for seeing, tongue consciousness for tasting, nose consciousness for smelling, ear consciousness for hearing, and body consciousness for touching or feeling. Here, it looks like five different consciousnesses, but there is only one mind, and that mind is reaching the objects through one of the five doors, one at a time. It is as if you place a monkey in a house with five windows. The monkey looks out of one window and then looks out another window, and you might think that there are five monkeys, but in fact there is only one monkey, who goes around and looks through the different windows.

(7) Mind consciousness. In the earlier stages, your mind first saw the objective fields and then saw clearly the particular field of the particular sense. Now, for the first instant, there arises a concept or thought (rTog Pa) of apprehending what the mind is seeing in general, as a general (idea of) object (gZungs Ba), thinking, "This is this"; and simultaneously there is formed the apprehender (or grasper), the subject ('Dzin Pa).

(8) Defiled mind consciousness. As soon as we have a dualistic concept of "This is this," there follows all the detailed or analytical concepts (dPyod Pa) of being tall, good, bad, my, your—with emotional afflictions of liking, disliking, or neutrality.

So the association of these eight consciousnesses formulates the process of a dualistic and discriminative concept with emotional afflictions, and this completes the formation of a karma.

Among these, the consciousnesses of mind and the five senses are the means or tools to create karma. The consciousness of defiled mind, that is, virtuous, unvirtuous, and neutral mind, is the creator of karma. The consciousness of the universal ground provides the space or chance to create, increase, or decrease the karma. The universal ground is the place where the karmas are stored or preserved until they are exhausted by being experienced, or purified through opposite karmas.

So, when we say the karmas of body, speech, and mind,

now this is easy to comprehend. The karma of the universal ground is the karma that is stored in the universal ground or, according to Khenpo Ngagchung,[91] it is the karmas created by the consciousness of the universal ground, which has dualistic concepts (an intellectual obscuration) with traces.

THE FOUR OBSCURATIONS (sGrib Pa bZhi)

This category is concerned with the purification of the impurities of our channels, air or energies, essence, and intellect. First we will talk about the channels, air, and essence.[92]

According to the scriptures, the physical channels are the most important aspect of the body, like the ground, foundation, house, or road. The air or energy causes changes, progress, increase, or decrease in the power of the expressions, like the aspect of dwelling in the house or moving the vehicle on the road. The essence is the thing that needs to progress, like the master who is dwelling in this house and traveling on the road. In tantric practices the enlightened essence (Bodhichitta) is to be refined, realized, and perfected through the path of purified channels by the right force of air or energy.

1. Channels (rTsa): The body is a composite of the channels. Whether these particular channels exist physically in the body of an ordinary person or are the creation of meditation is a question. Jigme Lingpa terms them the channels developed by meditation (sGom Byung Gi rTsa). For a highly accomplished meditator, these channels become real channels in the body, and they bring esoteric power and realization.

There are three principle channels, the uma at the center, roma on the right, and kyangma on the left. For women kyangma is on the right and roma is on the left.

The uma goes straight from the head to the genitals. The two channels are on its right and left. (According to esoteric practices, the roma and kyangma are tied around the uma with twenty-one knots, and when the knots are untied through the force of practice, realization will be achieved. But here we should just see them as straight, without the uma being tied.) There are five chakras (wheels or centers) around the three channels, like the spokes of an umbrella. At the crown of the head is the great-bliss chakra with thirty-two petals, at the throat is the enjoyment chakra with sixteen petals, at the heart is the dharma chakra with eight petals, at the navel is the chakra of formation with sixty-four petals, and at the genitals is the bliss-maintaining chakra with seventy-two petals. (There are also practices using six or seven chakras.)

The structures and numbers of the channels and chakras depend on the particular practice (or text) that you are following. For Vajrasattva purification, Paltrul Rinpoche's commentary instructs one to visualize the uma with the first four chakras. In phowa practices, the uma is visualized as ending below the navel.

The uma possesses four qualities. It is light blue; very thin, like the petal of a lotus; clear, like the light of a lamp; and straight, like a bamboo arrow.

On the right is the roma, white, filled with semen. On the left is the kyangma, red, filled with blood. These channels are half the size of the central channel. They go straight up and then, curving around the ear, come through the nostrils. At the bottom, four finger-widths below the navel (i.e., about two inches below the navel), they meet in the uma, forming a shape similar to a Tibetan "ch'a" letter. They pass through five chakras (or four chakras, six chakras, or seven chakras).

For ordinary people, these three channels are the symbols of three poisons: uma is ignorance, roma is desire, and kyangma is hatred. In their pure character, they are the three Buddha bodies: uma is Dharmakāya, roma is Sambhogakāya, and kyangma is Nirmāṇkāya.

2. Air (rLung): Air is like a tool that causes or permits things to change, move, decrease, or increase. Air is the vehicle of speech. The channels are described as being like a road, the air or energy like a blind horse, and the essence, which is associated with the mind, like a lame person. So air forces the essence to change and to travel through the channels. Air can be categorized into three aspects: outer, inner, and secret energies.

Outer air is the common view of air as explained in the Tibetan medical system. There are five kinds of air: (1) Life force, which sustains or maintains life, is stationed at the heart. (2) Upward-moving air, which is the aspect of breathing and the voice that moves upward, is situated in the upper body. (3) Pervasive air pervades and sustains every part of the body. (4) Heat air, which provides warmth and digestion, is situated at the navel. (5) Downward-clearing air, which helps to relieve things, is situated in the lower part of the body.

Inner air is described in the scriptures as being five kinds of air according to five colors. The five-color air goes back to the original stage, as we discussed in the case of the five colors of light. The five-color air corresponds to the five ele-

ments and five emotions. The earth element and the emotion
of pride is in the form of yellow air. Water and hatred are in
white. Fire and desire are in red. Air and jealousy are in green.
Space and ignorance are in blue.

Secret air is the air of the five wisdoms. The five colors of
air signify the self-appearing colors, as we discussed in the
case of light. The yellow is the wisdom of equalness—the
state of sameness, oneness, and impartiality. White is the mirrorlike wisdom, manifesting all as self-appearances, as a mirror provides all things the possibility of appearing as reflections. Red is the discriminating wisdom, knowing all and
each simultaneously, without confusion. Green is the wisdom
of accomplishment, the Buddha actions that fulfill all needs.
Blue is the wisdom of the ultimate sphere, totally pure and
open, like space.

Also, in meditation, there are three kinds of meditative air
or breathing. They are the air of inhaling, holding, and exhaling in the cycle of meditation.

(3). Essence (*Thig Le*): This is the essence of the physical
body as well as the essence or experience of spiritual enlightenment (Bodhichitta), the union of bliss and emptiness. It is
like the master or the passenger in the vehicle of energy on
the road of the channels. In relative truth it is the basis of
mind, and in absolute truth it is the enlightened mind itself.
It has two aspects, relative essence and absolute essence.

Relative essence is the gross essence—the white and red
fluids. The channels of the body are filled with either white
or red essence.

Absolute essence are the channels of pure lights (as discussed above) filled with the five-wisdom air on energies (of

five colors), the pure-light essence of wisdom in five colors. The essence (as well as the channels and air) of the five lights is the five Buddha wisdoms, the nondual presence of Buddha nature and its self-manifesting power. That means that the essence of the five-color pure light is the Buddha wisdoms.

Regarding the practice of this, see and visualize the uma, the central channel, in the center of the body, and on its right and left are the roma and kyangma channels, starting from the nostrils and ending at the uma below the navel. Visualize a HAM letter in the form of a white essence with a blissful nature at the top end of the uma. See it as if the HAM letter is almost melting and dripping with bliss. Visualize a red ĀH letter at the place where the roma and kyangma channels meet in the uma. It is of the nature of a wisdom-flame—a flame with heat. The white HAM letter represents the divinity of the male, and the red ĀH of fire represents the divinity of the female. The red ĀH of fire has four characteristics—it is a flame with bliss, heat, clarity, and a sharp pointed flame at the top. Also, the flame is not a burning or destroying fire, but a flame of the warmth of bliss and purification.

By inhaling air through the roma and kyangma, this blows on the flame of bliss, and the flame becomes bigger and bigger. The flame goes up and touches every part of the body, sending waves of bliss-heat, and touches the white HAM letter. As the HAM letter is almost melting and dripping with bliss by nature, the touch of the flame turns it upside down, and an inexhaustible stream of white essence-nectar of bliss flows or drips from the top of the HAM. Slowly it fills the five (four, six, or seven) chakras, generating the wisdom of fourfold bliss: bliss, supreme bliss, extraordinary bliss, and innate bliss. When the nectar fills the head chakra, you experience the wisdom of bliss. When it fills the throat, you feel the wisdom of supreme bliss. When it fills the heart chakra, you feel extraordinary bliss. When it reaches the navel chakra, you experience innate bliss. Or, when the nectar comes from the head chakra to the throat chakra you feel bliss, from the throat to heart chakra supreme bliss, the heart chakra to navel chakra extraordinary bliss, and from the navel chakra to secret chakra innate bliss.

Also, send lights of bliss to all the Buddhas as offerings, and receive back their blissful blessing lights, merging them into the HAM letter of bliss. Send lights of bliss to the whole world, and let them blaze in the oneness of great bliss, the union of bliss and emptiness.

In Ngöndro, we are not expected to practice meditation on the channels, air, and essence as I have explained; but as we receive the blessing lights, we see and feel that all the impurities in them are totally purified and that they have become pure and capable of being vessels of practicing the esoteric trainings.

4. Intellect (*Shes Bya*): This is the purification of the obscuration of intellect. Intellect is the dualistic mind, or it is also described as the view that conceives of things having three characteristics: subjective, objective, and action. The intellectual obscuration is one of the two obscurations, the other being the obscuration of emotional afflictions. Emotional obscurations are grosser and easier to recognize and purify, but intellectual obscuration is harder, as it is the aspect of dualistic concept, which is subtle and the root of all mundane concepts. When we are free of both obscurations,

we transcend karmic effects, reach Buddhahood, and become omniscient.

THE FOUR VAJRA BLESSINGS (rDo rJe bZhi)

These four vajras are the receiving of the blessings of vajra body, vajra speech, vajra mind, and vajra wisdom of Guru Rinpoche, the Buddha.

Vajra body (sKu rDo rJe) is the two form bodies of the Buddha. They are the pure form of the enjoyment body and the impure form of the manifested body. While you are practicing, you see this in the form of a light, powerful, and inspiring image, with pure perception and faith in it as the absolute source of purifications and empowerments. Here, we are not only practicing our seeing and having faith in the vajra body of Guru Rinpoche as the Buddha body, but the whole universe as the pure land of Buddha, in the form of pure lights.

Vajra speech (gSung rDo rJe) has the sixty harmonious qualities. In relative truth, it is truthful, peaceful, enchanting, enlightening, everlasting, all-pervading, and all Dharma expressions. In absolute truth, it is the natural presence, spontaneously accomplished and self-arisen sound, which is not separate from the wisdom of the ultimate nature itself.

Vajra mind (Thugs rDo rJe) has the nature of the two purities—pure in its primordial nature and pure from any adventitious or sudden impurities.

Vajra wisdom (Ye Shes rDo rJe) is a twofold knowledge—knowing the ultimate truth of all as it is and knowing every happening in relative truth simultaneously as it appears.

(Next are actually the four empowerments themselves, but we will discuss them at the end, as the conclusion.)

The Four Tantric Practices

The empowerments enable us to practice and accomplish the following four practices. They are the practices of the development stage, recitation, bliss-emptiness heat yoga, and the Great Perfection. Among these four, the first is the development stage, and the other three constitute the perfection stage of the two stages of tantric practice.

1. Development stage (*bsKyed Rim*). In this practice you see or create all phenomena as three purities or transformations (*Dag Pa gSum* or *'Khyer So gSum*): You perceive, feel, and believe the forms of beings to be the forms of the Buddha, and the land or nature to be the pure land of the Buddha. You hear sounds as the pure sound of the Buddha, the sound of the expression of teachings, prayers, mantras, peace, joy, and wisdom. You realize thoughts as pure thoughts of the Buddha, the thoughts of purity, peace, compassion, joy, openness, oneness, bliss, wisdom, and light. So all these are the three practices that constitute the development stage.

Generally, we might think that the development stage consists of visualization. This is both true and not true. Visualization is an important part of it, but it is not just the visual images that mind creates to see over there as an object to play with and enjoy. When our minds visualize, see, and realize the forms, sounds, and thoughts as pure and concentrate on or unite with those visualized pure forms, sounds, and thoughts, then because of the pure perception of our minds, the whole world becomes the world of Buddha wisdoms, peace, openness, and light. If we have compassionate minds, the whole world becomes a world of compassion. If we have joyful minds, the whole world becomes a world of joy. So if we have the pure perception and experience of it, the whole world in front of us will become a world of Buddha wisdom. It is not just a matter of perception; it is the realization of the truth brought about by pure perception, as the natural display of the absolute nature of the mind.

What is the perfection stage (*rDzogs Rim*)? The perfection stage (dissolution or completion stage) is the fruition aspect of the esoteric training—the experience or realization of absolute truth, the great bliss and innate wisdom.

There are many kinds of wisdom. But here we are concerned with the two wisdoms, the causal symbolic wisdom (*dPe'i Ye Shes*) initiated by the empowerment, and the resultant meaning-wisdom (*Don Gyi Ye Shes*), realized, developed, and perfected through the path of clear light and fourfold bliss by properly using the channels, air or energy, and the essence of one's own vajra body. The perfection stage has two means of training: the path of liberation (*Grol Lam*) and the path of skillful means (*Thabs Lam*).

In the general trainings on the perfection stage, you use the channels, air, and essence of the vajra body because they are very effective and powerful means, and they are intimate to you, in order to bring about the result, the union of bliss and emptiness.

2. Recitation (*bZlas brJod*). Recitation is an inadequate term in this context. Here we repeat mantras, but it also involves doing visualizations, invocations, purifications, and having the experiences again and again; and these are the exercises in generating, increasing, and strengthening the medita-

tive experiences and the realization of the wisdom. So "recitation" is an important part, and this part is named as such,
but it is more than reciting.

In many tantric practices (not in the Guru Yoga), you are
visualizing yourself as the main deity, with the heart syllables
(or seed letter) in your heart encircled by the rosary of mantra letters. By exhorting with the recitation of the mantra,
energies are emitted and generated in the form of blessing
lights or nectars from the mantra rosary at your heart, like
electricity generated from the revolutions of a motor, and
they transform the world into a pure land of bliss and light.
This involves the total dedication of yourself to the practice
ceaselessly, completely, and perfectly, as well as bringing
the whole world into it. Recitation has four categories, as
follows.

Nyenpa (*bsNyen Pa*): This is mainly concentration on the
mantra. First visualize yourself as the deity. On a disc at
your heart visualize the mantra rosary. Concentrating on that
mantra one-pointedly, recite the mantra again and again.

Nye-nyen (*Nye bsNyen*): Reciting the mantras, visualize
beams of light coming from the rosary of mantras. They go
out of your mouth and enter into the mouth of the consort
and, channeling through the body of the consort, they return
into your body through the point of union. Its circling forms
a ring of light, like a firebrand (*mGal Me*).

Or, visualize the wisdom deity (the actual deity, *Ye Shes Pa*)
in the sky in front of you and, from the mantra rosary inside
you, the samaya deity (visualized deity, *Dam Tshig Pa*), beams
of light circle through you and the wisdom deity (instead of
the consort).

Drubpa (*sGrub Pa*): Reciting mantra, visualize that from the rosary of mantras, lights are projected in all directions and touch all the Buddhas, and they are filled with bliss. Then they send back blissful lights as their blessings, which merge into you. Feel bliss and believe that you, the samaya deity, have received all the blessings of all the Buddhas. Again, you send out lights and touch all sentient beings and the whole world. The whole world is filled with great bliss and transformed into the mandala of the deity.

Drupchen (*sGrub Ch'en*): Then from your samaya-deity body and from the mantra rosary, infinite rays of light are emitted in all directions and transform the forms of the whole world into the forms of the deity, all sound into the sound of mantra, and all thoughts into the wisdoms of bliss, clarity, and no-thought. Recite the mantra with the oneness of oneself and the whole universe as the mandala of the deity.

3. Union of bliss and emptiness and the heat yoga (Tib. *bDe sTong*, Skt. *chandālī*): As I mentioned earlier, in the purification of the four obscurations, this is the practice that brings the realization of the union of bliss and emptiness through the means of fourfold bliss by exerting the channels, energy, and essence of the vajra body with the fierce force of the blissful flame at the navel.

4. Great Perfection (*rDzogs Pa Ch'en Po*): In Great Perfection the important point is to distinguish or separate mind and the intrinsic nature of the mind, the Buddha nature. First, by searching with exercises and by the power of a highly realized person, one can be awakened or introduced to the true nature of mind; and at that moment you get a glimpse of the nature of the mind. Then you should contemplate that

experience of the glimpse of the nature of the mind. As a result, the realization of the glimpse of the nature of the mind will be perfected into an everlasting and totally awakened freedom. Then, not just the nature of the mind, but the true nature of the whole universe, will be unified into that oneness, and that is the Great Perfection.

In the Great Perfection there are two major divisions of practice: Thregchö (*Khregs Ch'od*) is the meditation on and realization of the intrinsic nature of the mind, which is primordially pure, by cutting off all dualistic concepts. Thögal (*Thod rGal*) is the meditation on and perfection of all appearances as the spontaneously accomplished pure light, which is one with the manifesting power of Buddha wisdom (the bodies and pure lands of Buddha), through the path of the direct approach of the six lamps or lights (*sGron Ma*) and attainments of the four stages of visions (*sNang Ba*).

In Ngöndro, you are not expected to do the four tantric practices I explained above, but by receiving the blessing lights, see, feel, and believe that you have become capable of practicing those esoteric trainings.

THE FOUR STAGES OF ATTAINMENT (*Rig 'Dzin bZhi*)[93]

In the sūtric tradition of Buddhism there are ten stages and five paths to go through to reach Buddhahood. In tantric traditions the stages are divided or classified in different ways. Most of the Nyingma tantric scriptures have four attainments, called "knowledge-holders" (Tib. *Rig 'Dzin,* Skt. Vidyādhara).

1. The Knowledge-holder with residues (*rNam sMin Rig 'Dzin*): This attainment is with karmic residues.

rm of being, such as human beings, animals, birds, and fish.
his form could appear as a good person, bad person, nice
rson, ugly person, or beautiful person, and in any kind of
rm and trade; but they all end up helping others. Tibetan
ulkus belong to this manifestation.

The supreme manifestation (*mCh'og Gi sPrul sKu*) is in the
rm of an enlightened being, like Shākyamuni Buddha. He
kes birth as an excellent being, goes through all the proper
perfect processes of spiritual life, manifests his highest
alization, and then teaches that to others and shows a su-
eme manifestation as an excellent model for others. A su-
eme manifestation is always in a perfect and Dharma form.

2. Enjoyment body (Tib. *Longs sKu*, Skt. Sambhogakāya):
his is the pure form or actual form of the Buddhas. It is a
ontaneously present or self-present form, and it can be
en only by the Buddhas. "Seen" means not through subjec-
ve and objective duality, but in oneness. The enjoyment
ody possesses the quality of five certainties (*Nges Pa lNga*):
he pure land is the infinite, limitless, and dimensionless ul-
mate sphere. The teachers or body is eternal and enlight-
ed pure light. The retinues are nondual, as all the teacher
d retinues are oneless. The teachings are all-pervasive, su-
eme Dharma. The time is timeless, as it is beyond the con-
tions of time.

3. Ultimate body (Tib. *Ch'os sKu*, Skt. Dharmakāya): This
the omniscient nature of the Buddha wisdom. There are
o Buddha wisdoms—the wisdom of knowing the absolute
ue nature of all as it is and the wisdom of knowing all and
ery relative phenomenon simultaneously, without con-
sion.

Here people might think that this attainment is not a good
one, and a negative attitude might be flickering. But, in fact,
this is a very high attainment and hard to attain for people
like us, who are not even able to realize the meaning of impermanence at the inner or spiritual level, and who could not
dedicate much of our minds and lives to such spiritual
meaning.

It is important to be inspired by high-sounding attainments, but equally or even more important to be realistic and
practical. Here, I would like to tell a story. When I was living
at Shantiniketan in India, I met a retired professor, seventy
to eighty years old, a well-known artist. He was not much of
a meditator, but was a very difficult person for anybody to
get along with. One day, I heard him asking seriously: "In
which bhūmi (stage of realization) am I?" He seemed honestly expecting to be quite a highly realized person. If you
said to him, "You are a Knowledge-holder with residues," he
might be offended. We, too, might have that kind of mentality, which only causes a laugh now and then.

The Knowledge-holder with residues has three characteristics. His mind has been perfected or matured as the deity,
but the residues of karmic effect on the gross physical body
have not yet been renounced, and immediately after release
from the mortal body (death) he will attain the Knowledge-
holder of great sign, the third attainment, which we will discuss below.

(Even in the case of Shākyamuni Buddha there are debates.
According to Hīnayāna tradition, Shākyamuni Buddha was
with residue until he attained mahāparinivāna, because until
the attainment of mahāparinirvāna he was with his gross

body, which is, they say, a residue of his karmic effects. Mahā-yānists disagree.)

2. Knowledge-holder who has control over life (*Tshe dBang Rig 'Dzin*): In this, not only has the mind been perfected as the deity, but even the gross body has been perfected. He also has the qualities of freedom from the four contaminations (*Zag Pa*). The four contaminations are the afflicted emotions of wrong views, loss of the body (death) without control or choice, no control over the harmony of the elements of the body (health), and taking rebirth according to karma, without control or choice.

Both the attainment with residues and the attainment with control over life are equal in terms of succeeding. It is not necessary to attain one after another. If you are a less capable person you will achieve the Knowledge-holder with residue, and then you proceed to the third attainment, Knowledge-holder of great sign. If you are a more capable person, you could achieve the Knowledge-holder who has control over life and then move to the third Knowledge-holder.

Both these first and second Knowledge-holders are equivalent to the path of insight (*mThong Lam*), the third of the five paths, and the first stage of the ten-stage system of sūtric traditions. In this, you abandon the obscurations of emotional afflictions (*Nyon sGrib*), the first of the obscurations, the other being the intellectual obscurations.

3. Knowledge-holder of great sign (*Phyag rGya'i Rig 'Dzin*): His base body (or main form) is in the form of the deity. For the benefit of beings, it has the capacity to project various emanated forms. The power of his foreknowledge and so forth is clearer, purer, and more stable than that of the

Knowledge-holder who has control over life[...] not equal) to the qualities of the enjoymen[...]

This is the equivalent of the realization[...] stage and the path of meditation, the fou[...] tradition.

4. Knowledge-holder of the spontaneou[...] (*Lhun Grub Rig 'Dzin*): This is the final st[...] before instantly becoming a fully enlight[...] forms are similar to those of the enjoym[...] realizations and activities are similar to tho[...]

This attainment is equal to the tenth[...] fourth path, the path of meditation, of sūtr[...] in these last two attainments, you abando[...] obscurations with their traces.

THE FOUR BUDDHA BODIES (*sK[...]*

After completion of the attainment of[...] edge-holders, you become a fully enlighter[...] Buddhahood consists of four Buddha bodie[...]

1. Manifested body (Tib. *sPrul sKu*, S[...] This is the manifested form that appears in[...] benefit of others, according to the percept[...] appears due to the power of the aspiration[...] of the Buddha and because of the good k[...] beings. This is in an ordinary gross form, [...] three categories:

The form of art (*bZo*) is any kind of[...] nature, such as an image, statue, trees, an[...] beneficial.

The form of rebirth (*sKye Ba*) is the m[...]

There are the simple but amazing events of near-death experiences, which portray oneness, timelessness, and so on. For example, in the books of Dr. Raymond Moody and according to what I have heard from other sources, there are people who had near-death experiences for a few minutes, and in that brief period they remembered everything in detail—whatever happened in their lives, from birth till the near-death experience. But they did not have to go through each of those experiences one by one, and they did not even have to see, hear, or think with their eyes, ears, or minds since everything was present in their minds as one. That means that they had an experience of a different dimension of perception and of knowing many things simultaneously.

In Buddhahood you can see everything simultaneously, as your mind is in the nondual state, and there are no limitations, restrictions, and hindrances.

4. Natural body (Tib. *Ngo Bo Nyid sKu*, Skt. Svabhāvika-kāya): This consists of the two purities of the Buddha. First, Buddhahood is pure in its primordial nature. The purity of Buddhahood is not something that was not pure but has become pure, or that underneath somewhere has residues of an impure presence. It is primordially and totally pure. Second, Buddhahood is pure from adventitious defilements. Various conceptual and emotional defilements arise for us all the time; they suddenly come up from somewhere or nowhere and obscure our nature. But in Buddhahood there are no arisings of sudden or adventitious defilements.

THE FOUR EMPOWERMENTS

This has two aspects. The first is the receiving of the four empowerments or blessing powers of Guru Rinpoche. The second is the unification of your mind with the Buddha mind of Guru Rinpoche. Within the explanation of the four empowerments, I would like to include the whole meaning of the lines involved in the receiving of the four empowerments, which we have discussed earlier.

The most important means for receiving the empowerments is faith in and devotion to Guru Rinpoche—in our training and in yourself. It is the faith in Guru Rinpoche: seeing him as the embodiment of all the Buddhas, Bodhisattvas, saints, sages, and the ultimate pure nature and energy of the universe, with compassion, power, and wisdom. It is the faith in our practice: viewing it as the most meaningful and powerful means of training, which leads us to the ultimate goal. It is the faith in yourselves, by seeing and feeling the good fortune, spiritual potential, and enlightening qualities that you have. With such faith and devotion, receive the blessings in the form of lights from the vajra centers of Guru Rinpoche with total belief that this is not just a light, but pure light, the blessing power from Guru Rinpoche, and feel the warmth, heat, bliss, energy, power, openness, and peace of the light. Then let the blessing lights, yourself, and the spiritual experiences (or the attainments) merge as one. And bathe in the union of openness, clarity, and the all-pervasiveness of that very oneness, in which there is no concept of duality or grasping, and there are no emotions of craving or aggression.

In the Ngöndro we are not necessarily going to pursue directly the practices of the categories involved in the four empowerments, which we have discussed before, such as the four tantric trainings and four attainments. Then why did I explain the four empowerments in such detail? If you have an urge to know the meaning of the various references mentioned but in reciting and practicing Ngöndro, the thought might flicker in you, "I don't know this stuff! What is this?" That kind of mentality forms a negating and resisting blockage in your spiritual growth and generates unhealthy energies in your mind. I have explained them so that we could have a sense of relief and understanding about these points.

However, knowing the details sometimes brings another kind of hindrance—conceptualizing too much in a rush, thinking, "This is this; this is that. This has three. That has four, etc." Then, instead of bathing in the experience of peace, joy, and blessing—the power of the empowerments— you might become a spiritual accountant or aesthetician, too conceptual and too intellectual, and it could derail the progress of your spiritual experiences. So the important thing is to use the information to create a balance, knowing enough not to worry about the meaning of the terms and not turning the information into a maneuver in rush-hour traffic.

1. Vase Empowerment: This is the receiving of the power or empowerment of the vajra body of the Buddha—in this case the vajra body of Guru Rinpoche—in our bodies.

Visualize, see, feel, and believe that the blessings in the form of a beam of white light come from the white OM letter at the forehead, the vajra body center of Guru Rinpoche. It enters the crown of the head, the body center, and fills the whole body with warmth, bliss, peace, and openness. It purifies all the unvirtuous karma of your body and the impurities of your channels. You have received the vajra-body power of Guru Rinpoche. You have received the empowerment of vase, the vajra-body maṇḍala of Guru Rinpoche. You have turned into a proper vessel for the practice of the development stage. The seed of the attainment of the Knowledge-holder with residues is sown in you. The capacity for attaining the manifested body of the Buddha is established in you.

Khenpo Ngagchung writes that the goal of the Vase Empowerment is to generate the wisdom of the union of appearances and emptiness, and to liberate all the appearances, sounds, and thoughts into forms of deities, sounds of mantra, and the wisdom of Guru Rinpoche.[94]

2. Secret Empowerment: This is the receiving of the empowerment of the vajra speech of Guru Rinpoche.

Visualize, see, feel, and believe that the blessings in the form of a beam of red light come from the red ĀḤ letter at his throat, the vajra-speech center of Guru Rinpoche. It enters into your throat, the speech center, and fills the whole body with warmth, bliss, peace, and openness. It purifies all the unvirtuous karma of your speech and the impurities of your air or energy. You have received the vajra speech power of Guru Rinpoche. You have received the secret empowerment, the vajra-speech maṇḍala of Guru Rinpoche. You have turned into a proper vessel for the practice of recitation. The seed of the attainment of the Knowledge-holder who has control over life is sown in you. The capacity for attaining the enjoyment body of the Buddha is established in you.

Khenpo Ngagchung writes that the goal of the Secret Empowerment is to generate the wisdom of the union of clarity and emptiness, and to liberate inhaling, exhaling, and holding the breath into the cycle of mantras.[95]

3. Wisdom Empowerment: This is the receiving of the empowerment of the vajra mind of Guru Rinpoche.

Visualize, see, feel, and believe that the blessings in the form of a beam of blue light come from the blue HŪM letter at his heart, the vajra-mind center of Guru Rinpoche. It enters your heart, the mind center, and fills the whole body with warmth, bliss, peace, and openness. It purifies all the unvirtuous karma of your mind and the impurities of your essence. You have received the vajra-mind power of Guru Rinpoche. You have received the wisdom empowerment, the vajra-mind maṇḍala of Guru Rinpoche. You have turned into a proper vessel for the practice of bliss and emptiness and heat yoga. The seed of the attainment of the Knowledge-holder of great sign is sown in you. The capacity for attaining the ultimate body of the Buddha is established in you.

Khenpo Ngagchung writes that the goal of the wisdom empowerment is to generate the wisdom of the union of bliss and emptiness, and to liberate all concepts into the nature of the union of bliss and emptiness.[96]

4. Verbal Empowerment: This is the receiving of the empowerment of the vajra wisdom of Guru Rinpoche.

Visualize, see, feel, and believe that the blessings in the form of a blue HŪM letter come from the blue HŪM letter at his heart, the vajra-wisdom center of Guru Rinpoche. It dissolves into your mind, and you feel peace and openness. It purifies all the unvirtuous karma of the consciousness of the universal ground and the intellectual obscurations that discriminatively conceptualize subject, object, and action. You have received the vajra-wisdom power of Guru Rinpoche. You have received the verbal empowerment, the ultimate truth. You have turned into a proper vessel for the practice of Great Perfection. The seed of the attainment of the Knowledge-holder of spontaneous accomplishment is sown in you. The capacity for attaining the natural body of the Buddha is established in you.

Khenpo Ngagchung writes that the goal of the verbal empowerment is to generate the spontaneously arisen innate wisdom, the absolute meaning of the empowerment.[97]

5. The unification: This is the unification of your mind with the vajra mind of Guru Rinpoche, the Buddha mind, and to be one in oneness.

Unification is not an empowerment in the sense of receiving the power or blessing that enables us to practice and realize an accomplishment, such as the realization of the Great Perfection, but it is the actual meditation on Great Perfection as the result of purification, devotion, and realization generated by the four previous empowerments. Great-Perfection meditation must be taught according to the needs and capacities of the individual practitioner. It is not helpful to talk about the meditation of Great Perfection as a lecture to a group of minds of different natures.

For the meditation of unification, you can see the source of the empowerments in either of two ways.[98] First, see that all the Buddhas, Bodhisattvas, deities, Ḍākinīs, and Lamas who are around Guru Rinpoche in front of us are of one mind with Guru Rinpoche in the concentration of bestowing the empowerment of unification. Second, all of them have melted into lights and have merged into Guru Rinpoche.

Then, the energy of strong devotion to Guru Rinpoche

opens up your mind and body as the vessel for receiving the empowerments, and it invokes the compassionate mind of Guru Rinpoche. Guru Rinpoche, smiling joyfully, sees you with his loving wisdom eyes and instantly, from his heart, a red light with heat, bright as the rising sun, comes toward you and touches your heart. Feel that your mind and body are filled with the heat of bliss. You are gradually melted into a red light of bliss, the size of a pea, from the top of your head and the soles of your feet toward your own heart center. This tiny sphere of light is the union of your mind and energy (rLung), and it is the vitality of your devotion. Then, like a spark, it shoots up and dissolves into Guru Rinpoche's heart. See and feel that you are merged into his heart, the vajra-mind center of Guru Rinpoche, with the force and energy of faith and devotion. Believe that your mind and Guru Rinpoche's enlightened and compassionate mind have become one! Then, instantly, let go of all thoughts and relax there, in Guru Rinpoche's mind, until thoughts come up. Do it again and again. If you have any individual instructions from an authentic and uncommercialized Great-Perfection master, then follow that. Otherwise, keep doing this in a relaxed way. Then, see what experiences you feel. Do not create any expectations of achieving good things or any fears of facing bad things. Just relax. Relax in openness and the light of clarity. More instructions are needed, when individuals make more progress.

In the off-meditation periods, like a fish jumping out of water, make yourself arise in the form of Vajrayoginī again, and maintain the view of the three points of taking (all into practice), i.e., seeing all as the pure manifestations of Guru

Rinpoche, hearing all as pure expressions of his speech or mantra, and thinking all as his enlightened visions.

Also, you are not just receiving the empowerments, but, thereafter, you can and should dedicate yourself to the tantric practices to which you have been initiated by the particular empowerments. The training for the Vase Empowerment is the development stage of peaceful and wrathful forms of Guru Rinpoche. The training for the Secret Empowerment is the practice of energy (*rLung*; air, energy, or breathing) and heat (*gTum Mo*). The training for the Wisdom Empowerment is the practice of skillful means (*Thabs Lam*). The training for the verbal empowerment is the meditation on thregchö (*Khreg Ch'od*, cutting through all into original purity) and thögal (*Thod rGal*, the direct approach to spontaneous accomplishment).

∘ I 3 ∘

A BRIEF MEDITATION
ON GURU RINPOCHE,
PADMASAMBHAVA

RELAXATION

EXHALE three deep breaths, thinking and feeling that all the energies of worries, pressure, and pain are being expelled; they are totally expelled from your body and mind with the breath. Feel that your body and mind become free from pressures. Feel peaceful, relaxed, and strong. Relax by bathing in that healing peace for a couple of minutes.

PRELIMINARY

Develop Bodhichitta, the attitude that we will meditate for the sake of all the mother beings, in order to bring peace, happiness, and enlightenment to all of them.

MAIN PRACTICE

Visualize Guru Rinpoche in front of you and above, in the totally clear, empty, pure, vast, open, and unobstructed blue sky. He is sitting on a clear and shining moon disc, above a bright and warm sun disc, in the center of a huge thousand-petaled lotus—fresh with moisture, blossoming with brilliant color, and perfumed with sweet fragrance.

Guru Rinpoche is in a body of luminous wisdom lights, attired in colorful silk and brocade, like robes of lights. The lights are beyond the traces of gross, rigid, restricted, hindering, and changing characteristics.

Guru Rinpoche appears youthful, as if sixteen years old. His face is filled with a smile of joy, and his eyes of compassion and power see, reach, enlighten, and empower every movement and state of our minds and every cell and atom of our bodies, and they bring the feelings of love, peace, bliss, strength, and openness. He is the embodiment of all the Buddhas, saints, and sages, with their love, power, and wisdom. His majestic presence of power, peace, beauty, and warmth brings us comfort, peace, joy, and openness, as if we were sitting by a fire in the cold of winter.

SOME DETAILS OF THE VISUALIZATION AND THEIR MEANING

Guru Rinpoche is visualized in the blue sky, which symbolizes emptiness or openness, the basis of the universe. He sits in the majestic royal-enjoyment posture on sun and moon discs, which are flat as a cushion, in the center of a thousand-petaled lotus. These attributes symbolize that he was born of immaculate birth in the Lotus Buddha family (lotus) out of the union of wisdom (sun) and skill (moon).

Guru Rinpoche is in a body of wisdom lights, since light has no trace of an earthy, gross, or changing character. He is sixteen, as he is beyond the realm of change and aging. His face is filled with a smile of joy, as he is untouched by pain and sorrow. His eyes are unblinking, loving, clear, wide-open, and powerful.

He is attired in robes[99] of light of different designs and colors, which symbolize his perfection of various disciplines. The white inner robe (*gSang Gos*) and the red gown (*'Dung Ma*) symbolize the perfection of the disciplines of the Bodhisattva. The blue outer gown (*Phod Ch'en*) symbolizes the perfection of the disciplines of tantra. The monastic shawl (*Ch'os Gos*) symbolizes the perfection of the disciplines of the prātimokṣha. The brocade cloak (*Ber Ch'en*) stands for the disciplines of all the yānas as one. His hat, brocade cloak, and shoes also symbolize his power of attainments, as they were offered to him by the King of Zahor, along with his daughter and the kingdom, when Guru Rinpoche transformed the fire that was to burn him into water.

Guru Rinpoche holds implements to symbolize his attainments and power. The golden vajra in his right hand symbolizes his indestructible skill or power, the male principle. The skull filled with nectar in his left hand symbolizes the union of appearances/bliss and emptiness. In this skull, the long-life vase ornamented with a wish-fulfilling tree symbolizes his attainment of immortality.

The trident staff in the crook of his left arm represents his consort or wisdom, the feminine principle, with the following symbols. Its three sharp points symbolize the three true natures of the mind—emptiness, clarity, and compassion (power). The three heads in skeletal, old, and fresh forms symbolize the three Buddha bodies—the Dharmakāya, Sambhogakāya, and Nirmāṇakāya. The nine iron rings symbolize the nine yānas of training. The five-colored silken hangings symbolize the five Buddha wisdoms. The locks of hair symbolize the power attained as the result of esoteric trainings in charnel grounds.

Thus, Guru Rinpoche's majestic presence, endowed with teachings, power, peace, beauty, and warmth, overwhelms the whole universe, as it is the vajra manifestation of absolute Buddhahood, the vajra nature of the universe.

His boundless love and compassion are totally open to the whole universe and reach every being, just as the love of a mother for her only child. His limitless wisdom knows every happening in the universe, simultaneously, without distracting from the absolute nature as it is—unrestricted, undiscriminating, all-reaching, and total openness. His limitless power provides all the benefits and pacifies all the turmoil of the universe and of every being, if they are open to that opportunity, as he is the perpetual source of fruition and healing.

Guru Rinpoche is not just a great eighth-century sage with amazing powers, but he is the embodiment of all the Buddhas, saints, and sages, since in whatever form and way we see, take, and use him, he becomes such. It is the power of the mind that is creating all the circumstances. The Buddha and Buddha fields are the nature of the realized mind and its power, and the impure mundane world is mere designations and experiences of the dualistic mind.

He is the reflection or manifestation of the Buddha mind, the true, pure nature of our own minds, since in true nature all appearances are absolutely pure-appearing lights of the true nature, the sole openness of peace.

Relying on Guru Rinpoche is nothing but a skillful means for realizing and empowering ourselves with the phenomena of our own pure, joyful, and powerful perceptions and experiences, which arise from our own peaceful and open Buddha nature that we all have inherited.

There are many benefits of visualization. It inspires you toward spiritual goals, it generates a habit of thinking in a disciplined and positive way, it cultivates a contemplative and stable character in the mind, and it channels the blessings and attainments of spiritual energies and realizations.

See that the whole earth is filled with all kinds of beings, with devotional hearts, cheerful faces, and joyful eyes, and that all are looking at the loving, beautiful, and powerful face of Guru Rinpoche. All are saying the mantra in one voice, with the loudest and sweetest melody, as a prayer to or invocation of Guru Rinpoche, as a means of healing our problems, as an exercise of our mental and physical energies, as a celebration of the presence of Guru Rinpoche with us, and as a meditation on the pure sound—the sound of mantra in the nature of oneness, oneness of the whole universe in the sound of prayer.

See, feel, and believe that the visualization and prayers have opened or warmed our body and mind in devotion, warmth, peace, joy, and openness, and now they have become the proper vessels for receiving Guru Rinpoche's blessings.

As a result of the prayers that invoked the enlightened mind of Guru Rinpoche, beams of powerful blessing lights of various colors come from Guru Rinpoche and touch different parts of your body. By their mere touch, feel the sensation of warmth, heat, bliss, and openness in our body and mind.

Experience that feeling and relax. Then, through every pore and door, the beams of blessing light enter into our body, dispelling all our worries, stress, and pain, like darkness dispelled by sunlight. See that our whole body is transformed into a blessing-light body, and all our feelings become blissful, open, and strong.

Believe that we have received Guru Rinpoche's body, speech, and mind blessing power and that all our mental and physical problems have been totally pacified. Relax there in the oneness of the feeling of warmth, bliss, and openness—the universal nature, absolute Guru Rinpoche.

If we believe, then Guru Rinpoche will always be with us. He is not an individual person of a particular time or place. He is (or represents) the Buddha, the Buddha nature and its expression. In other words, he is the true nature of the universe and the pure character or expression of that universe. Whenever we allow our mind to connect with our inner truth, that truth will always be there to be reached, and then the manifestations or expressions arisen from that truth will always arise as pure and divine manifestations or appearances. If we let ourselves be inspired and see that very ultimate peace and truth, which we all have, through the support of and/or as Guru Rinpoche, we will realize and become Guru Rinpoche and his qualities and expressions.

Finally, see and feel that Guru Rinpoche comes closer to you and merges into you, physically and mentally, as water into water and light into light. You become one with him. With the energy of that feeling and belief, without any more concepts, just relax there, relax there, and relax there.

CONCLUSION

With compassion, from the depth of the heart, dedicate all the merit, the powerful blessing energies that we have received, to all the mother beings for the sake of their happiness and enlightenment. See and feel that they have received the merit of blessing lights.

Dedication of merit is a great practice. No merit is too small to dedicate. Even if it is a small merit, if you dedicate it, that merit will become a great merit, for the dedication itself is a powerful way of increasing merit, as it opens our minds in the openness of generosity toward all without discriminations or attachments. Dedication loosens the tightness, discriminations, or closed character of the mind and strengthens the energy of openness.

Here are a few more pointers: Try to visualize, but do not struggle too much for details or the perfection of this. Sometimes, if it is difficult to visualize at all, just feel the presence of Guru Rinpoche and feel the blessing lights; be one with it and relax in the feeling of peace, warmth, and openness.

When you are meditating, do what you are doing—stay in the present, without worrying about the results in the future. Otherwise, the distance you need to go can only cause discouragement and a mental block.

If you have done practice in the early morning and have felt peace and warmth, then during the day, as many times as you can, bring back the feelings of that energy, again and again, for a second or two. Also, try to keep that feeling alive, as the foundation or basis "underneath" your daily activities.

Then you will not only be maintaining your practice but making it progress, turning your daily life into spiritual experiences, even while you are working.

Do not expect a flow of energy or inspiration. Do not be afraid of a lack of inspiration and drive. Just do it as a part of your daily chores or as an elephant walks. If you do it with fewer expectations and concepts, slowly things will improve naturally, as part of getting used to, training in, and being strengthened by the practice.

THE PRAYER MANTRA OF GURU RINPOCHE

In Sanskrit:

OM ĀḤ HŪṂ VAJRA-GURU-PADMA-SIDDHI HŪṂ

In Tibetanized Sanskrit:

OM AH HUNG BADZAR GURU PADMA SIDDHI HUNG

or

OM AH HUNG BEDZAR GURU PEMA SIDDHI HUNG

THE MEANING

TRANSLATION

(The Embodiment of) the body, speech, and mind (of the Buddhas), O Vajra Master Padma(sambhava), please grant attainments
[or: please bestow your blessings (upon us), may there be the attainments, or may the attainments be accomplished].

| OM | seed syllable of Buddha body |
| ĀḤ | seed syllable of Buddha speech |

HŪM	seed syllable of Buddha mind
VAJRA	diamond (adamantine), Dharmakāya (absolute body)
GURU	master (prosperity), Sambhogakāya (enjoyment body)
PADMA	lotus (pureness), Nirmāṇakāya (manifestation body)
SIDDHI	attainments, common and uncommon results, accomplishments
HŪM	Please grant. May it be. Supplication.

RECOLLECTION OF THE QUALITIES OF GURU RINPOCHE
THE GREATNESS OF THE QUALITIES

General Qualities

OM ĀH HŪM are the seed syllables of the three vajras (vajra body, speech, and mind) of all of the enlightened ones.

OM: For the general meaning, it is the heart syllable of the vajra body of all the enlightened ones. Its special meaning is the heart of the great blissful, spontaneously accomplished primordial wisdom, arisen in the character of the illusory net, which is the united body of appearances and emptiness.

ĀH: For the general meaning, it is the heart syllable of the vajra speech of all the enlightened ones. Its special meaning is the essence of the indescribable union of awareness and emptiness, and it is its appearance in the form of sound. As such it becomes the foundation of all speech.

HŪM: For the general meaning, it is the heart syllable of the vajra mind of all the enlightened ones. Its special meaning is the essence of the vajra Rainbow Body, the self-arisen primordial wisdom, and the union of awareness and emptiness, the original purity.

Guru Rinpoche is the embodiment of the qualities of all these three vajras of the enlightened ones.

Particular Qualities

VAJRA-GURU: Prosperous with qualities of the vajra (indestructible, adamantine, and essence). VAJRA: The very adamantine primordial wisdom of the basis through the skillful means of the vajra path, perfected into the nature of the spontaneously accomplished three vajras. GURU: Prosperous with qualities, "master."

The Name, the One Who Possesses These Qualities

PADMA: His name denotes that he is born in a lotus; he belongs to the Buddha family of Padma. He attained the Vajradhara state by the support of the padmas of the vajra Ḍākinīs. He is like a lotus in the mind in that he appeared in saṃsāra but was not stained by saṃsāric defilements.

PRAYING TO BESTOW THE WISHES AND ATTAINMENTS

The Wishes

SIDDHI: For the general meaning, it is the attainment of happiness and success, both worldly and spiritual. Its special meaning is to perfect the paths and stages of the vajra path without any hindrance, and to attain the state of Vajradhara by the stairs of the four Vidyāhara practices.

The Attainments

HŪṂ: It has three letters—H, Ū, and Ṃ. This is for the invocation of the three vajras. Also, HŪṂ is the vajra mind, and it is the means of invoking the mind of Guru Rinpoche to bestow the attainments.

IN BRIEF

The body, speech, and mind (of the Buddhas): O Vajra Master Padma, please grant attainments.

or

O Padma (Padmasambhava, Lotus-Born)—prosperous with vajra virtues, (the embodiment of the) body, speech, and mind (of the Buddhas)—please bestow (upon us the common and uncommon) attainments.

A Short Meditation

When you do not have much time or energy, you could practice for just ten or fifteen minutes, or even less. Take one or two deep breaths, thinking and feeling that you are expelling all the dead energies. Feel relaxed. Then see Guru Rinpoche above in the beautiful, clear sky, as the embodiment of all the Buddhas and the virtues of the universe. Feel the heat of the presence. Chant (vocally or in your mind's voice) the mantra with the energy of inspiration and the devotion of your body and mind. Receive and be one with blessing lights, and feel the heat, warmth, bliss, and openness. Finally, just relax; relax again and again in the feeling of warmth, bliss, and openness. Dedicate the merit to all the mother beings.

You could practice when you have just woken up in the early morning, before falling asleep, while resting, between work, or any time. And enjoy it.

° 14 °

EVALUATING THE
PROGRESS OF DHARMA
PRACTICE

IN ORDER TO EVALUATE our spiritual progress, it is essential to recognize our goal, the path leading to that goal, and the ground where we are presently standing on the path of our spiritual journey.

In Buddhism there are numerous paths of spiritual training. Each has its unique goal, purpose, and benefits for oneself and others. But in order to be able to benefit truly, it is very important to understand the principal purpose underlying these practices. If we take the wrong turn at a crossroads, every step we make will take us farther away from our destination. In the same way, if we fail to realize the nature of our spiritual goal and what our aim should be, our practice will not be beneficial, or at least not nearly as helpful as it could otherwise be.

The main focus of all of our training in Dharma is to

_____

A talk given at Maha Siddha Nyingmapa Temple, Hawley, Mass., on July 27, 1985.

benefit our minds. This may sound selfish, but it is not. Unless we improve ourselves we cannot really help others or do any Dharma activities. Without being equipped, the mere desire to help others could be like practicing archery without knowing how to shoot or without having a bow and arrow. Even if we put up a hundred targets, we will not turn into skilled archers.

Thus, I am not saying that we should be self-centered in focusing on ourselves. Rather, I am saying that we should aim our efforts in practice toward benefiting our minds, with a view to becoming open to others. The more we tame our wild thoughts and tumultuous emotions, the more peaceful, compassionate, and enlightened we become, and the freer we become from selfishness. So, our intention in disciplining our minds should be to transform them into the enlightened mind for the benefit of living beings.

The benefits of meditation practice are not limited to conceptual or intellectual understanding. They should include our feelings as well. The most important point of Dharma practice is to discipline or perfect the mind by bringing it to a state of utmost peace, relaxation, and clarity, protecting it from emotional affliction. To attain this state, we should cultivate peaceful feelings and experiences in our minds.

However, the problem we have with Dharma practice is that we do not integrate our understandings into our lives and do not apply what we have learned. Unfortunately, our understandings frequently remain in the realm of imagination, somewhere over there. Understanding becomes another object of the mind, not applied to the subject, oneself. That is why we often want to know many things, to study many things. But even if we spend ten or twenty years in study or practice, we may gain no more than a superficial understanding, a vague familiarity with the object of our study.

While our goal is enlightenment, that is something we cannot understand at this time, and it is not easy to explain. But, in a simple way, the goal of practice is to attain the mind of ultimate peace, the state that is most relaxed, strongly stable, and perfect. If we do not improve our minds, then regardless of how many understandings we have about the ten stages, the five paths, ceremonies, philosophies, and so forth, they will all become objects that we never apply to ourselves. It can be very simple, like when we are facing the right direction—every step will bring us closer to our destination. In the same way, when we start practicing—whatever practice we select—if we use it to benefit and train our minds, then even if it is a small and simple practice, even if it lasts no more than an hour or a single day, it will help us. But if we turn our practice into an object, a nice goody over there, it will not really benefit us. We may become a writer or scholar, able to parrot many different things; but this will not truly help us.

In the Buddha's lifetime, one of the sixteen Arhats or sages, named Chullapanthaka,[100] was extremely dull and could not memorize even four lines of teaching. So the Buddha instructed him to dust the assembly hall and the sandals of the bhikṣhus while repeating, "Dust is cleaned. Defilements are cleaned."

Chullapanthaka spent years just concentrating on cleaning and repeating these same verses. One day, he thought to himself: "What did the Buddha mean by the 'cleaning of the dust' and 'cleaning of the emotions'? Is the dust the defilement of the mind or of the hall and sandals?" At that very moment the following verses came into his mind:

> This is not the dust of earth, but the dust of desire, hatred, and ignorance.
> Dust is the name of desire, hatred, and ignorance and not of the earth.
> Learned ones who have cleansed the dust
> Attain confidence in the teachings of the Buddha.

Instantly he became an Arhat, an enlightened one. Why? Not because he had hundreds of different techniques. Not because he was a great scholar and found the esoteric path to reach the goal. Rather, keeping his mind in an utmost simple, peaceful, and joyful state, and doing meritorious work, he concentrated one-pointedly with awareness on what he was doing. He applied his whole mind to whatever he did physically and mentally, so he eventually become enlightened.

To become enlightened it is not necessary to know many things, nor is it necessary to do many kinds of practices. It does not matter if it is simple. Maybe it is better to keep it simple—the more we do, the more we are confused. So keep it simple and, most importantly, apply it to your mind.

If we know how to apply our practice properly and if we have an experience of meditation, strength, or some sort of realization, the next important step is to develop pure perception. The purpose of most Buddhist practices, whether exoteric or esoteric (sūtric or tantric) is to purify our perception. Usually we see and think in dualistic terms, with a subject and object. We usually think, "This is good," "This is bad," "She or he is my friend," "She or he is my enemy."

Because of this constant discrimination, we experience sadness and happiness, and create good and bad karma.

All of this is set in motion because of our wrong perceptions, because we discriminate in the wrong way. Sometimes, of course, there is validity to our discriminative labels, as when there is sickness or hunger. But most of the time our labels are the creation of our minds. For example, if Mr. C sees Mr. A, he may think, "He is my friend," and feel happy to see him. But when Mr. B sees Mr. A, he may think, "There is my enemy," and be unhappy, although in each case the person is the same. Our judgmental labels, "friend" or "enemy," can change from day to day, and our feelings will change accordingly, even though the person really remains the same. The cause is our own perception.

We are constantly filtering the world through the lenses of our own perception. When we wear dark shades, everything looks dark. But with clear glasses, that same world appears clear. This is why it is important to change the way we perceive things. Pure perception is the Buddhist method of seeing things positively and as they are.

As we know, pure perception can be interpreted at many levels. In tantric practice, everything is seen as a Buddha pure land. The trainee transforms phenomena into the support of practice and spiritual life through pure perception. But that is another topic.

For fully enlightened Buddhas, regardless of what form or body appears before them, they will have no dualistic concepts or emotional afflictions. They will not feel pain or excitement.

For highly realized adepts, too, physical circumstances

have no emotional or conceptual negative impact on them. Adepts may look like they are in great pain, but their minds will remain serene and joyful. In fact, sickness can be a source of happiness and peace for them.

An example of this is provided by the story of Zhang Rinpoche,[101] a great Kagyupa Lama and yogī, who practiced great bliss all his life. One day he hit his head really hard on the wall of his cave. Even though he was seriously injured and his head was bleeding terribly, he felt bliss, not pain. Why? After all, he was made of the same flesh and blood as all of us. The history of Tibetan Buddhism is replete with great Lamas who displayed miracles to prevent and transform calamities coming to them. But Zhang Rinpoche did not need to display physical miracles to prevent injuries. Because of his inner mental state and perception, he experienced bliss instead of pain. This was due to the power of his pure perception and his realization of the wisdom of great bliss. That kind of result might be beyond us, but we can at least try to train ourselves in seeing people as friends, not enemies—not just one or two people, but everybody, by meditating on compassion and other meditations.

A story about the first Dodrupchen according to the autobiography of Jigme Gyalwe Nyuku (1765–1843) provides another powerful example of how highly accomplished adepts who have realized perceptions transform their experiences. Jigme Gyalwe Nyuku once journeyed from Eastern Tibet to Central Tibet, where he met the first Dodrupchen at Samye. The first Dodrupchen sent him with a letter to Jigme Lingpa in Tsering Jong. He saw and received teachings from Jigme Lingpa and then returned to Dodrupchen at Samye. At that time, Dodrupchen was quite well-known but not yet famous, and Jigme Gyalwe Nyuku was around twenty and not yet well-known. Together they began a pilgrimage to Western Tibet to meet several great Lamas.

One day, Dodrupchen said he was going back to Lhasa and then to Kham. Jigme Gyalwe Nyuku said, "No, you cannot go alone. I will help you go up to Lhasa." They argued and at last agreed to go together. Dodrupchen got sick on the way, and Jigme Gyalwe Nyuku carried both of their backpacks. As they were trying to cross a high mountain, Dodrupchen could not walk up the steep slope. They had only one little piece of animal fat, a little oil, and no tsampa (roasted barley flour, a dietary staple in Tibet). They would rest after walking very short distances and could barely make any progress.

After a while Dodrupchen could not even get up, so Jigme Gyalwe Nyuku had to pull him up after every rest. Yet, although Dodrupchen was so sick physically, no sadness or feeling of pain entered his mind. Dodrupchen said, "Today I am having a little opportunity to experience austerity in the practice of Dharma by burdening our bodies and experiencing mental hardships—little sacrifices in the practice of the holy Dharma." He celebrated his suffering, saying, "Through such offering, I am achieving the fruits of the precious human life with the eighteen qualities and the glory of four great wheels (living in a harmonious place, having a holy person as a teacher, making good aspirations, and accumulating merit). So this kind of experience is, without any doubt, the result of my accumulation of merit and the purification of defilements in my past lives." Jigme Gyalwe Nyuku then continues, "And so Dodrupchen had great joy in his mind, and it was so wonderful to see it. This Lama really is following the Buddha's words, 'By crossing flames and razor fields, you should seek Dharma for the ultimate goal.'"

So there are two points here. First, if you have joy, regardless of how serious your situations is, you can easily transform it into practice. Second, even if you cannot transform it into practice, this will make it easier to tolerate even the most horrible experiences. So, although Dodrupchen Rinpoche was physically in critical condition, he was so happy because he could celebrate the opportunity to experience his suffering for a meaningful purpose and for a wonderful future.

For us ordinary people it is important to have a simple but positive and realistic view, thinking that every single living being has been our parent and friend. If we can see things this way, we will have love and compassion for everyone. We will have a peaceful and relaxed mind. If our mind is peaceful and cheerful, we can apply it to transform any situation into something positive, a source of more peace and joy.

How do we evaluate our practice and determine whether we are improving or not improving, going backward or forward? The first problem is that many of us do not really want to see our own shortcomings. Or, even if we see them, we cannot bear to acknowledge them because of weakness of mind, lack of self-confidence, and a sensitive ego. We take refuge in blaming somebody else or something else and get a false sense of comfort by hiding behind a security blanket. In Tibetan literature it is always said that it is important to have a mirror to see our own face, not just the eyes to see the faults on others' faces. So, instead of looking for a scapegoat, we should learn to look at our own mental behavior and then at our physical acts. We are here today as living proof of whether we have progressed.

Even if we find only shortcomings in ourselves, we should be happy, thinking, "Now that I can see my problems, I can turn onto the right track." If we have made any spiritual progress, no matter how modest, we should acknowledge it, feel it, and celebrate. Then, the energy of our rejoicing will strengthen and multiply the power of our spiritual progress. Being happy about our improvements helps us maintain the progress we have made and energizes our future efforts.

When I lived in India, I met an important Indian scholar and leader who was born in a lower-caste family. He received a good education and become a doctor and, later, the governor of a state in northern India. During his whole life, he fought against the caste-discrimination system. But once he told me, "Although I say I am against the caste system and have spent my whole life fighting against it, I am not honest. If someone from a caste even lower than mine were to ask for my daughter's hand, I would feel hesitant. That means that I actually hate and am jealous of the higher-caste people, and am not for overall justice as far as the entire caste system goes."

Whenever I remember these words, I experience a feeling of celebration for his wisdom, openness, and honesty. Of course, I am not saying that political discrimination is okay; but this Indian scholar's ability to face his faults honestly is remarkable. If we can see and accept our own failings, changing them will be easy. I think we are all guilty of the same kinds of things. The difference is that many simply do not want to think about them and cannot bear to accept them.

Many of us are against rich people, thinking, "I hate the rich because they do not help the poor." However, when we have something, we rarely share it with those who are less fortunate. We hardly ever volunteer social services even when we have free time. So why do we find fault with the rich? In reality, we are jealous of them and hate them. Many of us have trouble being generous to our own parents, children, relatives, or Dharma siblings, whose care is our prime responsibility. Only if, like Mother Teresa, we devote our lives to sharing whatever we have, can we criticize those who are not so giving. We all have our own views—"This system is bad. That system is worse"—but our feelings are usually based on our own emotional reactions. Rarely are they based on true ethical or spiritual understanding. It is important to understand this.

To evaluate our spiritual progress we need to check whether our meditation is grounded properly in our lives. We need to make sure that we used the practice to discipline our own minds, and that we did not just lean on it as a tradition. We need to ask ourselves whether we have been using the practice as an intellectual goody and as an excuse to hide some of our failings. If so, we will not have applied the practice to our own minds. This is the time to wake up and set out on the right path.

If we are meditating on compassion, for instance, we might find it easy to generate compassion for someone who is distant and not connected to us. If we do not know Mr. Smith in London, who is perhaps sick or something, it is relatively easy to develop compassion for him. But the important question is whether we can practice compassion and pure perception for the people we do know—family members, father, mother, children, husband, wife, coworkers, fellow Sangha members, and our enemies—all those with whom we are connected. If we cannot have compassion toward those who are close to us, then talking about compassion for living beings is the biggest joke and shame.

If we are meditating on impermanence and have really carried the practice far, one of the eventual results will be that we will not have anger toward others. No one is our enemy—it is just transitory. Whoever is an enemy today will be a friend tomorrow and something else the next day. If we really know impermanence, we know there is no reason to feel attachment or hatred, since there is no such thing as a lasting enemy or friend. We should cultivate equanimity to all living beings and have compassion for all those who are fighting with each other because of their ignorance. So, even practice on impermanence, if done properly, will totally change us. Of course, if we have done higher stages of practice properly there is no question about the power of their effects. However, even if we have practiced even the simplest or most ordinary aspect of our teachings from the heart, it will benefit us enormously.

It is not necessary for us to be told whether we are doing well. We are our own best indicators. We must always check ourselves to see if we have made any improvement in our minds. It does not matter if we have memorized and learned many things. If our minds have not become disciplined and peaceful, we have to look at ourselves seriously for our own benefit and growth.

The big problem for us is the emotions. Intellectually we can go into philosophy, higher meditations, and intellectual observations. But practically, we are frequently overwhelmed by negative emotions. What can we do with these emotions? As discussed above, the first step is to recognize them.

Next, we should use our meditation experiences to pacify them. For example, sometimes we get angry. But anger is just a fabrication of our minds. Anger and hatred are the product of dislike, which is simply the creation of our imagination. Attachment is also our mental fabrication. We think, "That's beautiful. That's wonderful. I would like to have it," or "That is delicious." We become attached in this way and start grasping and clinging. Then all the other emotional afflictions follow. Anger and hatred are a leading problem for a large number of Orientals and Tibetans, as jealousy is for Americans. Jealousy is something we develop from childhood, conditioned by school, games, parents, and competition. It has even become a compliment: "Oh, your dress is gorgeous; I feel so jealous."

We must not approve of or justify our emotions by thinking, "I am angry, but that's my right. I should be angry; that's good." No, that's wrong. The flames of emotions will burn us to ashes. Some of us excuse our anger, saying, "Everybody is angry, so why not me?" However, just because other people are in a pit of fire does not mean we have to jump in too. If we want to improve, we should try not to have these emotions. That is why we choose Dharma practice.

We have to see negative emotions as bad and ugly. For

example, if we hate or are attached to someone, we can think, "I have all these emotions in me. I am like a filthy bag of garbage." Do not think, "I am angry; but since I am educated or rich, it is my right." This will only make our emotions grow further.

Seeing our emotions as negative and ugly is very important. When we are mean, say bad things about someone, or speak harshly, we should imagine that we are vomiting, or that we are a poisonous snake hissing and flicking our tongues. If we are doing something hurtful to someone, we should think of ourselves as a frightful monster, burning with flames, trying to eat everybody. Even though we may be good-looking physically, when we become possessed by emotional afflictions, we turn into monsters. If we see ourselves as monsters, what will happen? We will not want to live in that kind of situation any longer.

After becoming aware of our emotional afflictions and seeing them as negative, we should use our Dharma training to cleanse and transform them into practice. The antidote for anger is to generate compassion for beings by thinking that they are our mothers. The antidote for jealousy is to rejoice over the well-being of all mother beings. The antidote for attachment is to understand impermanence and the suffering nature of saṃsāra. The antidote for ignorance is to realize the true nature and interdependent causation of phenomenal existents.

In one way, it is difficult to discipline our minds because they change easily and are constantly flickering. But this is also what makes them so easy to train. To change the shape of a solid table, we need to work very hard. But changing our way of thinking is much easier—it can be done almost instantly. If we take care not to let our minds fall under the control of anger, attachment, jealousy, etc., then they will naturally be in an open, relaxed, and peaceful state.

Once, on television, I saw a piece on someone who developed the technique of juggling to treat mental patients. While we are not in the category of the mentally disturbed, many of us have excessively sophisticated, complex minds, to say the least. It is essential to release all of these negative views and emotions, to get our minds back to a relaxed natural state (I'm not referring to high natural states, just an ordinary natural state), like going back to a child's state of mind.

You might think that because a child's mind is not educated it is undesirable. Intellectually yes, but everything has two sides. The mind of a child is much less emotional. Maybe children will cry when hungry or cold, but they do not analyze: "This is my enemy because of this and that" or "This is my friend because of this and that." They fabricate less. Even if we are old, playing children's games, like juggling, can bring us back to the innocent, open state of mind of childhood.

So, if we could have open, relaxed, and simple minds, like those of children, and if we could apply the knowledge and experiences of a skillful meditator, we are on the right path to both peace and awareness. Also, if our minds are relaxed in openness, our conceptual and emotional bonds will spontaneously be loosened, and the experience of peace and realization wisdom will arise naturally through little meditation. So the first crucial point is to open the window of the mind widely, in order to welcome the light of spiritual dawn in our hearts. If we have taken any step in this direction, then we are making progress. Rejoice over it.

A PRAYER SONG TO THE ABSOLUTE LAMA

I N THE CENTER of the palace, the primordially pure absolute sphere,
Dwells the spontaneously present Lama, embodiment of all
the Buddhas.
We pray to you with changeless faith.
We shall achieve the attainment, the blessing of his inexhaustible kindness.

In the absolute nature of uncontrived mind, in which every-
thing appears naturally,
Dwells the self-arisen absolute Lama, free from elaborations.
We pray to you through the power of nondual awareness.
We shall get the fortunate opportunity to realize the intrinsic
awareness Dharmakāya (the ultimate body).

A translation of a prayer written in Tibetan. *Lama* means excellent, supreme, and spiritual teacher. The absolute Lama refers to the true nature
of the mind or the absolute reality of the universe. Absolute Lama in the
sense of spiritual teacher refers to the person who guides one to the
realization of Buddha nature.

In the absolute nature of the variously appearing, manifesting
power of intrinsic awareness
Dwells from the beginning the unmodified intrinsic-aware-
ness Lama.
We pray to you by taking the six consciousnesses as the path.
We shall set out on the path that liberates all existents as
Dharmakāya.

In the absolute nature of the illusory play of various plays
and players
Dwells the Lama of dharmatā (the absolute state), unmoving
from the beginning.
We pray to you by understanding the nature of whatever
arises.
We shall achieve the result of liberation in the natural state
of whatever arises.

In the absolute nature of countless illusory manifestations of
peaceful and wrathful divinities
Dwells the absolute wisdom divinity, the omnipresent Lama.
We pray to you by condensing hundreds of deities into one.
We shall achieve the various attainments simultaneously,
without effort.

In the absolute nature of the hosts of thoughts, experiencing
varieties of happiness and suffering,
Dwells the stainless and blissful vajra Lama.
We pray to you through the (union of) bliss and emptiness,
free from association and separation.
We shall liberate the cause and effect of emotions and suffering into the natural expanse of great bliss.

In the sphere of the way of existing of the true mode, the
  ultimate nature,
Dwells the Dharmakāya Lama, free from elaborations and
  originally pure.
We pray to you by realizing the absolute nature.
We shall dissolve all the phenomenal appearances of relative
  truth into the ultimate nature.

In the absolute nature of the recollecting song of the absolute
  Lama
Dwells the blessing of the Lama, the power of our faith.
With these virtues we make aspiration for the eternal happi-
  ness of all living beings.
We shall unite inseparably in the nature of Universal Good-
  ness (Samantabhadra).

NOTES

1. EL 124.
2. BP 33a/5.
3. On the Ngöndro of Longchen Nyingthig, there are other publications in English: *The Wish-Fulfilling Jewel* by Dilgo Khyentse (Boston & London: Shambhala Publications, 1988); *Kün-zang La-may Zhal-lung*, 2 vols., translated by Sonam T. Kazi (Upper Montclair, N.J.: Diamond-Lotus Publishing, 1989 & 1992); *The Dzogchen Innermost Essence Preliminary Practice* by Jigme Lingpa, translated with commentary by Tulku Thondup (Dharamsala: Library of Tibetan Works and Archives, 1989); *The Short Preliminary Practice of Longchen Nyingthig* by Kunkhyen Jigme Lingpa, compiled by the Fourth Dodrupchen Rinpoche (Hawley, Mass.: Mahasiddha Nyingmapa Center, 1992); *The Words of My Perfect Teacher* by Paltul Rinpoche, translated by the Padmakara Translation Group (New York: Harper Collins, 1994); *Tantric Practice in Nyingma* by Khetsun Sangpo Rinbochay, translated and edited by Jeffrey Hopkins and Anne Klein (Ithaca, N.Y.: Snow Lion).
4. Dharma—the eternal truth of the universe, which is expressed in the teachings of the Buddha.
5. Saṃsāra—the continuous cycle of earthly existences.
6. KD 22a/2.
7. Karma: the law that states that every action one performs has a commensurate effect in this and future lives.
8. Bodhisattva: a Buddha-to-be, who defers final liberation for himself or herself in the interest of helping others to attain enlightenment.

9. BP 47a/5.

10. YD 4b/2.

11. BP 3b/2.

12. KZ 273/15.

13. DC 5a/2.

14. BP 97b/2.

15. GN 32/4.

16. BP 96a/4.

17. BP 52a/5.

18. The dates for King Srongtsen are based on DPM 18b/5 and DPM 69a/3.

19. The dates for Thrisong Detsen are based on DPM 79b/4 and DPM 155a/3.

20. Bardos of life (birth), dream, absorption, dying, ultimate nature, and becoming.

21. Please look for these most detailed and powerful teachings in the original esoteric scriptures of Tibetan Buddhism.

22. GG 1a/6.

23. Life-accompanying, upward-moving, pervasive, fire-accompanying, and downward-clearing energy (air/wind).

24. This is the common interpretation, but according to TRD 224b/1 and GG 1b/5, the dissolution is explained on many levels of the five elements (such as outer, inner, secret, and perfect qualities of each of the five elements), and also each dissolves into its own element, e.g., the energy (*Nus-Pa*) of outer earth dissolves into inner earth and so on.

25. According to NS 389b/4 (based on *Thal 'Gyur tantra*), consciousness dissolves into space, and space dissolves into luminosity.

26. In DM 10b/6 and KZM 2a/4, in the first and second experiences the order of the whiteness and redness visions is reversed. In some texts, the cessation of emotions are interchanged.

27. See NS 192b/2.

28. Dissolution of attainment into luminosity is based on KZM 2b/1 and GG 2b/1.

29. BN 2/9.

30. PM 1b/1.

31. See SGG: 403a/2.

32. GG 2b/1 and NS 192b/2.

33. An Oriental ritual hand-held mirror.

34. BN 3/4.

35. GG 4a/2.

36. SR 10a/6 (translation: BM 333/23).

37. This is the reason that sur (*gSur*, food burning) offerings are usually dedicated to a deceased person for many weeks after his or her death.

38. According to accounts by Tibetan Delogs (*'Das Log*, "Returners from Death").

39. *Thos Grol* ("Liberation by Hearing") is a series of texts (*Bar Do Thos Grol, The Tibetan Book of the Dead,* being one of them) discovered as Ter by Karma Lingpa. *See* DM 32b/6.

40. According to Buddhism, every being goes through the transmigration of an infinite number of successive lives. So, in the process of our numerous past lives, each of the infinite number of beings has been our own parents and spouses as well as enemies numerous times. So, as mother is the symbol of love and care, Buddhist teachings see and illustrate every being as a "mother being" in order to bring the spiritual openness of gratitude and love in us toward all beings without any discrimination.

41. See chapter 8 and HTT for details.

42. DC 7b/5.

43. CD 84b.

44. KD 22a/2.

45. NG and HTT.

46. NG 4b/2.

47. NG 30b/4.

48. *gSol 'Debs Le'u bDun Ma* discovered by Rigdin Gödem.

49. NS 80b/4.

50. Based on NS and others, which are based on Ashvaghoṣha's text on root infractions.

51. Based on NS and others, which are based on Nāgārjuna's text on gross infractions.

52. Based mainly on DN, NS, and others.

53. NCC 11B-12B.

54. DN 13a/6.

55. See chapter 7 of this book.

56. See chapter 11 of this book.

57. See chapter 9 of this book.

58. BP 2b/3.

59. GR 88a/2.

60. See chapter 6 of this book.

61. GR 88a/2.

62. See chapters 4 and 5 for the significances of spiritual objects.

63. According to the Dodrupchen lineage, KZ 283/11, and TS 85a/1, Guru Rinpoche or Ogyen Dorje Chang (Guru Vajradhara) is in the usual form of Guru Rinpoche (see chapter 13 in this book for details), except that he is in union with Yeshe Tsogyal, who is white in color, holding a curved blade and skull. According to NLS 8a/6 and KT 87/1, Guru Rinpoche is blue in color, in union with Yeshe Tsogyal, white in color, and both are in Sambhogakāya costumes.

64. According to KDN 4a/2.

65. See chapter 2 of this book.

66. KZ 409/15.

67. According to KDN 7a/4.

68. See chapter 9 of this book.

69. In this training, Vajrasattva means both male and female Vajrasattvas, but as they are indivisible, at most places they are referred to in the singular.

70. According to KT 102/14, Khyentse Wangpo instructed

Nyagla Sögyal that one could visualize the letters and their lights in white color also.

71. According to the Dodrupchen lineage, KZ 507/13, and TS 141b/1: she is red, naked, with a curved blade in the left hand. According to NLS 15a/5 and KT 122/4: like Vajrayoginī, she is naked in red color, stands on a lotus, sun, and corpse seat, with bone ornaments, holding a curved blade in the right hand, blood-filled skull in the left hand, and a trident in the crook of the left arm.

72. For details, read chapter 13 of this book.

73. See chapter 11 of this book for the meaning of this prayer.

74. See chapter 13 of this book for the meaning of this mantra.

75. See chapter 12 of this book for the explanation of receiving the four empowerments.

76. See KZZ 189a/5 and chapter 12 of this book.

77. The assembly (*Tshog 'Khor*) comprises Rigdzins (Skt. Vidyādharas), Siddhas, Pawos (Skt. Ḍākas, Heroes), and Khadromas (Skt. Ḍākinīs).

78. AH KA SA MA RA TSA SHA TA RA SA MA RA YA PHAṬ.

79. See chapter 8 of this book or HHT for details.

80. Tib. *dPa' Bo*, Skt. *Ḍāka* (male) and Tib. *mKha' 'Gro*, Skt. *Ḍākinī* (female) sages and deities.

81. The absolute certainties of place, teacher, disciple, teaching, and time.

82. *Dang Ba'i Dad Pa:* faith that cleanses the mind. *'Dod Pa'i Dad Pa:* faith that inspires the devotee to accomplish the same attainment as the object of his or her faith. *Yid Ch'es Kyi Dad Pa:* faith that produces full confidence in the object of faith.

83. *Sems Nyid:* the ultimate nature and the essential nature of mind, of which *Sems* (mind) is the deluded mode. In this text, Mind with a capital *M* denotes the *Sems Nyid*.

84. Primordial wisdom of the ultimate sphere, mirrorlike primordial wisdom, primordial wisdom of evenness, discriminating primordial wisdom, and all-accomplished primordial wisdom.

85. *Ngo Bo* is translated here as "essence." Generally, *Ngo Bo, Thig Le* of light, and *Thig Le* (semen) of physical body all could be translated as "essence," and it is therefore confusing. So in this text I am translating the *Ngo Bo* as "essence," *Thig Le* of physical body in the perfection stage as "essence," and the *Thig Le* of light of Thögal as "thig-le."

86. "May I realize" is the significance of "Please come" in the prayer. Being a quotation from *Pramāṇavārttika* in Mipham Rinpoche's text, *Shegs* ("to come") has the meaning of "realization" (*rTogs*).

87. The inseparability of *Ngo Bo* and *Rang bZhin, sTong Pa* and *gSal Ba, Ch'os sKu* and *Longs sKu, Guru* and *Padma*.

88. Vajra body, vajra speech, vajra mind, and vajra primordial wisdom of the Buddhas.

89. KZZ 199a/4.

90. Based mainly on SCI: 85a/6 and 83a/5.

91. KZZ 199b/3.

92. Based on NS and DD.

93. Based on DD 58a.

94. KZZ 199a/5.

95. KZZ 199b/1.

96. KZZ 199b/2.

97. KZZ 199b/4.

98. TS 152b/5 and KT 140/2.

99. According to KZ and TS. But it is not always certain that all the Guru Rinpoche images have the same attire as that mentioned here, for in some texts the red gown is not given.

100. RD 244a/6.

101. KDD 27b/4.

KEY TO ABBREVIATIONS OF WORKS CITED

BG   *Bla Ma'i dGongs rGyan,* Lushul Khenpo Könchog Drönme (1859–1936).

BM   *Buddha Mind: An Anthology of Longchen Rabjam's Writings on Dzogpa Chenpo,* Tulku Thondup Rinpoche (Ithaca: Snow Lion Publications, 1989).

BN   *Zab Ch'os Zhi Khro dGongs Pa Rang Grol Las, Bar Do'i sMon Lam rNam gSum,* discovered as Ter by Karma Lingpa (fourteenth century).

BP   *Byang Ch'ub Sems dPa'i sPyod Pa La 'Jug Pa,* Shāntideva (seventh century). Dodrup Chen monastery, Tibet, xylograph edition.

CD   *'Phags Pa Ch'os Thams Chad Yang Dag Par sDud Pa,* Kanjur, Dege edition, mDo sDe, vol. Zha, f.1a–99b.

DC   *rDzogs Ch'en (Thor Bu),* Jigme Tenpe Nyima.

DD   *dPal gSang Ba'i sNying Po'i rGyud Kyi sPyi Don Rin Ch'en mDzod Kyi lDe'u Mig,* Jigme Tenpe Nyima (1865–1926). Dodrupchen Sungbum, vol. I. Published by Dodrupchen Rinpoche, India.

DM   *Bar Do sPyi'i Don Dran Pa'i Me Long,* Natsog Rangtrol (1608–?). English translation: *The Mirror of Mindfulness,* Tsele Natsok Rangdrol, trans. Erik Pema Kunsang (Boston & Shaftesbury: Shambhala Publications, 1989).

DN   *Rang bZhin rDzogs Pa Ch'en Po'i Lam Gyi Ch'a Lag sDom gSum rNam Par Nges Pa,* Pema Wangi Gyalpo (1487–1542). Published by Khamtrul Rinpoche, India.

DPM   *Gangs Chan Bod Ch'en Po'i rGyal Rabs 'Dus gSal Du bKod Pa sNgon Med Dvangs Shel 'Phrul Gyi Me Long* from the Collected Writings and Revelations of H. H. Bdud-'Joms Rin-Po-Che 'Jigs-Bral-Ye-Ses-Rdo-Rje. Vol. 3. Published by Dupjung Lama, Delhi, 1978.

EL   *Enlightened Living,* trans. Tulku Thondup (Boston & London: Shambhala Publications, 1990).

GG   *Bar Do'i sMon Lam dGongs gChig rGya mTsho,* Khyentse'i Özer (Jigme Lingpa, 1729–1798). Nyingthig Tsa Pod, vol. 2. Published by Dilgo Khyentse Rinpoche, India.

GN   *Grub Thob brGya Chu rTsa bZhi'i rNam Thar,* Mijigpa Jinpapal. Tenjur, Narthang edition, rGyud 'Grel, f. 1–64.

GR   *'Phags Pa rGya Ch'er Rol Ba,* Kanjur, Dege edition, mDo sDe, vol. Kha.

HTT   *Hidden Teachings of Tibet,* Tulku Thondup Rinpoche (London: Wisdom Publications, 1986).

KD   *Kyai rDo rJe Zhes Bya Ba rGyud Kyi rGyal Po [brTags Pa gNyis Pa].* Kanjur, Dege edition, rGyud, vol. Nga, f. 1a–29a.

KDD   *Dri Ba Lan Du Phul Ba sKal bZang dGa' Byed bDud rTsi'i 'Dod 'Jo,* Tsele Natshog Rangtrol. Tibetan xylograph edition.

KDN   *Klong Ch'en sNying Thig Gi sNgon 'Gro'i Khrid Yig Dran Pa Nyer bZhag,* Jigme Lingpa. Nyingthig Tsa Pod, vol. 3. Published by Dilgo Khyentse Rinpoche, India.

KNR   *sNga' 'Gyur Ch'os Kyi Byung Ba mKhas Pa dGa' Byed Ngo mTshar gTam Gyi Rol mTsho,* Ngawang Lodrö (Guru Trashi; completed in 1873). Published by Mirig Petrunkhang.

KT   *sNgon 'Gro Kun Las bTus Pa,* Yukhog Chatralwa Chöying Rangtrol (d. 1952/3). Published by Sönam Nyima, Serta, Kham, Tibet.

KZ   *rDzogs Pa Ch'en Po Klong Ch'en sNying Thig Gi sNgon 'Gro'i Khrid Yig Kun bZang Bla Ma'i Zhal Lung,* Ogyen Jigme Chökyi Wangpo (Paltul, 1808–1887). Published by Sithron Mirig Petrunkhang.

KZM   *sKu gSum Zhing Khams sByong Ba'i sSol 'Debs sMon Lam,* Khyentse'i Özer (Jigme Lingpa). Nyingthig Tsa Pod, vol. 2. Published by Dilgo Khyentse Rinpoche, India.

KZZ   *Klong Ch'en sNying Thig Gi sNgon 'Gro'i Khrid Yig Kun bZang Bla Ma'i Zhal Lung Gi Zin Bris,* Ngawang Palzang (Khenpo Ngagchung, 1879–1941). Tibetan xylograph edition.

LST *Yon Tan Rin Po Che'e'i mDzod Kyi dKa' gNad rDo rJe'i rGya mDud 'Grol Byed Legs bShad gSer Gyi Thur Ma,* (Sogpo) Tentar Lharampa (1759–?). Published by Jamyang (Dilgo) Khyentse, India.

NCC *gZhi Khregs Ch'od Kyi Zin Bris sNyan brGyud Ch'u Bo'i bChud 'Dus,* Padma Ledrel Tsal (Khenpo Ngagchung). Manuscript.

NG *Las 'Phro gTer brGyud Kyi rNam bShad Ngo mTshar rGya mTsho,* Jigme Tenpe Nyima.

NL *Klong Ch'en sNying Thig Gi sNgon 'Gro rNam mKhyen Lam bZang,* Jigme Lingpa, compiled by Jigme Thrinle Özer (1745–1821). Doncha collection. Published by Dodrupchen Rinpoche, India.

NLS *Klong Ch'en sNying Thig Gi sNgon 'Gro rNam mKhyen Lam bZang gSal Byed,* Khyentse Wangpo (1820–1892). From Nyingthig Doncha collection. Published by Dodrupchen Rinpoche.

NS *Yon Tan Rin Po Ch'e'i mDzod Las 'Bras Bu'i Theg Pa'i rGya Ch'er 'Grel rNam-mKhyen Shing rTa,* Jigme Lingpa. Adzom edition, reproduced by Dodrupchen Rinpoche, India.

PM *'Pho Ba Ma bsGom Sangs rGyas,* Jigme Lingpa. Nyingthig Tsa Pod, vol. 3. Published by Dilgo Khyentse Rinpoche, India.

RD *'Dul Ba'i Gleng gZhi Rin Po Che'e'i mDzod,* Gedundrub, the first Dalai Lama. (Delhi, India: 1970) Neychung & Lhakar.

SC *Sems Nyid Ngal gSo'i 'Grel Ba Shing rTa Ch'en Po,* Longchen Rabjam (1308–1363). Adzom edition, reproduced by Dodrupchen Rinpoche, India.

SG *Shes Bya Kun Khyab 'Grel Ba Legs bShad Yongs 'Dus Shes Bya mTha' Yas Pa'i rGya mTsho,* Yönten Gyatso (Kongtrul, 1813–1899), 3 vols. Published by Mirig Petrunkhang.

SGG *gSang sNgags Lam Rim 'Grel Ba Sangs rGyas gNyis Pa'i dGongs Pa'i rGyan,* Rigdzin Gyurme Tsewang Chogdrub. Dar-rtse-mdo xylograph edition, reproduced by Padma-chos-ldan, Leh, 1972.

TRA *Tibetan Religious Art,* Loden Sherab Dagyab. (Wiesbaden: Otto Harrassowitz, 1977).

TRD *Theg mCh'og Rin Po Ch'e'i mDzod*, Longchen Rabjam. Adzom
edition, reproduced by Dodrupchen Rinpoche, India.

TS *Klong Ch'en sNying Thig Gi sNgon 'Gro'i Khrid Yig Thar Lam gSal
Byed sGron Me*, Drodul Pawo Dorje (Adzom Drugpa, 1842–
1924). Tibetan xylograph edition from Kham.

TY *gTum Mo'i 'Bar 'Dzag Yig Ch'ung*, Jigme Lingpa. Nyingthig Tsa
Pod, vol. 3. Published by Dilgo Khyentse Rinpoche, India.

YD *Yon Tan Rin Po Ch'e'i mDzod dGa' Ba'i Ch'ar*, Jigme Lingpa.
Adzom edition, reproduced by Dodrupchen Rinpoche, India.

YG *Lam Rim Ye Shes sNying Po'i 'Grel Ba Ye Shes sNang Ba Rab Tu
rGyas Pa*, Lodrö Thaye (Kongtrul, 1813–1899). Terdzö collection.